ISLAMIC PHILOSOPHY A–Z

Volumes available in the Philosophy A–Z Series

Forthcoming volumes

Islamic Philosophy A–Z

Peter S. Groff
with
Oliver Leaman

Edinburgh University Press

© Peter S. Groff, 2007

Edinburgh University Press Ltd
22 George Square, Edinburgh

Reprinted 2008

Typeset in 10.5/13 Sabon by
Servis Filmsetting Ltd, Manchester, and
printed and bound in Great Britain by
Antony Rowe Ltd, Chippenham, Wilts

A CIP record for this book is
available from the British Library

ISBN 978 0 7486 2216 0 (hardback)
ISBN 978 0 7486 2089 0 (paperback)

Contents

For my Mother and Father

Series Editor's Preface

Islamic philosophy is like all philosophy when tied in with a religion in having indistinct parameters and requiring an understanding of the religion as well as of philosophy. Peter Groff explains a good deal about Islam in his book, and in particular the range of theoretical issues that arose in the religion. Many of these are more theological than philosophical, or so one might think, but really the distinction is rather artificial in Islamic philosophy. So many of the theological debates had and indeed continue to have profound philosophical significance. Over time philosophy was often under attack in much of the Islamic world and went to ground, as it were, in the guise of theology, and it is important for those coming to the subject for the first time to bear in mind the strong links that exist between Islamic philosophy and Islam itself. This book is designed to be appropriate for those coming for the first time both to the religion and to the philosophy, and the entries are linked to other entries and to further reading to help those readers broaden their understanding of what they find here. The Arabic terms are carefully explained and it is important to know the context in which Islamic philosophy flourished. But it would be a mistake to represent Islamic philosophy as exotic. Readers familiar with philosophy in general will recognize many of the issues debated here, and readers familiar with Islam will also see how that religion quite naturally can be taken to raise and then deal with philosophical issues. Readers familiar with neither will be interested to discover what an intriguing form of theoretical thought is represented by Islamic philosophy.

Oliver Leaman

Introduction

This book offers a series of inroads into the rich tradition of Islamic philosophy. Those familiar with this tradition have long recognized its profound influence on medieval Christian and Jewish thought, as well as the pivotal role that Islamic philosophers played in preserving and transmitting the legacy of classical Greek thought to Europe. True as this picture is, it is incomplete, because it overlooks the intrinsic value of Islamic philosophy. This is a vital, flourishing tradition in its own right, one that needs to be approached not just from the perspective of its European beneficiaries, but on its own terms as well.

The tradition of Islamic philosophy is remarkably diverse. Far from being monolithic or homogeneous, it comprises a wide range of positions and approaches, and brings with it a lively history of disputation. In this book, we have tried to do justice to the many different ways in which philosophy has expressed itself within the Islamic context. The reader will find entries on Greek-influenced Peripatetic thinkers and their major ideas, various schools of theology, Isma'ilis, Sufis, Illuminationists, and later synthetic developments such as the School of Isfahan, as well as some modern thinkers. We have also included a handful of Jewish and Christian philosophers whose work was profoundly influenced by, and in some cases contributed significantly to, the Islamic intellectual tradition. Finally, we have tried to convey some sense of the traditionalists' critique of philosophy, which can be quite sophisticated and powerful, and which is essential to a proper understanding of the relative place of philosophy within the larger intellectual life of Islam.

It is important to recognize the permeability of philosophy and religion within the Islamic tradition, a fact that may at first be perplexing to the contemporary student of philosophy. As moderns, we often assume that these two approaches to the good and the true are by their very nature distinct and antagonistic towards one another. Yet this is a relatively recent development, and a rather culturally specific one at that. At the same time it would be a mistake to see Islamic philosophy as identical with, or somehow reducible to, Islam as a religion. Islamic philosophy has no uniquely 'Islamic' essence. It might simply be described as philosophy that emerges within a context predominantly informed by the religious, social, political and cultural dimensions of Islam. As such, its presuppositions and conclusions may or may not be Muslim. Even when philosophy begins by reflecting upon the revealed truths of Islam, it can move in decidedly different directions. Sometimes it preserves and clarifies and defends these insights, sometimes it appropriates but radically reinterprets them, and sometimes it rejects them altogether.

Thus, while recognizing the ways in which philosophy and religion are intertwined in the Islamic tradition, we have tried to keep the focus on the former rather than the latter, delving into theology, Sufism and the traditional sciences only when they had some crucial bearing on points of philosophical interest. We have also opted for longer rather than shorter entries on the whole, in order to (1) uncover the questions, disputations and assumptions that gave rise to the major claims, (2) capture something of the rationale or argumentative force behind them, (3) show what is at stake philosophically, and (4) convey some sense of their abiding universal interest.

Such an approach, combined with the necessarily limited scope of a small introductory reference volume such as this, has required that we leave out certain figures and concepts. Given the intrinsic constraints of the work, our choices about what to include were made with an eye to the student or newcomer, rather than the specialist. If this book helps those readers to appreciate the vital insights and resources of the Islamic philosophical tradition – and perhaps even prompts them to want to learn more about it – it will have succeeded in its modest task.

Using This Book

Should the reader wish to delve deeper into any particular figure, school or topic, we have listed several additional sources at the end of each entry as suggestions for further reading: primarily book-length studies, occasionally specific articles, and wherever possible, translations of primary sources. We have included only works in English, but of course the reader fluent in other languages can discover a world of first-class scholarship by consulting their bibliographies. Apart from the translations, book-length studies and articles we have cited, there are numerous historical overviews, anthologies and reference works, many of which may profitably be consulted for virtually every entry in this book. For the sake of economy, we have not listed these works over and over again in the entries themselves, but encourage the reader to consult them as well – in some cases first – should he or she wish to pursue particular figures or ideas further. Although they are included in the general bibliography, we will mention a few such resources here.

First, for more detailed accounts of individual thinkers, schools, topics and such, we strongly urge the reader to seek out the anthology edited by S. H. Nasr and O. Leaman, *History of Islamic Philosophy* (Routledge, 1996), as well as M. M. Sharif's earlier two-volume collection, *A History of Muslim Philosophy* (LPP, 1961/99). Both of these collections comprise top-notch essays by outstanding authorities in the field. A recent addition to this genre – also excellent, albeit somewhat

xiv   **USING THIS BOOK**

less comprehensive – is *The Cambridge Companion to Arabic Philosophy*, ed. P. Adamson and R. Taylor (Cambridge, 2005). There are a number of very good encyclopedias worth consulting as well. The most immediately useful will be the comprehensive two-volume *Biographical Encyclopaedia of Islamic Philosophy*, recently compiled by O. Leaman (Thoemmes Continuum, 2006). After that, I would recommend Brill's new edition of the *Encyclopedia of Islam*, ed. P. J. Bearman et al. (Brill, 1960–2005), which also contains many articles on Islamic philosophy and theology, all of the highest quality. The first edition (1913–38, reprinted 1993) still contains many classic, definitive articles. The *Encyclopedia Iranica*, ed. E. Yarshater (Routledge Kegan and Paul, 1985ff.) can be a very useful source too, as well as the *Routledge Encyclopedia of Philosophy*, ed. E. Craig (Routledge, 1998), which includes numerous entries on the Islamic philosophical tradition by major scholars in the field. Finally, two good book-length historical overviews can be found in H. Corbin's *History of Islamic Philosophy* (Kegan Paul International, 2001) and M. Fakhry's *A History of Islamic Philosophy* (Columbia University Press, 1970/2004). O. Leaman's *An Introduction to Classical Islamic Philosophy* (Cambridge University Press, 2001) offers a somewhat more selective account, but is a fine entry into key debates in the tradition.

We have included transliterated Arabic terms for many of the key concepts, in order to give the reader some sense of the actual technical vocabulary of Islamic philosophy. We have also included Arabic (and in some cases, Persian) titles of books, along with their English translations, since the latter can vary a bit. There are a number of ways in which Arabic can be transliterated into English. We have employed the modified *Encyclopedia of Islam* system, with a few qualifications. First, because of the non-specialist nature of this book, we have opted for minimal transliteration: all diacritics (macrons and dots) have thus been omitted, while the left apostrophe (') represents *'ayn* and the right apostrophe (') represents *hamza*. Second, in the interests of comprehension we have occasionally opted for an alternative transliteration of a term or name, if it is more commonly encountered and more easily recognizable. Third, for the sake of clarity, we have as a rule retained Orientalist word endings (e.g. Mu'tazilite, Shi'ite, Hanbalite), but again, where the Arabic word ending has become more commonplace, we have opted for that (e.g. Sunni, Isma'ili, Sufi). Capitalization has been kept to a minimum and is generally used only for formal names of persons, schools of thought or places. Traditional names, titles or standard descriptions of God such as the Creator, the Originator, the Necessary Existent, the First Cause and the One are capitalized; 'divine' entities such as the forms, active intellect or universal soul are not. Use of the masculine pronoun when referring to God is used simply out of deference to traditional usage. With regard to dating, most figures are listed first according to the Islamic calendar (AH, i.e. *anno Hegirae),* then according to the Gregorian calendar (CE, i.e. Common Era). For example, 1266–1323/1849–1905 means 1266–1323 AH/1849–1905 CE; references to whole centuries follow the same general formula. The few exceptions to this are the dates of (1) the Prophet Muhammad, whose birth date (570 CE) precedes the beginning of the Islamic calendar (622 CE), (2) ancient Greek philosophers (listed as BCE, i.e. Before the Common Era) and (3) Jewish philosophers who worked in the Islamicate milieu (only listed as CE, because precise AH dates were not always available). Within each entry, words in **bold** signal a cross-reference, so that readers may chase down figures or concepts that strike their interest.

Acknowledgements

I would like to thank Oliver Leaman for his patience, encouragement, practical wisdom and generous assistance in the writing of this book. He helped out in the final stages by writing entries on the following topics: **aesthetics, afterlife, creation vs. eternity of the world, epistemology, essence and existence, ethics, God's knowledge, God (unity of), Illuminationism, language, law, logic, modern Islamic philosophy, mysticism, Nasr (Seyyed Hossein), political philosophy, prophecy, science** and **Sufism.** The entry on **Islamism** is a collaborative effort. I am responsible for all other entries, and of course, any errors or lacunae that might be found there. I'd like to express my appreciation to a few other folks, too: my colleagues in the Bucknell Philosophy department, as well as philosophical interlocutors from other departments and institutions, my former teachers, and my students, all of whom have helped me keep thinking and growing. Special thanks go out to Abdur-Rahman Syed and Kaley Keene, who generously read through the manuscript and made many thoughtful suggestions regarding translation and transliteration, and to Laury Silvers, who offered so much helpful advice along the way. Finally I would like to thank my family and friends for their good-humored patience and support, and especially my love Valerie, who is in my heart, whether she's in Pennsylvania, Switzerland or Belgium.

Islamic Philosophy A–Z

A

'Abduh, Muhammad (1266–1323/1849–1905): An Egyptian
jurist, philosopher, religious scholar and liberal reformer,
'Abduh played a pivotal role in the nineteenth-century
Renaissance (*nahda*) of **Islam**. Along with his teacher **al-
Afghani**, he is responsible for founding the Salafi reform
movement, which strove to recover Islam from its decadent
state by returning it to the spirit of its pious forefathers
(*salaf*). However, like al-Afghani and unlike the later
salafiyya, his sympathies were ultimately more **rationalist**
than **traditionalist**. 'Abduh saw Islam as an essentially
reasonable and pragmatic religion, one that was not
necessarily at odds with the modern scientific worldview. Indeed, despite his reservations about the West, he
embraced **science** and technology as crucial to the revivification and autonomy of Islam. In his attempt to recover the
true spirit of Islam, 'Abduh inveighed against the uncriti-
cal acceptance of dogma based purely on religious authority (*taqlid*, lit. 'imitation' or **obedience**) and defended the
irreducible importance of **independent judgement** in religious and legal matters. He recuperated elements of
Mu'tazilite rationalism as well (e.g. figurative **interpretation** of ambiguous Qur'anic passages, emphasis on **God's
transcendence**, affirmation of human **free will**) and
attempted to purge Islam of **Ash'arite** predestinarianism

and **occasionalism**, which he saw as hostile to the principle of **causality**, and thus to modern science in general. 'Abduh's main philosophical work, the *Theology of Unity* (*Risalat al-tawhid*), proceeds in this vein, but is primarily known for its rationalist **ethics**. According to 'Abduh, revealed **law** does not *make* things good or evil, but rather reveals to us what is naturally good or evil. Siding with the Mu'tazilites and the *falasifa*, he argued that human reason is in principle capable of perceiving good and evil without the aid of **revelation**. However, revelation is still necessary because (1) not all people have the same intellectual capacity to differentiate between good and evil (or to grasp the existence and nature of God, the **afterlife**, etc.) and (2) for most people, reason alone will not provide the specific practical **knowledge** necessary to realize a happy life. At the heart of 'Abduh's life and thought was the desire for reform, whether religious, legal, moral or educational. For this reason, he eventually parted ways with the more radical al-Afghani and distanced himself from his erstwhile teacher's pan-Islamist project. He had a great impact on subsequent religious, social and philosophical reformers (e.g. Rashid Rida, Qasim Amin and Mustafa 'Abd al-Raziq), as well as influential twentieth-century nationalist and revivalist movements that did not always share his commitment to reason and gradual reform.

See **al-Afghani; Ash'arites; Islamism; modern Islamic philosophy; Mu'tazilites; rationalism; traditionalism**

Further reading: 'Abduh 1966/2004; Adams 1933; Amin 1953; Hourani 1983

active intellect (*al-'aql al-fa"al*): The concept of the 'active' or 'agent' intellect plays a pivotal role in Islamic **metaphysics** and **psychology**, particularly in the **Peripatetic** tradition. Its origins can be traced back to the Aristotelian notion of *nous poietikos* in *De anima* III.4–5. Expanding upon the doctrine that 'that which thinks and that which is thought are the same', **Aristotle** draws a distinction between a passive, potential intellect which *becomes* all things and an active, productive (ostensibly eternal and divine) intellect which *makes* all things. Aristotle posits this 'active intellect' in order to account for the possibility of thought, which stands in need of an explanation because it is a kind of process or movement, and as such, is characterized by change. All change requires an efficient **cause** to bring it about, so there must be some efficient cause by which the transition of intellect from potentiality to **actuality** is effected. It is also described by Aristotle and his commentators as a kind of illuminative principle which sheds light upon universal forms, making them intelligible to the human intellect. In Islamic **philosophy**, this notion of the active intellect is taken up and typically situated within a **Neoplatonic** cosmology (the tenth and final intellect to arise through the process of **emanation**, often associated with the moon and the angel Jibril), as a kind of link between the human and the divine. It plays a pivotal role in several respects. First, it functions as a principle of both intelligibility and intellection by providing form to the sublunary realm and actualizing potential human intellect, enabling us to extract and disjoin intelligible forms from objects of sense perception and ultimately grasp them independently of it. Second, it makes possible the perfection of human nature, the attainment of highest **happiness**, and the immortality of the **soul**. As the human intellect is transformed from its initial state of pure potentiality to one of pure actuality, it becomes more like the immaterial, eternal active intellect, and is ultimately assimilated to it. Finally, the active intellect explains the possibility of prophetic **revelation** – as the reception of intelligibles by the **imagination** – within the context of an Aristotelian/ Neoplatonic worldview.

See **Aristotle; causality; al-Farabi; Ibn Bajja; Ibn Rushd; Ibn Sina; metaphysics; prophecy; psychology.**

Further reading: Davidson 1992; al-Farabi 1973; Ibn Rushd 2007; Ibn Sina 1952/1981; Netton 1989/95; Rahman 1958

actuality and potentiality (*fi'l, quwwa*): see **metaphysics; psychology**

adab (etiquette, refinement, culture): Initially, the Arabic term *adab* seems to be a virtual synonym for *sunna* (custom, tradition), insofar as it has to do with a norm of habitual conduct founded by ancestors or other exemplary persons. This notion was gradually magnified and embellished, particularly during the 'Abbasid empire, and by the heyday of Islamic **humanism** in the second half of the fourth/tenth century under the Buyids, the term had taken on a panoply of social, ethical and intellectual connotations. Due to the increasing refinement of bedouin customs by the introduction of **Islam**, as well as by exposure to Persian, Greek and Indian civilization, *adab* had come to signify a kind of ethical perfectionism that encompassed good manners, etiquette, elegance, education, urbanity, *belles-lettres* and culture in general. More specifically, it referred to the sort of **knowledge** necessary to produce refined, well-cultivated people. In this sense *adab* can generally be seen as the secular complement to *'ilm* (**science**, knowledge), which has more to do with religious sciences such as tradition (*hadith*), **jurisprudence** (*fiqh*), Qur'anic exegesis (*tafsir*), etc. It comprises knowledge of poetry, rhetoric, oratory, grammar and history, as well as familiarity with the literary and philosophical achievements, the practical-ethical wisdom and the exemplary individuals of the pre-Islamic Arabs, Indians, Persians and Greeks. It can be said to encompass the natural sciences as well, although its primary focus is always on the human. The semiotic field of *adab* would eventually shrink and reify, referring merely to the specific knowledge required for the performance of a particular office, or signifying literature in a narrow sense. But at its apex, the *adab* tradition – at least as interpreted by Islamic humanists such as Abu Sulayman Muhammad al-Sijistani, al-Tawhidi and Miskawayh – gave rise to the cosmopolitan ideal that wisdom and moral exemplars could be drawn from many cultures, and that their insights were the collective birthright of humankind.

See ethics; humanism; Miskawayh; al-Sijistani (Abu Sulayman Muhammad); al-Tawhidi

Further reading: Goodman 2003; Kraemer 1986a/93

aesthetics (*'ilm al-jamal*, lit. 'science of beauty'): Neoplatonism had a lasting influence on Islamic aesthetics during the classical period. Al-Kindi argued that beauty must be linked with perfection, and since God is the most perfect being, He must also be the most beautiful. Other things are beautiful in proportion to their perfection. Perfection was seen very much as being in line with things like the motion of the heavenly spheres, and so acts as an objective guide to beauty. This idea was taken up by the Sufis and their followers, and they argued that there is a natural beauty in certain shapes, sounds and movements since these replicate very basic and perfect aspects of reality. In later philosophy the concept of imagination comes to be used more often, and beauty becomes something that we observe when we mix our ideas up in ways that delight us. Imagination is very much a function of our role as material creatures, and this is emphasized in aesthetics, where different individuals with different experiences and backgrounds often have different ideas of the aesthetic value of a particular thing.

One of the themes in Islamic aesthetics is the analysis of poetry (*shi'r*), a particularly important art form in Arabic culture. It is generally taken to follow a syllogistic form, i.e. it is like an argument, albeit with the conclusion that the audience should be moved to action or emotion, not some statement of fact. Imagination is significant in reflecting our experiences and feelings while at the same time also linking our thinking with more abstract ideas and so extending or broadening those experiences from the purely subjective into something more abstract that can be communicated to others. Art is a function of our nature as emotional creatures, as beings that are not just rational, and we need to find ways of persuading people to see the world, and have the same experiences as we do. The idea of art as following the pattern of reasoning or argument is designed to explain how it is possible to do this, since it is certainly a fact that we can sometimes get others to think as we do after coming into contact with an artistic product that we have created or experienced.

See **logic**; **political philosophy**; **prophecy**; **Sufism**

Further reading: Black 1990; Kemal 1991; Leaman 2004

Afdal al-Din Kashani (d. 610/1213–14): Baba (or 'Papa') Afdal, as he was affectionately known to his students and intellectual progeny, was one of the few Islamic philosophers to write almost entirely in Persian. While other Iranian authors (e.g. **Ibn Sina, Nasir-i Khusraw, al-Suhrawardi** and **Mulla Sadra**) wrote works in Persian as well, most expressed their definitive statements in Arabic, which had long been considered the scholarly *lingua franca* of the Islamic world. Not so with Baba Afdal, whose clear, straightforward and elegant Persian prose made a synthesis of **Neoplatonic-Aristotelian** and **Sufi**

ideas intelligible to a wider audience, many of whom would have found the uncompromising and sometimes unwieldy technical precision of Arabic philosophical texts forbidding. Among his major philosophical works are *The Book of Displays* (*'Ard-nama*), *The Book of the Everlasting* (*Jawidan-nama*) and *The Rungs of Perfection* (*Madarij al-kamal*). The overriding concern of these books is how to achieve salvific knowledge of the self (*dhat*, *huwiyya*) by means of rational inquiry and ethical cultivation. When one realizes one's own everlasting self as **intellect** (*khirad*, *'aql*) – according to Baba Afdal, a kind of radiance of **God** – one perfects or actualizes one's own nature. Although Baba Afdal does not concern himself with many of the topics that obsessed other Islamic philosophers – the divine **attributes**, God as the **Necessary Existent**, etc. – he develops an elaborate ontology and cosmology, which while Neoplatonic in its general contours, has no obvious, specific precedent. It might be said that Baba Afdal's **metaphysics** are rooted in, and unfold from, his **epistemology** of the self. For the human being as a microcosm of the universe contains within itself all the lower levels of existence, i.e., all the actualized potentialities presupposed by its own living **soul**. The actualization of human **existence** (*wujud*) in particular – which Baba Afdal characterizes as 'finding' (*yaftan*) rather than just 'being' (*budan*) – consists in the full self-awareness of the intellect. It is through this perfection of self-knowledge that the soul awakens from its forgetfulness and separates itself from the body in preparation for death. But on a macrocosmic level, it is through the flowering of the human being (as microcosm) that the potentialities of the universe as a whole can ultimately be actualized and the return or ascent of creation to God can be effected. What makes Baba Afdal's thought particularly interesting and compelling is its eminently practical conception of **philosophy** as a way of life, aimed at salvific self-realization and the perfection of our nature, and the stylistic verve and clarity with which he presents this project. Apart from Baba Afdal's many philosophical works, he is highly regarded for his poetry, also in Persian.

See **Neoplatonism; psychology; Sufism**
Further reading: Chittick 2001; Nasr 1996

al-Afghani, Jamal al-Din (1254–1314/1838–97): An enormously influential nineteenth-century philosopher, journalist, orator and political activist-leader, al-Afghani was the chief architect of both Islamic modernism and the pan-Islamist movement. His modernism consisted in an attempt to reform and revitalize **Islam** by retrieving its original moral force and essential rationality, while at the same time appropriating modern western **science** and technology. His aim was to negotiate a middle way between the more fatalistic, authoritarian and anti-intellectual elements of the Islamic tradition and the seemingly atheistic and nihilistic worldview of the modern West. The pan-Islamist movement that he kick-started aimed at mobilizing and empowering Muslim nations with modern science and technology in order to resist European imperialism and colonialism. Ultimately he hoped to unite Muslim nations into a single autonomous caliphate, thus re-attaining the glory of Islam. Philosophically, al-Afghani's most important contribution is *The Refutation of the Materialists* (*al-Radd 'ala al-dahriyyin*). The work begins with a philosophical-scientific critique of materialism from Democritus to Darwin, then offers a social-ethical criticism of materialism (which, he argues, has a corrosive, degenerative effect on civilization), and concludes with a defense of the value of **religion** (in particular, Islam) for the health of individuals and societies and the progress of humanity in general. However, far from being a **tradition-alist** attack on the pretensions of **reason**, the *Refutation* clearly manifests a commitment to the power of the intellect and the importance of free inquiry, and holds religious belief to a fairly rigorous standard of rationality. Indeed, al-Afghani's critical stance towards Darwin softened over time (e.g. he accepted a version of natural selection) and at times he appears to privilege **philosophy** and science over religion when they conflict (e.g. his famous defense of Islam against the French positivist Ernest Renan). Al-Afghani had a profound impact on thinkers such as Muhammad **'Abduh**, Rashid Rida and Muhammad **Iqbal**, to name just a few. However, his greatest influence would be felt through subsequent developments in Islamic reformism and Islamist movements such as the *salafiyya* and the Muslim Brotherhood, who also sought to purify Islam, albeit in a more fundamentalist direction.

See **'Abduh (Muhammad); Iqbal (Muhammad); Islamism; modern Islamic philosophy; rationalism; traditionalism**

Further reading: Keddie 1968; 1972; Kedourie 1966

afterlife (*ma'ad*, lit. 'return'): The **Qur'an** provides a graphic account of a physical afterlife that is going to occur to everyone, either in Paradise or in Hell. **Al-Ghazali** objects to philosophers such as **al-Farabi** and **Ibn Sina** because their account of the afterlife is of something entirely spiritual, while the Qur'an describes the afterlife as a very corporeal realm. There are two difficulties with this objection, and one actually occurs to al-Ghazali when he analyzes the afterlife from the perspective of **Sufism**. Some religious language is to be taken literally, and some only allegorically, and perhaps the afterlife should be interpreted in the latter way. Careful examination of the

Qur'anic verses mentioning women or houris might note their ordering in the text, since this reveals a transition from the material to the more spiritual. In the first Meccan period (from the first to the fifth year of the Prophet's mission, 612–17 CE) we find references to very desirable young ladies awaiting the virtuous as part of their reward, but by the time of the Medinan period (622–32 CE) the language has changed to such an extent that they are identified as 'purified spouses' (2.25, 3.15 and 4.57). The pagans of Mecca needed the crude physical language used during that period, it might be argued, while by the time of the Medinan revelations a more refined and spiritual form of description could be used. This accords with the role of **religion** in al-Farabi's philosophy of **language**, where religion is explained in imaginative language and imagination is important to motivate us given that we are material creatures. We can gradually perfect our thinking, and one can see this happening with the changing role of the houris. At first they were described in ways that would resonate with an audience motivated by material images and appetites, but once the public became more refined in its thinking, no doubt due to the influence of religion, it could be told about houris' real and more spiritual nature.

Thinkers like **Ibn Rushd** pushed the envelope even further. On his account, the afterlife is not only not physical, it is not even personal or individual. According to his Aristotelian **psychology**, when the body dies the intellect blends together with other immaterial intellects into one thinking thing, brought together through their contemplation of an abstract subject matter.

See **al-Farabi; al-Ghazali; Ibn Rushd; Ibn Sina; interpretation; psychology**

Further reading: al-Ghazali 1997/2000; Ibn Rushd 2007; Leaman 2006a; McAuliffe 2001–6

al-ʿAmiri, Abu al-Hasan Muhammad ibn Yusuf (d. 381/992): Like his intellectual forebear **al-Kindi**, al-ʿAmiri sought above all to show the harmonizability of **Islam** and **philosophy**, while granting primacy to the former. Although his best–known work, *Exposition of the Merits of Islam* (*al-Iʿlam bi manaqib al-Islam*), presents an argument for the superiority of Islam over rival religious traditions, the overarching concern of al-ʿAmiri's work was the rational defense of divine **revelation** against philosophers who valorized the power of unaided human **reason**. In his *Book on the Afterlife* (*Kitab al-amad ʿala al-abad*), he argues in a **Neoplatonic** fashion for the individual immortality of the **soul** and its reward or punishment in the **afterlife**. This is ultimately determined by the actualization or completion of the human **intellect** in this life. However, the actualization of the intellect is impossible without right action, which tempers the physical faculties and directs the intellect towards the divine. Here we see the indispensability of revelation for al-ʿAmiri, since (1) it provides us with an unerring guide to right action and (2) it plays a necessary role in the actualization of the human intellect. For although Greek philosophers posited the immortality of the soul and its reward or punishment in the afterlife, they did not acknowledge the resurrection of the body. Revelation thus provides us with essential information about the fate of the soul, which is inaccessible to the intellect alone. In spite of his emphasis on the primacy of revelation over reason, al-ʿAmiri is sometimes associated with the school of **al-Farabi** because of his emphasis on the soteriological function of metaphysical **knowledge**.

Al-ʿAmiri is also known for his interventions on the question of predestination, *Deliverance of Humankind from the Problem of Predestination and Free Will* (*Inqadh al-bashar min al-jabr wa al-qadar*) and *The Determination of the Various Aspects of Predestination* (*al-Taqrir li-awjuh al-taqdir*). Anticipating **Ibn Sina**'s system, he attempts to resolve the problem by distinguishing between **God** as the only **Necessary Existent** and all other existents as contingent or merely possible beings. Insofar as contingent beings depend up on the Necessary Existent for their sustained existence, they are determined or preordained. However, insofar as contingent beings are related to one another, they are not, which opens up the possibility of individual responsibility. Al-'Amiri's treatment of the problem of predestination provides a nice example of his conciliatory approach to **philosophy** and Islam: by employing an **Aristotelian** model of **causation**, he arrives at a theologically respectable intermediate position which avoids the extremes of both divine compulsion and unrestricted human **free will**. Although quite influential in its time, al-'Amiri's Kindian approach to the relation between revelation and philosophy would soon be overshadowed by **Ibn Sina**'s approach, which while also conciliatory, would in many ways privilege the latter over the former.

See **afterlife; al-Farabi; free will and predestination; Ibn Sina; al-Kindi; psychology**

Further reading: Rosenthal 1975/94; Rowson 1988/96

annihilation of self (*fana'*): see **Ibn al-'Arabi**

anthropomorphism: see **assimilation; God (anthropomorphic descriptions of)**

Aristotle (Aristutalis, Aristu) (384–322 BCE): In the Islamic tradition, Greek philosophy is virtually synonymous with the name of Aristotle, who was traditionally known as both 'the Philosopher' and 'the First Teacher'. Indeed, one of the most influential schools of Islamic **philosophy** in the classical period was the *mashsha'un* – the 'Walkers' or **Peripatetics** – among whose ranks can be counted **al-Farabi, Ibn Sina** and **Ibn Rushd**, along with many others. The *mashsha'un* sought to appropriate and build upon Aristotle's philosophical achievements, and their systems are generously infused with myriad elements from his thought, e.g. his conception of (and arguments for the existence of) **God**, his notions of the **eternity** of the world, the **active intellect, actuality and potentiality**, form and matter, the four **causes, necessity and possibility, essence and existence** (at least implicitly), and the demonstrative syllogism. However, Islamic Aristotelianism was by no means purely Aristotelian, at least in its earlier stages. Despite the fact that most of his considerable corpus had been translated into Arabic (excepting the *Politics*, the *Eudemian Ethics* and the *Magna Moralia*), Aristotle's system was initially interpreted through a **Neoplatonic** lens. Indeed, for a number of centuries, two influential Neoplatonic texts were mistakenly attributed to Aristotle: *Aristotle's Theology* (a translation of a paraphrase of Books 4–6 from Plotinus' *Enneads*) and the *Book of the Pure Good* (a translation of selected and rearranged chapters from Procus' *Elements of Theology*, known subsequently to the Latins as *Liber de causis*). However, this Neoplatonizing of Aristotle was not unique to the Islamic philosophers; to some extent they inherited it from the Greek Neoplatonic commentators themselves, whose works were also translated into Arabic, and who were wont to posit an essential harmony between the philosophies of **Plato** and Aristotle. It was not until **Ibn Rushd**'s monumental commentary project in the latter half of the sixth/twelfth century that Aristotle's thought was effectively retrieved and fully disentangled from Neoplatonic ideas. However, by then Aristotle's influence within the Islamic tradition had already begun to wane, due to the **Ash'arite** theologians' assault on

Greek-influenced philosophy and the emergence of **Illuminationism,** a school of philosophy that rejected key aspects of Aristotelian **logic** and **metaphysics.** In many ways, Christian Latins profited more from Ibn Rushd's scholarship than subsequent Islamic philosophers did: it played a pivotal role in the West's rediscovery of Aristotle's thought, which would breathe new life into medieval Christian philosophy and remain the dominant philosophical and scientific influence until the rediscovery of Plato and the emergence of mathematical physics at the dawn of modernity.

See **active intellect; Ash'arites; causality; creation vs. eternity of the world; al-Farabi; God; humanism; Ibn Rushd; Ibn Sina; Illuminationism; logic; Neoplatonism; philosophy; Plato**

Further reading: Aristotle 1984; Peters 1968a, 1968b; Walzer 1962

Ash'arites (*ash'ariyya*): The Ash'arite school of **theology** was founded in the early fourth/tenth century by Abu al-Hasan al-Ash'ari. Originally a theologian of the **Mu'tazilite** persuasion, al-Ash'ari ultimately rejected his former school's privileging of reason after a series of visions and returned to a more robust **traditionalism.** Specifically, he embraced the traditionalist vision of **Sunni Islam** put forth by Ahmad ibn Hanbal. However, although al-Ash'ari avowedly subscribed to the tenets of Hanbalism, unlike the **Hanbalites** themselves (and much to their chagrin) he defended those tenets via rational argumentation. Ash'arism thus staked out a relatively moderate middle ground in the conflict between Mu'tazilite **rationalism** and Hanbalite traditionalism. In part because of this, in part because of the originality and resourcefulness of its major thinkers, it quickly established itself as the dominant school of *kalam.* From the mid-fifth/eleventh century on, the Ash'arites' principal doctrines came to be virtually synonymous with mainstream, orthodox Sunni theological thought. The Ash'arites' theological stance is best understood through its opposition to Mu'tazilism. First, contra the Mu'tazilites, they maintained that the **Qur'an** is uncreated. Indeed, they claimed that God's speech – like all other traditional divine **attributes** (e.g. **God's knowledge**, sight, etc.) – is eternal and distinct from His essence. Second, the Ash'arites generally rejected the Mu'tazilites' figurative **interpretation** of traditional Qur'anic attributes without at the same time retreating to the **literalism** of unreconstructed traditionalists. Following Ibn Hanbal, they held that expressions such as 'God's hand' or 'God's face' should be read *bila kayf*, 'without [asking] how', that is, they accepted them as real attributes whose exact nature could not be grasped by human reason. They applied this strategy as well to crucial eschatological passages in the Qur'an, such as the vision of God, the basin, the bridge, the balance, intercession by Muhammad, etc., which had been denied or rationally reinterpreted by the Mu'tazilites. Finally, contra the Mu'tazilites' emphasis on God's justice (i.e., on the centrality of human **free will**), the Ash'arites gave primacy to God's omnipotence. They radicalized the Mu'tazilites' **atomism** and insistence on the contingency of all created things, fashioning it into a kind of **occasionalism** in which God is the direct **cause** of all that occurs, whether good or evil – even the choices and acts of human beings. According to the doctrine of acquisition (*kasb*), God creates the acts of human beings by creating in them the power to perform each act. It would seem that the Ash'arites' insistence on divine omnipotence undermines the possibility of free will and implies some sort of fatalism. This is indeed how their opponents understood it, particularly the Mu'tazilites. However, the Ash'arites themselves understood this position as a mean between the **Jabrites'** privileging of divine compulsion and the **Qadarites'** and Mu'tazilites privileging of free will.

The Ash'arite school produced more than its share of outstanding thinkers. From a philosophical perspective, the most important Ash'arite theologians were **al-Ghazali**, **al-Shahrastani** and Fakhr al-Din **al-Razi**. All three men undertook extensive study of the philosophers, learning their doctrines and adopting their syllogistic methods of argument in order to refute them. Particularly as a result of al-Ghazali's pivotal *Incoherence of the Philosophers*, the tide started to turn against Greek-inflected **philosophy** in the late fifth/eleventh century and it was soon overwhelmed by *kalam*. However, Ash'arism itself was ultimately transformed by its victory over rationalism: after such an extensive engagement with the doctrines and tools of the philosophers, theology took on a considerably more philosophical cast.

See **al-Ghazali**; **God (attributes of)**; **Hanbalites**; **interpretation**; **Jabrites**; **al-Juwayni**; **Mu'tazilites**; **occasionalism**; **philosophy**; **Qadarites**; **al-Shahrastani**; **al-Razi (Fakhr al-Din)**; **theology**

Further reading: al-Ash'ari 1953; al-Ghazali 1997/2000; Watt 1948, 1973

assimilation (*tashbih*, lit. 'making similar'): The act of comparing **God** to His creatures, thus conceiving of Him as corporeal, finite and imperfect. Although there are numerous Qur'anic passages in which God is described in rather human terms, anthropomorphizing God is seen as a kind of paganism or idolatry. It is thus a grave sin in **Islam**, and one that ultra-**traditionalists** were sometimes accused of. Philosophers and more **rationalist**-oriented theologians tended to interpret such passages figuratively and emphasize God's radical otherness and **transcendence** – a theme that also has its basis in the Qur'an – sometimes to the extent of denying that God has any **attributes** at all, above and beyond His unitary essence (*tawhid*). But this too is a sin (*ta'til*, lit. 'stripping' or 'divesting' God of His attributes), because it ostensibly leads to atheism. Thus the believer had to tread a subtle path between crude theological **anthropomorphism** and a destructively thorough-going transcendentalism.

See **God** (**anthropomorphic descriptions of; attributes of; imitation of**); **interpretation**; *shirk*; **theology**

Further reading: van Ess 2006; Watt 1948

atomism: see **al-Ghazali, occasionalism, theology**

attributes, divine (*sifat Allah*): see **God** (**attributes of**)

Averroës, Averroism: see **Ibn Rushd**

Avicenna: see **Ibn Sina**

B

Baba Afdal: see **Afdal al-Din Kashani**

Batinites (*batiniyya*): A term applied to those who emphasize the inner (*batin*) meaning of a text over its external or apparent (*zahir*) sense. It is sometimes loosely applied to thinkers who opt for a figurative **interpretation** (*ta'wil*) in order to avoid absurd or superficially literal readings of scripture, e.g. the **Mu'tazilites**, the *falasifa* or the **Sufis**. However, it is primarily reserved for the **Isma'ilis**, for whom the distinction between the apparent and esoteric or hidden meaning of **revelation** is paramount. The

Isma'ilis went beyond the metaphorical approach to Qur'anic exegesis preferred by rationalist theologians, philosophers and mystics, insisting on elaborate symbolic and allegorical readings of even seemingly straightforward passages. Finding meaning in numbers and letters, they disclosed through their interpretations an elaborate, mythologized **Neoplatonic** cosmology, along with a cyclical but eschatological conception of history. For the Isma'ilis, interpretation was absolutely essential to the attainment of truth, rivalling even revelation (*tanzil*) itself in importance. Like revelation, it was seen as imminently rational, albeit not discoverable by universally distributed, unaided human **reason**. Proper understanding required divine assistance of sorts: the true import of scripture could only be discerned and passed on in the form of an authoritative teaching (*ta'lim*) by divinely guided **imams** descended from the family of the Prophet **Muhammad** himself, who were invested with **knowledge** by the first originated being, the intellect. However, the esoteric truths of the imams and their missionaries were deliberately concealed from common believers (*'amm*), who, in their ignorance, might misunderstand or abuse them. Indeed, they were jealously guarded and only revealed, in a decidedly secretive, exclusionary, hierarchical and gradual manner, to the elite (*khass*). The Isma'ilis extended the Shi'ite idea of precautionary **dissimulation** (*taqiyya*), interpreting it as an obligation not to disclose the *batin*, rather than simply as a means of escaping religious and political persecution. Even the observation of Islamic **law** in its *zahir* form could be understood as a kind of dissimulation. While the Isma'ilis' radical hermeneutics introduced a system of great richness and sophistication into the Qur'anic worldview, it also understandably intensified **Sunni traditionalists'** wariness towards what they saw as over-interpretation, and reinforced their penchant for a more sober and conservative, if not entirely **literalist**, approach to scriptural exegesis.

See **interpretation; Isma'ilis**

Further reading: Corbin 1993; Daftary 1990

being/existence (*wujud*): see **essence and existence; metaphysics**

belief, faith (*iman*): In the formative period of Islam, an early theologico-political controversy emerged around the question of what qualifies a person as a Muslim. Answers ranged from the bare act of witnessing ('I declare there is no god but God and that Muhammad is the Messenger of God'), to external performance of the divine **law**, to having proper **knowledge** and right intention in the heart. The outcome of this debate, and the subsequent mainstream position, comprised a fusion of all three to some extent. A closely related issue concerned the status of sinning Muslims, specifically, whether they ceased to be Muslims altogether. The **Kharijites** in particular defended this radical stance, which however soon gave way to a range of more moderate, 'intermediate' positions.

It was not unusual for philosophers to be charged with **freethinking** or heresy (*zandaqa*) or, more dramatically, outright unbelief (*kufr*) by the more **traditionalist** elements within **Islam**. The **Hanbalites** in particular were quite free with such accusations, but perhaps the most important instance of it is associated with the great **Ash'arite** theologian and **Sufi**, **al-Ghazali**, who in his *Incoherence of the Philosophers*, charged **Peripatetics** like **al-Farabi** and **Ibn Sina** with seventeen counts of heretical 'innovation' (*bid'a*) and three counts of unbelief (*kufr*). The three major philosophical conclusions that al-Ghazali characterized as incompatible with Islam are (1) the **eternity** (rather than createdness) of the universe,

(2) the claim that **God** knows things only insofar as they are universals (and not temporal particulars), and (3) the denial of the resurrection of the body (i.e. conceiving the 'return' [*ma'ad*] in purely spiritual or intellectual terms). Although **Ibn Rushd** responded forcefully to these charges in his *Decisive Treatise* and *Incoherence of the Incoherence*, al-Ghazali's portrayal emerged triumphant historically, and philosophy as a self-sufficient way of knowing over against theology and **mysticism** declined dramatically in the **Sunni** world. Although philosophers in the **Shi'ite** milieu confronted their own share of such accusations (e.g. **Mulla Sadra**), they were never quite as devastating, perhaps because the later Persians' approach was more synthetic and informed by the vital concerns and commitments of the Islamic tradition.

See **freethinking; al-Ghazali; Ibn al-Rawandi; Ibn Rushd; Ibn Taymiyya; Kharijites; Mulla Sadra; Mu'tazilites; al-Razi (Abu Bakr)**

Further reading: al-Ghazali 1997/2000; Hallaq 1993; Ibn Rushd 2001a

bila kayf ('without how'): see **Ash'arites; God (anthropomorphic descriptions of); Hanbalites**

al-Biruni, Abu Rayhan Muhammad (362–440/973–1048): One of the greatest and most original scientists in the Islamic tradition, the Persian-born al-Biruni made vital and lasting contributions to the fields of astronomy, mathematics, geodesy, geography, mineralogy, pharmacology, history and chronology. He is accordingly known as 'the Master' (*al-ustadh*). His seminal study, *The Book Confirming What Pertains to India, Whether Rational or Despicable* (*Kitab fi tahqiq ma li al-hind*), written while accompanying the Ghaznawid sultan Mahmud during his military conquest of India, is considered by many to be the first great work of comparative **religion** and **philosophy**. It offers a serious, charitable examination of key religious and philosophical doctrines in classical Indian thought (including Samkhya, Yoga and Vedanta), set in dialogue with Greek and Islamic insights. Many of al-Biruni's philosophical ideas are woven throughout his scientific works. His chief extant philosophical text is *Questions and Answers* (*As'ila wa al-ajwiba*), a record of his correspondence with **Ibn Sina**, which offers a powerful, multi-pronged critique of Aristotelian natural philosophy. Although al-Biruni's metaphysical commitments sometimes align with the Islamic theologians in surprising ways (e.g. he rejects the **eternity** of the world in favor of its originatedness and opts for *kalam* **atomism** over Aristotelian hylomorphism), his natural philosophy is rooted primarily in his own scientific observations and inductions. This can be seen in his exchange with Ibn Sina about **Aristotle**'s inadequate model of the heavens, his dynamic, developmental model of the natural world (in which the possibilities inherent in the nature of things unfold gradually, becoming actualized) and his philosophy of history (which, based on geological evidence, inferred tremendous cataclysms in the past and posited a cyclical model of history, in which civilizations become increasingly corrupt and materialistic, until they are destroyed by a natural disaster and then renewed by a divinely sent prophet). Al-Biruni's qualified admiration of his predecessor, the unpopular freethinker Abu Bakr **al-Razi**, is thus not entirely surprising, since despite their sharply differing opinions regarding religion, they shared a deep respect for empirical observation.

See **creation vs. eternity of the world; Ibn Sina; al-Razi (Abu Bakr); science**

Further reading: al-Biruni 2003–5; Nasr 1964/93; Nasr with Aminrazavi 1999

Brethren of Purity (Ikhwan al-Safa'): Designating themselves
with the Qur'anic sobriquet 'Sleepers in the cave of our
father Adam', the Brethren of Purity were a secretive and
mysterious group of philosophers centred on the cosmopolitan city of Basra. Their actual membership is still
a matter of dispute, as are their exact religio-political
commitments (some scholars believe they were **Isma'ilis**).
The only thing that is relatively certain is that they lived
and wrote in either the fourth/tenth or fifth/eleventh centuries and collectively produced fifty-two remarkable
Epistles (*Rasa'il*) that ranged over mathematics, astronomy, geography, music, **logic**, the natural sciences, magic,
astrology, **psychology**, **metaphysics** and religious **law**.
The Brethren offered up a syncretic system that drew
from diverse Greek philosophers, the **Qur'an**, and even
divergent systems of belief such as Judaism, Christianity
and Hinduism. They employed **Aristotelian** concepts in
their metaphysics (matter and form, substance and accidents, the four **causes**, **actuality and potentiality**), but
wove them into an elaborate **Neoplatonic** hierarchy in
which being emanated from the Creator, to the **intellect**,
to the universal **soul**, and on down through prime matter,
nature, the absolute body, the spheres, and the four elements to the beings of our world. With such a hybrid **philosophy**, it is hardly surprising to encounter certain
tensions in the Brethren's writings; what *is* surprising is
that they make little effort to reconcile explicit contradictions (e.g. between the unknowable, impersonal **God**
of Neoplatonism and the concerned, guiding God of the
Qur'an). However, the Brethren did not pursue 'actual
knowledge' as an end in itself; for them it ultimately
served a practical, soteriological function. In conjunction
with asceticism, mutual assistance and virtuous living, it
purified the soul, helping the Brethren and their interlocutors to free themselves from the body and ascend

from the material world to Paradise. The Brethren thus presented themselves as a 'ship of salvation', and in fact their eclecticism and tolerance was a deliberate strategy in the salvation of the soul, seizing upon practically efficacious **wisdom** wherever they found it.

See **afterlife; Aristotle; Isma'ilis; metaphysics; Qur'an; Neoplatonism; psychology**

Further reading: Brethren of Purity 1978; Nasr 1964/93; Nasr with Aminrazavi 2001; Netton 1982/91, 1989/95

C

causality; cause (*sabab, 'illa*): Islamic **theology** generally employs a weak conception of causality. According to the traditional model, a thing's cause is simply the occasion (*sabab*, i.e. 'channel' or 'intermediary') for its **existence** – that which permits it to occur without fully determining or necessitating it. Although this idea can be found in philosophical circles as well, the more common term there is *'illa*. This corresponds roughly to **Aristotle**'s notion of *aition* as the 'explanation' for *why* a thing is what it is. Islamic philosophers such as **al-Farabi** and **Ibn Sina** took up Aristotle's four-fold model of causality (formal, material, efficient and final), but added a **Neoplatonic** twist to it, by conceiving of cause as a kind of ontological ground that perpetually sustains the existence of its effect. On this model, **God** is the First Cause, from whom all things emanate necessarily and automatically, as if by a kind of logical entailment. Indeed, the relation between all causes and effects in the world is one of **necessity**, and this is precisely what renders the world intelligible to human **reason**. However, it is difficult to reconcile the Aristotelian-Neoplatonic model of causality with the Qur'anic notion of God's free **creation** of the world, not to mention the possibility of **revelation** or **miracles**. Furthermore, it raises hard questions about **free will**, moral accountability and divine reward and punishment. Anticipating David Hume's critique of causality by virtually seven centuries, the **Ash'arite** theologian **al-Ghazali** attacked the philosophers by arguing that it is impossible to demonstrate a necessary causal relation between natural events. One can certainly observe a repeated concomitance between two events, but this does not establish that one necessitates the other. Al-Ghazali articulated an alternative metaphysics of possibility, in which all things are the direct effect of God's free will and thus can always be other than they are. His so-called 'occasionalism' preserves God's freedom and omnipotence but, as **Ibn Rushd** and modern philosophers such as Muhammad '**Abduh** have argued, it also undermines the very possibility of **science**, since it rejects the idea that there is any real intelligible order or regularity hard-wired into nature (at best, it is simply a provisional function of divine habit or custom). Similarly, al-Ghazali recontextualizes the question of free will and moral accountability without adequately resolving it. For insofar as every event – human choices and actions included – is the effect of God's will, human agency seems subsumed if not obliterated by divine omnipotence. Ibn Rushd's reply to al-Ghazali pointed towards a purely Aristotelian conception of causality stripped of problematic Neoplatonic innovations, but by then the tide had turned against the philosophers.

See **Aristotle; free will and predestination; al-Ghazali; Ibn Rushd; Ibn Sina; Neoplatonism; occasionalism; science**

Further reading: al-Ash'ari 1953; Fakhry 1958; al-Ghazali 1997/2000; Goodman 1992a/2006; Ibn Rushd

1954/78; Ibn Sina 2005; Kogan 1985; Marmura 2005; Watt 1948; Wisnovsky 2003

creation vs. eternity of the world: A leading controversy in Islamic **philosophy** during its earliest few centuries concerned the status of the world as either created (*huduth*) or eternal (*qidam*). **Aristotle** had argued that the world should be regarded as eternal, since for him time is a function of motion, and before the world was created there was no motion, since motion requires a world to take place in. Since there is no motion, there is no time, and accordingly no time at which the world was created. Moreover, on the **Neoplatonic** developments of this theory the process of creation seems to be itself eternal, since the world exists as a result of a continuous **emanation** from the highest levels of reality down to this world, and there is no sense in asking the question when the process started. Most of the **Peripatetic** thinkers thus argued for the eternity of the world, and argued that it was co-eternal with **God**. The major exception was **al-Kindi**, who argues that there are no logical difficulties in accepting that God created the world at a particular time. His successors, though, such as **al-Farabi, Ibn Sina** and **Ibn Rushd**, all defended the eternity doctrine in one form or another.

One of the most strident critics of the eternity thesis was **al-Ghazali**, who attacked it on logical grounds, and pointed out that were the thesis to be valid then God really has a remote connection with the world. It cannot be that he created it when he wished to, nor even in the way he wished it to be. Yet this, al-Ghazali suggests, is very different from the Qur'anic account and gives God very little to do with respect to the world. Ibn Rushd countered by arguing that if the world was worth creating, and if God could always have created it, as He could due to His omnipotence, then why would He wait? We have to wait before bringing things about since we are weak and imperfect creatures, but God is very different and has no need to wait. So He would always have created the world, and that means that the world is eternal. Ibn Rushd acknowledged the significance of this debate, returning to it time and time again.

See al-Ghazali; God (also: arguments for the existence of); Ibn Rushd; Ibn Sina; metaphysics; Mulla Sadra; Neoplatonism

Further reading: Davidson 1987; Leaman 1999, 1985/ 2002

D

al-Dawani (or al-Dawwani), Jalal al-Din (830–908/ 1426–1502): Al-Dawani is most famous for his Persian ethical treatise, Lustres of Illumination on the Noble Virtues (Lawami' al-ishraq fi makarim al-akhlaq), more commonly known as the Jalalean Ethics (Akhlaq-i Jalali). Ironically this work, which is closely modeled on al-Tusi's more substantial and original Nasirean Ethics (itself an extension of Miskawayh's Refinement of Character, which in turn took Yahya ibn 'Adi's work of the same name as its template), does not really constitute al-Dawani's most important contribution to the Islamic philosophical tradition. Arguably, it is in his commentarial writings as a representative of the School of Shiraz, e.g. The Shapes of the Houris in Commentary on [al-Suhrawardi's] Temple of Light (Shawakil al-hur fi shahr Hayakil al-nur) and a supercommentary on al-Tusi's Abstract of Theology (Tajrid al-kalam), that his unique significance emerges. For commentaries of this sort were the dominant vehicle for philosophical work at that time and it is there that one sees most clearly his pivotal role as one of the first thinkers to blend the two great competing currents of Islamic philosophy: **Illuminationist** (*ishraqi*) and **Peripatetic** (*mashsha'i*) thought. In this respect, he might be seen as a kind of 'godfather' of the School of Isfahan, which would forge a robust new synthesis from the *mashsha'i*, *ishraqi*, **Sufi** and **Shi'ite** traditions.

Of particular importance is the ongoing debate he had with other seminal figures in the School of Shiraz, Sadr al-Din al-Dashtaki and his son Ghiyath al-Din. Both were Illuminationists who espoused a kind of radical essentialism that went far beyond al-Suhrawardi's famed insistence upon the **primacy of essence**. On al-Suhrawardi's position, **existence** as a generality is simply a mental abstraction, with no extramental reality at all. The Dashtakis pushed this conclusion a step further, arguing that existence did not even possess mental reality. Al-Dawani defended a position whose roots can be traced back through Fakhr al-Din **al-Razi** (and arguably to **Ibn Sina** himself, insofar as the 'modern' **Ash'arites** like al-Razi basically adopted a moderately Avicennan stance on the question of **essence and existence**). On his account, existence does have external or extramental reality, albeit as something singular, simple, undifferentiated and necessary – that is to say, **God**. It is individual entities that are not extramentally real; they are rather only contingent parts of existence conceived by the mind. The reality of the external world is thus made possible only by essences or quiddities. In this way, al-Dawani tempers Illuminationist essentialism, pushing it closer to an Avicennan model. This kind of compromise would in turn influence **Mir Damad**, who founded the School of Isfahan, but be subsequently rejected by **Mulla Sadra**, who formulated a more radical version of the **primacy of existence**.

See **Ibn Sina; Illuminationism; Mir Damad; al-Razi (Fakhr al-Din); al-Suhrawardi; al-Tusi**
Further reading: al-Dawani 1839/1977; Nasr 2006

demonstration (*burhan*): see **logic**

dhawq (mystical experience, lit. 'taste'): see **al-Ghazali**

dialectic (*jadal*): see **logic**

dissimulation (*taqiyya*): see **Twelver Shi'ites**

double truth: see **Ibn Rushd**

E

Eastern philosophy (*al-hikmat al-mashriqiyya*): In addition to his classic Aristotelian or **Peripatetic** (*mashsha'i*) works, **Ibn Sina** composed a small number of texts which he suggestively described as his 'Eastern philosophy' or 'Oriental wisdom'. The two most important of these works, *The Easterners* (*al-Mashriqiyyun*) and *The Fair Judgement* (*al-Insaf*), are no longer entirely extant. Of the former, only the introduction and the '**Logic**' (and possibly the 'Physics') remain; of the latter, all we now possess is a commentary on Book Lambda of Aristotle's *Metaphysics* and a partial recension of '**Aristotle**'s' *Theology* (i.e. Plotinus' *Enneads*). Other relevant texts are (1) the Prologue to *The Healing* (*al-Shifa'*), where Ibn Sina refers to *The Easterners* and describes its relation to his Peripatetic works, (2) his marginal notes on Aristotle's *De anima*, (3) his trilogy of 'visionary recitals', or initiatory allegories (i.e. *Living, Son of Awake* [*Hayy ibn Yaqzan*], *The Treatise of the Bird* [*Risalat al-tayr*] and

Salaman and Absal [*Salaman wa Absal*]), and possibly (4) the last portion of his encyclopedic *Remarks and Admonitions* (*Isharat wa al-tanbihat*), which deals with **Sufi mysticism**.

Over the last century, there has been considerable scholarly disagreement as to the precise nature of Ibn Sina's Eastern philosophy. According to one view (traceable to **Ibn Tufayl** and championed most recently by Henri Corbin and Seyyed Hossein **Nasr**), it constitutes an alternative, indigenous, esoteric and mystical system in which **philosophy** is re-envisioned as a kind of **wisdom** or **gnosis** (*'irfan*) and the cosmos is seen not just as an external object of theoretical understanding, but rather as a symbolic, interiorized reality to be experienced. According to this interpretation, Ibn Sina's Eastern philosophy is intended to supplement and even supersede his more rationalistic Peripatetic system, a system which is still true (so far as it goes), but ultimately limited and incomplete. Insofar as it infuses philosophy with Sufi mysticism and grants epistemological priority to intuition (*hads*), Ibn Sina's Eastern philosophy can be understood as a forerunner of the school of **Illumination** (*ishraq*), which would come to dominate Islamic philosophy after the decline of the Peripatetic school. This is indeed the way numerous Persian Illuminationist thinkers (from **al-Suhrawardi** to **Mulla Sadra** and beyond) understood their own relation to their predecessor. The etymological connections between *al-mashriq* (the East) and *al-ishraq* (illumination, light) made the family resemblance between these two philosophies seem even more natural (they share the same trilateral root, *sh-r-q*, which has to do with the rising or shining of the sun). Advocates of this view argue that Ibn Sina's place in the later history of Islamic philosophy is unintelligible if he is read simply as a Peripatetic *faylasuf* and not also as a proto-*ishraqi*.

Another major view, espoused most recently and force-fully by Dimitri Gutas, maintains that all this is predi-cated on a somewhat fanciful misreading of what Ibn Sina himself actually says. Viewing the history of knowl-edge in a developmental way, Ibn Sina strongly believed in the possibility of intellectual progress beyond one's predecessors, and made no bones about the ways in which he had revised and improved **Aristotle**'s system. The 'Eastern' philosophy refers not to some esoteric, indigenous alternative to western (i.e. Greek) thought, but simply the Khurasani school of Peripatetic philoso-phy (Ibn Sina hailed from the eastern part of the Islamic world). Nor does the philosophy of the 'Eastern' texts differ in any essential way from the philosophy set forth in his Peripatetic texts. Most crucially, it retains both the notion of the **active intellect**, which was a key Peripatetic idea, and the notion of intuition (*hads*), which, far from signifying some kind of super-rational mystical insight, has to do with the rational soul's ability to hit upon the middle term of a syllogism. Further, Ibn Sina acknowl-edges the epistemological legitimacy of Sufi gnosis (from the standpoint of a sympathetic outsider) in the *Remarks and Admonitions*, a text that belongs to his Peripatetic oeuvre. The main difference between his Peripatetic and Eastern works, as Ibn Sina himself suggests in the Prologue to *The Healing*, is their intended audience and manner of presentation: while his Peripatetic works offer a more involved, technical and comprehensive treatment of topics (addressing all the requisite traditional issues and pausing to consider and refute competing views), the Eastern texts simply opt for a more straightforward, sys-tematic and pithy presentation of Ibn Sina's own views, unencumbered by the usual scholarly apparatus.

Lacking the requisite texts, it is doubtful that this con-troversy will ever be settled to everyone's satisfaction.

See **Ibn Sina**; **Ibn Tufayl**; **Illuminationism**; **mysticism**;
Nasr (Seyyed Hossein); **Sufism**
Further reading: Corbin 1960/80; Gutas 1988; Ibn
Tufayl 1972/2003; Nasr 1964/93; Nasr with Aminrazavi
1999; Pines 1995

emanation (*fayd*, lit. '[over]flowing'): see **Neoplatonism**

epistemology: Words directly meaning knowledge or *'ilm*
appear twenty-seven times in the **Qur'an**, and *'alim*
(knower) 140 times. There are 704 references in the book
to words that come from *'ilm*. In addition, references to
knowledge such as the book, pen, ink and so on occur
very often, and the text itself starts with the phrase *iqra*
or 'read/recite', something that involves knowledge. The
first human being Adam was taught all the names of
things in the world, and the text frequently calls on its
readers and hearers to reflect on what they are told, to
consider how reasonable it is, whether it seems true and
so on, so knowledge is a constant theme in the text. A different term for knowledge, *ma'rifa*, is used to represent
mystical or hidden and deeper knowledge, knowledge
more like *hikma* (**wisdom**) and higher than *'aql* (**reason**),
and is popular in **Sufism**.

Al-Ghazali in his Sufi phase talks of three levels of
knowledge that correspond with three levels of faith.
The faith of the ordinary people is based on imitation
or **obedience** (*taqlid*); the faith of the theologians is based
on reason; and the faith of the mystics (*'arifin*) and saints
(*awliya'*) is based on the light of certainty (*nur al-yaqin*).

A basic distinction in **Peripatetic** epistemology exists
between *tasawwur* (conceptualization) and *tasdiq* (assent).
Conceptualization describes the way in which the
mind grasps particular essences or beings. Assent is the
act of the **intellect** which makes a judgement in terms of

truth value. To assent to anything we must first be able to form a concept of it, but the reverse is not the case, since we can have an idea about something without making any truth claim about it. We have experiences and combine them to bring out what they have in common, and our mind then forms an abstract idea that raises them from their material context. The **imagination** is both abstract and particular, it stretches our experience but also needs that experience to get started. The mind comes into contact with the **active intellect**, the source of our abstract ideas. Our mind moves from potentially knowing something to actually knowing it, and from actuality to reflection on that actuality, which the Peripatetics classified in terms of potential intellect, actual or agent intellect and acquired intellect. The last is called 'acquired' because it borrows ideas from higher celestial realms of existence, ideas that are not derived from experience at all.

Al-Farabi and **Ibn Rushd** argue that the mind is only eternal insofar as it has for its subject matter eternal objects, i.e. the abstract. **Ibn Sina** argues that the mind must be eternal as such since unless it was eternal in the first place it could not comprehend eternal objects, based on the same principle that the knower and the object of knowledge must be the same for knowledge to be possible.

See **active intellect**; **Ibn Sina**; **Illuminationism**; **logic**; **psychology**; **rationalism**; **science**; **Sufism**

Further reading: Davidson 1992; Ha'iri Yazdi 1992; Leaman 1999; Rosenthal 1970; Wan Daud 1989

esoteric/inner meaning (*batin*): see **Batinites**; **Isma'ilis**

essence and existence: **Ibn Sina** argued that existence (*wujud*) is secondary to essence (*mahiyya*, lit. 'whatness' or quiddity), because we can think about something and it need not exist. In any case, everything that exists only comes into existence because it is brought into existence by something else, with the exception of the ultimate existent, **God,** who is the only **Necessary Existent.** Many things might exist; they have essences or concepts that describe them, but unless something moves them from potential to actual existence, they will remain just ideas. So essence precedes existence. This view was disputed by **Ibn Rushd,** who argued that in an eternal universe anything that could exist would and indeed must exist, and the existence of a thing is not just a property added to it, but is a basic part of its meaning. **Al-Suhrawardi** suggested that if existence is just a property a thing has then essence or the concept would have to exist before the property was applied to it in order for it to be an essence, which leads to an infinite regress. So essence precedes existence since the latter is only an idea with no reality attached to it, whereas essence is real. This position is referred to as the **primacy of essence** (*asalat al-mahiyya*). **Mulla Sadra** argued against al-Suhrawardi that existence is more real than essence. This is because existence is a necessary aspect of what it is for something to exist and so there is no regress in regarding the concept as an attribute. Reality is existence, differentiated in a variety of ways, and these different ways look to us like essences. What first affects us are things that exist, and we form ideas of essences afterwards, so existence precedes essence. This position is referred to as the **primacy of existence** (*asalat al-wujud*).

The debate has implications for the nature of philosophy. For Ibn Sina and al-Suhrawardi, **philosophy** is the study of the essences or ideas of things, while for Ibn Rushd and Mulla Sadra, philosophy is a study of existing things. Ibn Rushd criticizes the doctrine of essentialism since it implies that something has to come from elsewhere to bring it to existence, and so the universe requires an external force to activate it. An essentialist uses thought experiments in philosophy, since the **imagination** can rule on what ideas are possible or otherwise. But for Ibn Rushd definitions are the basis of **knowledge,** not our imagination, and using the latter really does not tell us much about what is possible or otherwise.

See **al-Dawani; Ibn Rushd; Ibn Sina; metaphysics; Mir Damad; Mulla Sadra; al-Razi (Fakhr al-Din); al-Suhrawardi**

Further reading: Leaman 1997; Morewedge 1982; Nasr 1989

eternity (*qidam*): see **creation vs. eternity of the world**

ethics (*akhlaq*): There was a heated debate in Islamic **theology** between the **Ash'arites** and the **Mu'tazilites** over the nature of ethics, harking back to the Euthyphro problem of whether the good is what it is because of **God**'s commands, or whether God's commands are as they are because they are good. The Mu'tazilites argued that ethics is objective and so God has no alternative but to recommend the good and forbid the evil in the way that he does. The principles of justice represent how we ought to act, and God follows them in telling us what to do. For the Ash'arites this goes against God's freedom to do exactly what he wants, and for them He is entirely unlimited in what He can do, what He can demand we do and how He punishes or rewards us. The debate extended into the nature of the **afterlife** and whether our fate there was determined by our behavior during this life, or whether it was entirely up to God. The Ash'arites and **al-Ghazali** argued that God can do anything He likes on the Day of Judgement, and is not obliged to adhere to any objective sets of standards.

Two important works for ethics were the *Republic* of **Plato** and **Aristotle**'s *Nicomachean Ethics*. These texts dealt with the definition of justice and a virtuous society, and the idea of virtue as a mean. Both concepts were applied to an Islamic context, and the emphasis in the **Qur'an** on patience and moderation was seen as fitting in nicely with definitions of virtue as a mean. A perfect society could be seen as run by philosophers, as with Plato, who combined their intellectual skill with those of a religious authority or leader. **Religion** is seen as a way of explaining theoretical truths to everyone in the community, regardless of their background or intellect, and this applies particularly to morality. Most people would not be able to work out how to behave on the basis of their own **reason**, unlike the philosophers, and require the vivid and imaginative **language** of religion to inform them of their duties and why they should carry them out. Without this, they will not be able to perfect their natures to whatever extent possible and thus achieve happiness (*sa'ada*). **Al-Farabi** developed a highly influential theory of language according to which **philosophy** and religion both express the same truths, albeit in different ways. The philosopher appeals to human reason, religion to our emotions, and so the latter tends to use more material ideas than the former, since we are material creatures and regard that as the most important aspect of our lives. Both the ordinary member of the community and the philosopher can know their duties and be happy, but they will come to it in different ways. The discussion in Aristotle of the claims of different lifestyles as the best such as the contemplative, social, animal and so on was linked with the **Qur'an**. The book was seen as presenting just one desirable lifestyle for everyone, albeit one that could be understood in different ways by different people.

Many complex accounts of the moral personality were produced by thinkers such as **Miskawayh**, **al-Tusi** and al-Isfahani. They often employed both Greek ideas and themes from the Qur'an to develop close analyses of particular moral dispositions. Intriguingly, even the enemies of philosophy such as al-Ghazali acknowledged that there was no dispute between the philosophers and their opponents on what moral behavior actually was, only how it should be understood theoretically.

See 'Abduh (Muhammad); *adab*; Ash'arites; al-Farabi; free will and predestination; God (imitation of); Miskawayh; Mu'tazilites; political philosophy; al-Razi (Abu Bakr)

Further reading: Butterworth 1992; Fakhry 1991; Hourani 1985; Lerner and Mahdi 1963

existence (*wujud, anniya*): see essence and existence; Ibn Sina; metaphysics

F

falasifa (Greek-influenced philosophers): see philosophy

al-Farabi, Abu Nasr (c. 257–337/870–950): Dubbed the 'Second Teacher' (after Aristotle), al-Farabi is a crucial early figure who set the stage for much subsequent Islamic philosophy, specifically that of the influential Peripatetic (*mashsha'i*) school. He was held in particularly high esteem for his logical writings (both commentaries on Aristotle's *Organon*, as well as independent treatises) and credited with the codification and establishment of logic in the Arabic-speaking world as a science independent of grammar. In the field of metaphysics, al-Farabi is traditionally credited with drawing two crucial ontological distinctions – that between essence and existence, and that between possible and necessary existence – which would become a basic presupposition of Islamic metaphysicians (most notably **Ibn Sina**, and through him, Christian thinkers such as Aquinas). He articulated a complex and influential **Neoplatonic** emanationist cosmology as well, one in which the nature of **God** (as an absolutely unitary, necessary being) overflows in its superabundance, giving rise to a chain of successively dependent 'intellects' which ultimately generate our contingent physical cosmos of change and multiplicity. Particularly innovative was the way he fit Aristotle's concept of the *nous poietikos* into this scheme, linking the human intellect to the divine. The 'active intellect', which al-Farabi identified as the tenth and final intellect in his hierarchy of being, plays the role of (1) providing form to the sublunary sphere and actualizing human intellect, (2) making possible the soul's **immortality** (although al-Farabi's position on this question is ultimately ambiguous), and (3) explaining the phenomenon of **prophecy**. Al-Farabi is perhaps best known for his works on **political philosophy**, such as *The Virtuous City* (*Madinat al-fadila*), *The Political Regime* (*al-Siyasa al-madaniyya*) and *The Attainment of Happiness* (*Tahsil al-sa'ada*). He follows **Plato** in positing the necessary coincidence of political power and **philosophy** as a condition for the **happiness** of the city, while reshaping this teaching to address the new realities of **Islam**. For al-Farabi, the *true* philosopher must not only be knowledgeable and virtuous, but also a prudential political legislator and spiritual leader (**imam**), which means that he must be capable of taking complex philosophical truths and conveying them to the multitude via colorful images and persuasive speech. This is in fact the role of **religion**: an 'image' of philosophy, it nonetheless provides true belief – and thus happiness – to all, according to their capacity. In this way al-Farabi stressed the compatibility of Islam with the philosophy of Plato and Aristotle (which he also understood as forming a harmonious unity); however, unlike his predecessor **al-Kindi**, al-Farabi ultimately emphasized the primacy of **reason** over **revelation**.

See **active intellect; afterlife; Aristotle; essence and existence; language; logic; metaphysics; Neoplatonism; philosophy; Plato; political philosophy; prophecy; psychology; Qur'an**

Further reading: Colmo 2005; Fakhry 2002; al-Farabi 1963, 1969/2002, 1973, 1985, 2001; Galston 1990; Mahdi 2001; Netton 1989/95, 1992/99; Parens 2006; Strauss 1945/77

floating man argument: An argument that **Ibn Sina** makes to prove the substantiality of the **soul**. He calls upon the reader to enter into an introspective thought experiment, whereby we are to imagine a human being who has suddenly come into being, fully developed and perfectly formed, but bereft of any sensory experience of the world or even of his own body (the man is floating in space, with shrouded vision and no physical contact). Ibn Sina argues that such a being would nonetheless be conscious of his own **existence**; i.e. that the soul has a reflexive, unmediated knowledge of itself (and more generally, a prelinguistic awareness of being). Since the existence of self as consciousness/soul is conceivable without any awareness of the body, it must be separable from, and ontologically independent of, the body. As numerous modern commentators have pointed out, Ibn Sina's thought experiment anticipates Descartes' *cogito* argument in drawing attention to the indubitable, and thus foundational, fact of one's own existence as a thinking thing.

See **afterlife; epistemology; Ibn Sina; Illuminationism; psychology; al-Suhrawardi**

Further reading: Goodman 1992a/2006; Ibn Sina 1952/81; Marmura 2005; Wisnovsky 2001

freethinking (*zandaqa*): In Muslim heresiology, a sort of malleable gray zone between **innovation** and **unbelief**. **Al-Shahrastani** characterizes it in terms of 'the exclusive, willful use of [personal] opinion' (*al-istibdad bi al-ra'y*) rather than reliance upon **revelation**. He accordingly lumps all philosophers together under this rubric, along with Hindus, Sabeans and adherents of pre-Islamic Arab religions. More specifically, freethinking might be defined as independent thinking within an Islamicate context which (1) relies upon natural **reason** alone as a means to reach the truth, and (2) rejects the authority and veracity of revelation, **prophecy** and tradition. A freethinker may or may not reject the existence of **God**. Freethinkers are traditionally perceived as more radical and pernicious than garden-variety heretics, because of their skeptical and even hostile attitude towards revealed **religion**. However, although they often appear to fall outside the bounds of **Islam** altogether, they are not exactly unbelievers, at least in any strict sense. While the category of unbelief traditionally refers to non-Muslims (i.e. those who are members of some other tradition, religious or otherwise), the phenomenon of freethinking is deeply rooted in the Islamicate context and inextricably bound up with the religion of Islam, if only in an antagonistic way.

See **belief; Ibn al-Rawandi; Islam; prophecy; rationalism; al-Razi (Abu Bakr)**

Further reading: Stroumsa 1999

free will and predestination: The tension between human free will and **God's** predestination is a thorny issue in the Islamic tradition. Although one can find prominent strains of fatalism in pre-Islamic thought, concepts such as *dahr* or *zaman* ('time', which inexorably determines the general contours of each individual's fate), *aqdar* (the blind 'decrees' or 'powers' that impose upon human beings the myriad details of life that are beyond their control) and *qisma* (initially 'portion' or 'allotment', later 'destiny' or 'kismet') are not explicitly at odds with the idea of human agency and responsibility, since not all events were believed to be predetermined by these impersonal forces.

The problem first emerges in the context of early theological debates. Drawing on selective passages from the **Qur'an** and *hadith* that emphasized God's foreknowledge (and indeed preordinance) of all events, as well as His omnipotence, the **traditionalist Jabrites** upheld the doctrine of divine 'compulsion' (*jabr*), claiming that all events are ultimately determined by God's decree (*qadar*, lit. 'measure' or 'determination'). Their conclusion – that it is God alone who acts and that human beings have no power over their choices and actions – was strenuously rejected by another early theological movement, the **Qadarites,** who (in spite of their misleading name) upheld the centrality of human free will (*tafwid*, lit. 'delegation'). Not wanting to attribute evil to the Creator, they argued that God had endowed human beings with the capacity to choose between good and evil. Their main contention was that God could not justifiably expect us to do good and avoid evil unless it were genuinely within our power to do so. Although the Qadarites denied God's preordinance (and arguably, His omnipotence), many nonetheless admitted divine foreknowledge, maintaining that God foresees our actions before we perform them but does not cause them.

The **Mu'tazilites** took up the Qadarites' defense of human agency. On their view, God's perfect justice requires that the human beings He rewards and punishes be genuinely accountable and thus deserving of whatever fate is meted out to them. He thus has created a power (*qudra*) in human beings, endowing us with free will (*ikhtiyar*, lit. 'choice'), so that we can truly be said to be the 'inventors' or 'creators' of our own actions. The more traditional-minded **Ash'arites** were aghast at the Mu'tazilites' attempt to justify God in the eyes of human **reason**. They emphasized God's omnipotence rather than His justice, and formulated an **occasionalist metaphysics** in which God is the direct perpetual **cause** or creator of everything that occurs, whether good or bad – including the acts of human beings. Everything is fixed by God's eternal decree and its existential determination in time (*al-qada' wa al-qadar*). As it stands, this view appears to undermine the ontological basis of free will and thus human responsibility, but the Ash'arite theologians experimented with various subtle distinctions and qualifications in order to strike a mean between the two 'extremes' of Jabrism and Qadarism-Mu'tazilism. One influential attempt was the theory of 'acquisition' (*kasb, iktisab*), according to which God repeatedly creates in human beings the capacity (*istita'a*) to act. Our actions are thus created by God but performed by us. Yet even on this view, the nature of human agency and responsibility remains unclear. The question is whether there can be a real agent other than God. If not, can anyone other than God justifiably be held responsible for their actions?

Philosophers (particularly the **Aristotelian** school) recast the problem of free will and predestination in the guise of causal determinism. Taking up a **Neoplatonic** emanationist model of reality, they posited a universal causal sequence in which effects followed necessarily from their determining causes as if by logical entailment. This **logic** of **emanation** was typically associated with God's eternal **knowledge** or providence, neither of which left much room for human – let alone divine – freedom. The philosophers still spoke frequently of the power of spontaneous choice or deliberation (*ikhtiyar*); however, the idea is relatively naturalized. For **Ibn Sina,** choice can be a function of the lower (concupiscent and irascible) as well as higher (intellectual) faculties. It applies to the estimative faculties of animals as well as to the rational deliberations of human beings, both of whom are equally subject to universal causal necessity. In **al-Kindi,** it is even applied to the celestial spheres' obedience to God. In short, the notion of free choice in classical philosophical discourse typically retains little metaphysical, psychological or ethical weight. One might even say it becomes more of an epistemological affair, inasmuch as it ultimately has more to do with knowledge than with the unconditioned power of the will.

Al-Ghazali, unsatisfied with the existential determinism of the philosophers as well as his Ash'arite predecessors' occasionalism, put forth a new synthesis of the two. Although he rejected Ibn Sina's necessitarian **metaphysics,** he retained the idea that human choice is determined to some extent by the judgement of the **intellect.** Appropriating the Ash'arite notion of divine omnipotence, he argued that God is unlike creatures in this respect, in that His will is not constrained or determined by any motive or end for the sake of which he acts. Consequently freedom in the absolute, unqualified sense is reserved for God alone. It is not uncommon for subsequent philosophers (ranging from **Ibn Rushd** to Muhammad **'Abduh**) to maintain both God's causal centrality and human free will, without pretending entirely to resolve the tension between these two fundamental ideas.

See **Ash'arites; causality; al-Ghazali; God; Ibn Sina; Jabrites; Mu'tazilites; Neoplatonism; Qadarites**

Further reading: Burrell 1993; Goodman 1992a/2006; Ibn Sina 1985; Marmura 2005; Watt 1948

fundamentalism: see Islamism

Gersonides: see Levi ben Gerson

al-Ghazali (alternatively, al-Ghazzali), Abu Hamid (450–505/
1058–1111): Theologian, jurist, philosopher and Sufi
mystic, al-Ghazali is a towering figure in the history of
Islam and a pivotal thinker within its philosophical tradition. He is often blamed – somewhat hyperbolically – for
bringing Islamic philosophy to an untimely end. Born in
Tus, the Persian al-Ghazali studied with the great Ash'arite
theologian al-Juwayni and spent his early adult years lec-
turing on Islamic jurisprudence and refuting heresies at the
prestigious Nizamiyya *madrasa* in Baghdad. During
this productive period he wrote *The Intentions of the
Philosophers* (*Maqasid al-falasifa*), which offered a clear,
accurate exposition of the *mashsha'i* or Peripatetic
philosophers (first and foremost, Ibn Sina). This was soon
followed by his monumentally important *Incoherence of
the Philosophers* (*Tahafut al-falasifa*), which critiqued
twenty of their most problematic claims. According to al-
Ghazali, three philosophical theses in particular were
odious enough to qualify as instances of unbelief (*kufr*): (1)
the assertion of the pre-eternity of the world, (2) the claim
that God knows the temporal entities and events of this
world only as universals and not as particulars, and (3) the
denial of bodily resurrection. Not content to play the role
of the dogmatic Ash'arite theologian, however, al-Ghazali
went far beyond mere denunciation to refute the claims of
the Peripatetic philosophers in accordance with their own
intellectual commitments and preferred methods of proof.
On the first thesis, he points up various contradictions

generated by the eternalist model and argues for the conceptual possibility of the world's creation. On the second, he attempts to show that, contra the philosophers, God *can* have complete **knowledge** of temporal things without Himself being subject to change and multiplicity. On the third, he demonstrates that the much-vaunted principle of **causality** (which undergirded the philosophers' rejection of bodily resurrection) is in fact much less certain than they believe. Contrary to the **Aristotelian-Neoplatonic** conception of causality, al-Ghazali argues that there is no good reason for positing a necessary relation between 'cause' and 'effect' because the most we can actually establish is their repeated concomitance. Drawing upon Ash'arite **occasionalism**, according to which God is the only real cause of all events, he shows that the seemingly iron-clad regularity of natural events is not a function of necessity, but rather benevolent divine habit or custom, which God in His omnipotence is always free to abrogate, making miracles possible. The overall strategy of the *Incoherence* is thus to show that the philosophers continually fail to fulfill the conditions for demonstrative proof that they themselves stipulate in their logical works, and that the orthodox religious views al-Ghazali sought to defend are not decisively excluded by **reason**. Subsequent works on Aristotelian **logic** clarified this critique and closed the deal: the philosophers talked a good game, but were ultimately incapable of demonstrating the conclusions about which they seemed so confident and certain.

Al-Ghazali's intervention had wide-ranging, complementary consequences. On the one hand, it effectively dealt a death blow, if not to Islamic philosophy as such, then at least to Greek-inflected *falsafa* within the **Sunni** world (**Ibn Rushd**'s defense, though powerful and resourceful, never achieved anything close to a comparable influence in the East). At the same time, however, al-Ghazali's protracted engagement with the ideas and argumentative strategies of the philosophers left an indelible impression on his own thought, as well as on subsequent Ash'arite theologians, whose works became increasingly philosophical in content and method. Thus one might say that his attack on **philosophy** gave it a new lease on life, albeit in a rather unlikely place.

After four years of teaching in Baghdad, al-Ghazali underwent a profound spiritual crisis that led him to question the validity of both sense experience and reason and even temporarily rendered him unable to speak. He renounced his academic career and worldly ambitions and became a wandering Sufi before finally returning home, a development that is vividly portrayed in his spiritual autobiography, *The Deliverance from Error* (*al-Munqidh min al-dalal*). In this work al-Ghazali details his quest for certain knowledge of the truth about reality, which led him from theology to philosophy to the esotericism of the **Isma'ilis** to Sufi **mysticism**. It is only through the direct, intimate, experiential knowledge of the mystics (i.e. *dhawq*, lit. 'taste'), he concludes, that one can attain certain knowledge. Like his earlier engagement with philosophy, al-Ghazali's mystical turn had wide-ranging and complementary effects. On the one hand, his sober, responsible appropriation of **Sufism** made mysticism respectable in the eyes of orthodox **traditionalists**; on the other, it helped to revitalize the stultified Islam of his time. Al-Ghazali's magnum opus, *Revival of the Religious Sciences* (*Ihya' 'ulum al-din*) exemplifies this mutual enrichment.

See **Ash'arites**; **belief**; **causality**; **God** (also: **God's knowledge**); **Ibn Rushd**; **Ibn Sina**; **mysticism**; **occasionalism**; **philosophy**; **Sufism**; **theology**

Further reading: Frank 1994; al-Ghazali 1980/2004 1997/2000; Leaman 1985/2002; Marmura 2005; Shehadi 1964; Watt 1963

gnosis (*'irfan, ma'rifa*):   see **epistemology; Ibn al-'Arabi; mysticism; Sufism**

God (*Allah*):   The rich, impressionistic portrait of God that emerges in the **Qur'an** looms large over all subsequent discussions of the divine within the Islamic tradition. There Allah is pictured as absolutely unitary and unique, the one true reality and the ultimate source of all value, as well as the creator, sustainer and sovereign of everything that exists. This anticipates later philosophical concepts of the divine, as do the traditional Qur'anic attributes of eternity, omnipotence and omniscience. But the God of the Qur'an is no mere abstract explanatory principle; He is a person in the most robust sense, and His great character comes across powerfully through the many 'beautiful names' attributed to Him in the Qur'an: He is living, willing, hearing, seeing, speaking, grand, majestic, terrible, sometimes even haughty, but also just, merciful, generous, patient, etc. In spite of His radical otherness and **transcendence**, He is also intimately concerned with the affairs of His creatures and intervenes when necessary in the course of human history. The most important of these miraculous interventions is the revelation of the Qur'an itself, which sets forth the divine **law** according to which human beings should live and according to which they will ultimately be judged and rewarded or punished.

The *kalam* theologians attempted to defend and clarify this revealed idea of God by means of **reason**. They thus offered a more systematic, philosophical reconstruction of the poetic portrait found in the Qur'an, albeit one still deeply rooted in, and answerable to, **revelation**. The two major theological schools, the **Mu'tazilites** and the **Ash'arites**, both followed scripture in maintaining a *creatio ex nihilo* cosmology, as well as the world's radical contingency upon God. However, they emphasized diverse aspects of the Qur'anic portrait. The Mu'tazilites privileged God's transcendent **unity** and justice above all else, interpreting the Qur'an's **anthropomorphic** verses figuratively, denying the existence of God's **attributes** as something distinct from His unitary essence, and insisting upon the power of **free will** in human beings. The Ash'arites' particular *idées fixes* were divine omnipotence and freedom: while remaining cautiously agnostic about the true significance of the Qur'an's anthropomorphic descriptions, they posited God as a radically free agent – the only real agent, in fact – and fashioned an **occasionalist metaphysics** which eliminated horizontal **causality** altogether, casting all events (even human choice and volition) as the direct effect of God's will.

The **Isma'ilis** furthered the theologians' move away from a personalized conception of the Divine towards the increasingly abstract and intellectual. They adopted the Mu'tazilites' **rationalism** and penchant for allegorical **interpretation**, as well as their obsession with God's absolute transcendence, infusing it with a **Neoplatonic** emanationist metaphysics. From this matrix they developed a negative **theology** of sorts, which recast the divine attributes as hypostases or emanations, while maintaining the inscrutable mystery of God Himself. The ultimate unknowability of God would remain a common theme among many philosophers and mystics.

The Hellenistic *falasifa* creatively appropriated Neoplatonic emanationism as well, along with **Aristotle**'s metaphysics/theology. They cast God variously as the Unmoved Mover, First Cause and **Necessary Existent**, i.e. the self-sufficient ontological ground of the universe which sustains all otherwise merely possible beings. According to this account, God and the created universe are co-eternal, the latter arising necessarily and automatically through

God's nature, rather than having been created *ex nihilo* through an act of divine free choice. Further, the God of the philosophers seemed to have no interest in – nor any real epistemological access to – the concrete particularities of human history. The *falasifa* claimed that their demonstrative arguments had revealed the true import of the Qur'an's revelations, stripped of their figurative garb, and that the truths of **philosophy** and **religion** were essentially in harmony. **Traditionalists** remained unconvinced, however, denouncing the philosophers' conclusions as a heretical departure from the implicit theology of the Qur'an. And yet one could argue that the worldview of the philosophers was in its own way just as theocentric as that of the Qur'an and the theologians: for them, knowledge of God constituted the apex and culmination of metaphysics or knowledge of 'divine things' (*ilahiyyat*), the most difficult and important of all sciences. They touted its conclusions as therapeutic and even soteriological, effecting the transformation, actualization and perfection of the human **soul**.

If the philosophers tempered and even rejected the Qur'an's personalistic conception of God, the **Sufi** mystics embraced it wholeheartedly. Without necessarily denying the veracity of the philosophers' theoretical claims, they set aside discursive reasoning and focused instead on achieving an intimate, first-person experiential knowledge of God by means of various spiritual practices. Although the content of such mystical experiences is by definition ineffable and incommunicable, they were often interpreted as disclosing some kind of fundamental **unity** with the Divine in which created things have no real ontological density apart from the existence of God (e.g. the '**oneness of existence**'). The school of **Illumination** (*ishraq*) articulated their own particular version of this monistic ontology, casting God as the 'Light of Lights' and all created beings as continuous and co-eternal with the divine, insofar as they receive luminosity from this one original source.

See causality; creation vs. eternity of the world; free will and predestination; God (anthropomorphic descriptions of; arguments for the existence of; attributes of; unity of); Illuminationism; Isma'ilis; Neoplatonism; occasionalism; philosophy; Qur'an; Sufism; theology

Further reading: Burrell 1986; McAuliffe 2001–6; Netton 1989/95; Rahman 1980/94; Shehadi 1964

God, anthropomorphic descriptions of: Numerous passages in the Qur'an known as the ambiguous or anthropomorphic verses describe **God** in strikingly human terms. One finds anthropomorphic characterizations of (1) God's external appearance (e.g. God possesses a face, eyes, hands, etc.), (2) actions (God sees, hears, speaks, sits on His throne, etc.), (3) emotions (God feels mercy, wrath, satisfaction, etc.) and (4) perceptible qualities (God is visible, audible, etc.). Such passages posed a considerable problem for Islamic theologians and philosophers. When taken at face value, they seemed to imply that God is a corporeal being with the same physical aspects and constraints as finite, contingent, created beings. But not only is this conceptually incoherent, it leads to the sin of assimilating God to His creature (*tashbih*, lit. 'making similar'), which amounts to a kind of paganism or idolatry. Hence, extreme **traditionalists** who subscribed to this kind of **literalism** were sometimes pejoratively referred to as *mushabbiha* (those who make God similar [*tashbih*] to created things, e.g. human beings) or *mujassima* (those who attribute to God a corporeal body [*jism*]). In order to avoid these problems, **Mu'tazilite** theologians, **Isma'ilis** and *falasifa* tended to emphasize God's radical otherness (*mukhalafa*) and transcendence (*tanzih*, lit.

'removing' or 'withdrawal') – in a word, His incomparability to created beings.

Considered on a more fundamental level, the very idea that God possesses a plurality of **attributes** in the manner that created things do threatens to undermine His absolute **unity** (*tawhid*), and with it, His divinity, making Him similar to a created being. Thus, some thinkers went so far as to deny that God has any attributes at all, over and above His unitary essence. Both the rejection of anthropomorphic language and the denial of divine attributes as distinct entities required that they rely a good deal upon **interpretation** (*ta'wil*) in order to bring revelation into accordance with the claims of **reason**. However, traditionalists, as well as the relatively more moderate **Ash'arite** theologians, were quick to criticize this strategy, not simply because of the apparent primacy it granted to human reason, but because it amounted to stripping or divesting God of His attributes (*ta'til*), which itself is a sin and leads to atheism. Accordingly, they advocated the affirmation (*ithbat*) of God's attributes, although without necessarily construing them as essentially similar to human qualities and traits. Ostensibly anthropomorphic descriptions of God should be understood 'without (asking) how and without comparison' (*bila kayf wa la tashbih*), i.e. without further specifying their modality. While for **Hanbalites** and other traditionalists, such affirmation oftentimes veered dangerously close to a kind of literalism, Ash'arites sought to navigate a middle course between characterizing God in creaturely terms and overindulging in metaphorical interpretation, such that one divests God of attributes altogether. However, by the fifth/eleventh century, most orthodox theologians (excepting the Hanbalites) had abandoned the traditional *bila kayf* strategy and accepted metaphorical interpretations of anthropomorphic terms. Yet another conciliatory approach was put forth by Isma'ilis and *falasifa* such as **al-Farabi, Ibn Sina, Ibn Tufayl** and **Ibn Rushd**, who recast the question by distinguishing what was appropriate in common, popular discourse from what was appropriate in expert, learned discourse.

See **God (attributes of; imitation of; unity of); interpretation; Mu'tazilites; rationalism;** *shirk*; **theology; traditionalism**

Further reading: Abrahamov 1998; van Ess 2006; Watt 1948

God, arguments for the existence of: Although the **Qur'an** provides no strict proofs for the existence of **God**, it repeatedly urges us to consider the origin, harmonious order and sustained existence of the world, and to draw the appropriate conclusion. In this manner, it lays the groundwork for rational reflection on the existence of God. Islamic theologians and philosophers took up this challenge and produced numerous resourceful proofs. They had a particular fondness for the cosmological argument, although **Aristotle**'s seminal argument from **causality** – which posits God as the primary Unmoved Mover in order to explain the phenomenon of motion – never really gained the preeminence in the Islamic world that it had in the West. Two versions of the cosmological argument deserve particular mention here. The first argument, formulated in various ways by the *kalam* theologians, endeavors to prove the existence of God through the createdness or temporal originatedness (*huduth*) of the world. The early **Mu'tazilites** and **Ash'arites** did this by analyzing the world into atoms (sing: *al-juz'*) and accidents (sing: *'arad*), which, they maintained, have no spatial or temporal extension (i.e. the basic constituents of the natural world cannot in themselves subsist beyond an instant of time). From the temporality of the world's basic components they derived the temporality of the world itself. (*Mutatis mutandis*, one could use this same model to argue for the existence of a micro-managing creator God who perpetually creates and recreates the world, providing it with the order, stability and efficacy that it intrinsically lacks – which the Ash'arites did by means of their **occasionalist metaphysics**.)

Another popular argument for the createdness of the world (appropriated from the Christian apologist John Philoponus and employed by **Ibn Hazm**, **al-Ghazali**, Fakhr al-Din **al-Razi** and others), argued dialectically against the eternity of the universe by teasing out the seemingly absurd implications of an infinite temporal regress. Once the temporal origination of the world had been established, it was then just a matter of applying the principle of determination. According to this principle, prior to the world's coming-into-being, it did not exist and thus required some preexisting cause (*murajjih*) to determine its existence over its non-existence. What could this determining cause be but God? Recast by al-Ghazali in syllogistic form, the argument ran as follows: Everything that is temporally originated must have a cause; the world is temporally originated; therefore the world must have a cause, which is God.

The *kalam* theologians sought to establish the existential contingency (*jawaz*) of the world (i.e. its dependency upon God) by proving its temporal origin. Accordingly, they rejected the philosophers' thesis that the world is eternal, insofar as it seemed to imply the **necessity** of the world itself and thus reduced God to an unnecessary hypothesis. For them, eternalism was effectively equivalent to materialism and atheism. However, one finds among the philosophers powerful, atemporal versions of the cosmological argument that emphasize the dependency of the world upon God without presupposing its temporal createdness. Ibn Sina's formulation – the most important and influential of all – begins with an Aristotelian distinction between necessary (*wajid*) and merely possible or contingent (*mumkin*) **existence**. That which exists necessarily requires no cause: its existence is self-explanatory and cannot be denied without generating a contradiction. That which possesses only possible or contingent existence may exist, but it might just as easily *not* exist – no contradiction is involved either way. Since it does exist, there must be some cause that necessitates its existence over its non-existence. This determining cause must in turn be either necessary in itself or possible. If it too is merely possible, then it requires another more fundamental cause in order to explain its existence. And so forth. Either this explanatory chain goes on indefinitely, with possible beings being caused by other merely possible beings, or there is ultimately a **Necessary Existent** which provides the ontological ground for all merely possible beings, without itself requiring a cause. An infinite regress is impossible, since no entity in the series would ever be actualized and thus the bare existence of any possible being would be inexplicable. Therefore, there must be some Necessary Existent that bestows existence upon all otherwise merely possible beings, and that being is God. This demonstration was taken up by numerous Islamic philosophers and theologians, as well as Jewish and Christian thinkers such as **Ibn Maymun** (Maimonides) and Aquinas, and today is generally considered the most robust traditional form of the cosmological argument.

See **Ash'arites**; **causality**; **al-Ghazali**; **God**; **Ibn Sina**; **occasionalism**; **Qur'an**

Further reading: Davidson 1987; Fakhry 1958; Goodman 1992a/2006; Netton 1989/95

God, attributes of (*sifat Allah*): Various theoretical problems
are raised by the **Qur'an**'s portrait of **God**. One question
is how to reconcile its insistence on God's **transcendence**,
uniqueness and radical otherness with its oftentimes
human-like descriptions of His actions and characteris-
tics. Another more fundamental problem is how to
understand the ontological status of God's 'beautiful
names' (*al-asma' al-husna*), or as they came to be known
in theological and philosophical circles, God's attributes.
Certain attributes seemed relatively unproblematic
because they denoted 'negative' qualities that clearly
emphasized God's unquestioned transcendence, e.g. His
eternity (*qidam*), permanence (*baqa'*), dissimilarity to
the created (*al-mukhalafa bi al-hawadith*) and self-
subsistence (*qiyam bi al-nafsi*). However, other more positive essential attributes such as God's power (*qudra*),
knowledge (*'ilm*), life (*hayat*), will (*irada*), hearing (*sam'*),
sight (*basar*) and speech (*kalam*) did not square well with
the idea of divine **unity** (*tawhid*), regardless of whether
or not they seemed explicitly **anthropomorphic**. For how
could God be one and simple, yet at the same time possess
a multiplicity of attributes? To admit multiplicity within
God's essence would be in effect to efface His very
divinity, likening (*tashbih*) Him to an imperfect, finite
creature. The **Mu'tazilite** theologians, seeking to preserve
God's absolute oneness and transcendence (*tanzih*)
against such crypto-anthropomorphism, denied the independent reality of the divine attributes, arguing that they
signified nothing over and above God's unitary essence
(*dhat*). **Traditionalists** (committed to the unquestionable
veracity of **revelation** as well as a robust, personalistic
God) accused the Mu'tazilites and their ilk of stripping
(*ta'til*) God of His attributes, thereby reducing Him to a
vague, abstract unity without content or character, in
effect little more than an empty concept. While more

extreme, literal-minded traditionalists contented themselves with simply asserting the reality of God's attributes as expressed in the Qur'an, moderate traditionalists such as the **Ash'arite** theologians affirmed them as real in a more cautious, qualified way, 'without asking how' or specifying their modality, yet also without comparing them to human qualities (*bila kayf wa la tashbih*). Their general strategy was to deny that the notion of multiple divine attributes necessarily compromised God's essential unity. Later Ash'arites such as **al-Ghazali** and Fakhr al-Din **al-Razi** found subtle methods by which to have their cake and eat it too, e.g. the theory of modes (*ahwal*), according to which an attribute is attached to an existent but itself can be said neither to exist or not to exist. In this way the mainstream theologians attempted to uphold divine transcendence without allowing an overly enthusiastic human **reason** to divest God of His attributes altogether. In different ways, the **Isma'ili** and **Aristotelian** philosophers furthered the path initially laid down by the Mu'tazilites. The former interpreted the divine attributes as **Neoplatonic** hypostases or emanations of God (who remained the unknowable, mysterious One), while the latter generally resisted the idea that the divine attributes were ultimately something distinguishable from God's unitary essence. One philosophical strategy was to cast the apparent multiplicity of God's attributes as a function of human **epistemology** (i.e. the nature and limits of human knowledge) rather than any actual ontological multiplicity in God. **Ibn Sina** in particular argued powerfully against the notion of God as a composite being, since that would entail that He is somehow caused or conditioned – either by His components (final causes) or by that which composed Him (efficient **cause**). And to admit that God Himself is caused would be to admit that He too is a contingent (*mumkin*) rather than **Necessary**

Existent (*wajib al-wujud*). Indeed, in a bold effort to preserve God's absolute unity from being infected with multiplicity, Ibn Sina maintains that God as First Cause and Necessary Existent has no **essence** as traditionally understood, since even that would entail that He is caused. Unlike merely possible or contingent created beings, in whom essence (*mahiyya*) and **existence** (*wujud*) are distinct and separable, God's very essence is to be (*anniyya*, lit. 'thatness').

See **Ash'arites; God** (also: **anthropomorphic descriptions of; arguments for the existence of**); **Ibn Sina; Isma'ilis; Mu'tazilites; theology**

Further reading: Burrell 1986; van Ess 2006; Watt 1962/85; Wisnovsky 2003; Wolfson 1976

God, imitation of (*tashabbuh*): A characterization of **philosophy** that became influential among classical Islamic philosophers. The source of this definition seems to be Greek – specifically, **Plato**'s ideal of 'becoming like **God** so far as it is possible' (*Theaetetus* 176b–c; cf. *Symposium* 207e–209e and *Timaeus* 90a–d) – although one can find comparable, indigenous ideas within the Islamic tradition, e.g. the **Sufi** project of bringing one's character traits into accord with the character traits of God (*al-takhalluq bi akhlaq Allah*), i.e. assuming or manifesting the divine **attributes**.

In philosophical contexts there are at least three distinguishable ways in which the notion of the imitation of God gets interpreted. The most noteworthy is the moral-intellectual interpretation, according to which the philosopher imitates God by knowing the truth, cultivating or perfecting his character, and doing good. One finds variations on this idea in **al-Kindi**, Abu Bakr **al-Razi**, the **Brethren of Purity, Miskawayh** and **Ibn Tufayl**, among others. Less common is the political interpretation adopted by **al-Farabi** and **Ibn Maymun** (Maimonides), in which the philosopher-legislator (1) acquires a theoretical knowledge of God and the world, (2) constructs an ideal state as the counterpart of the universe, and (3) imitates the actions of God by endeavoring to establish the state in space and time, taking into consideration the prevailing cultural-historical conditions and constraints. Finally, there is what might be called the natural scientific interpretation advanced by Jabir ibn Hayyan, in which the philosopher imitates the Creator of the universe by acquiring the science of generation and ultimately learning how to produce minerals, plants, animals, and even an artificial man.

The project of assimilating oneself to God faces unique and potentially severe challenges within the Islamic tradition. It raises the problem of *tashbih* ('making similar', i.e. anthropomorphizing in a way that fails to recognize God's **transcendence**) and drifts dangerously close to the sin of *shirk* ('associating' or 'sharing', i.e. attributing divinity to things other than God). In part for this reason, the above interpretations typically have to do with imitating God's *actions* rather than His **essence**. In general, philosophers were understandably conservative in their claims about the extent to which one could really make oneself similar to God, emphasizing the qualification built into Plato's original formulation: 'becoming like God *so far as it is possible*.'

See **ethics**; **God (anthropomorphic descriptions of)**; **Ibn al-'Arabi**; **Plato**; *shirk*

Further reading: Altmann and Stern 1958/79; Berman 1961; Druart 1993

God's knowledge: It is generally accepted that **God** knows everything. Not only does God know everything that is visible, He knows everything that is secret and hidden. In his account of divine knowledge, **Ibn Sina** points to a problem which **al-Farabi** had also identified, and this is that God's knowledge is general knowledge, not knowledge of particular facts. The latter form of knowledge involves the senses and God would then be limited in space and time. He could know particulars whose particularity is unique, in that there can only be one of them given the conditions under which they arise, and Ibn Sina here gives the example of an eclipse. An eclipse has to take place at a certain place and a particular time given the causal laws that control the planets, and since God knows what those laws are, since He created them himself, He knows that the eclipse took place. But He does not know how it took place, since He could not watch it take place, having nothing to watch it with.

Al-Ghazali remarks that this implies that God did not know that **Muhammad** prophesied or what anyone does, and so does not know how to reward or punish people in the next life, if he sets out to treat them in accordance with their deserts. The **Qur'an** certainly suggests that God knows all these things, and reminds us of God watching us and being aware of what we do at all times and places. We ourselves are particular things and we might expect God to know who we are and what we do. According to al-Farabi and Ibn Sina, He does know all this but only in general terms, since without senses he cannot actually pick out ordinary objects. In any case, if He knew everything that happened in our world of generation and corruption He would be constantly changing His consciousness, and God is supposed to be unchanging, so the idea that God is aware of everything we do all the time cannot be understood as literally true. **Ibn Rushd** suggests that we can resolve the problem if we take God's knowledge to be the paradigm of perfect knowledge, and our knowledge is a weak reflection of that perfection. Then our knowledge of particulars is an imperfect version of the perfect knowledge that God has, and His knowledge is much more perfect than ours because He knows everything as part of a generalization. He knows everything about it, whereas we know what it actually looks like, or smells like, and so on.

See epistemology; al-Ghazali; God; Ibn Rushd; Ibn Sina

Further reading: al-Ghazali 1997/2000; Ibn Sina 2005; Leaman 1985/2002

God, unity of (*tawhid*): Islam places great emphasis on the unity of God, and this became an important theme in all the varieties of Islamic philosophy. It explains a motive for the attraction to Neoplatonism, which has as a central issue how there came to be many things in existence when really there exists only one absolute being or principle. For the Neoplatonists what happens is that the One thinks and through thinking brings other things into existence, since once it thinks it understands that it is a thinking thing, and this brings about a mental division in its perfect unity, and that leads to the production of a range of beings that exist either closer to or more distantly from it. The more perfect and abstract they are, the nearer, the less perfect and the more material are more distant. Another issue was how God related to the world. If God is identified with the One, then He creates the world by emanation, not production. God thinks about Himself and as a result other things are brought into existence, but it would be an interference with God's perfection and unity were He to know or think about any of these lesser things. The only thing He should think about is Himself, and the world comes about indirectly while the One contemplates the One. Since God is eternal, His thinking is also eternal, and so is what He thinks about, the world. The doctrine of unity then leads to implications that do not accord with the literal meaning of the **Qur'an**, and the philosophers spent a lot of effort in showing why this was not a problem.

Although the first employers of Neoplatonism were the **Peripatetics**, it was also much used by the **Isma'ilis**, **Illuminationists** and **Sufi** thinkers. The notion of emanation as holding the universe together could be reinterpreted in terms of light for the former, and the idea that the world really is just an aspect of divine unity proved very fertile ground for the last of these.

See **creation vs. eternity of the world; God** (also: attributes of); **Neoplatonism**

Further reading: Leaman 1985/2002; Watt 1962/85

Greek philosophy: see **Aristotle; Neoplatonism; Plato**

$\boxed{\text{H}}$

hadith (speech, report, tradition): see **traditionalism**

Halevi, Judah (c. 1075–1141): The greatest of Islamic Spain's Hebrew poets, Judah Halevi was also arguably the most important critic of **Aristotelian-Neoplatonic** philosophy in the Jewish intellectual tradition. Like **al-Ghazali**, his **traditionalism** was informed by a deep familiarity with the doctrines and methods of the philosophers, as well as a stringent commitment to the claims of **reason**. His one and only theologico-philosophical text, written in Arabic, was *A Defense and Argument on Behalf of the Despised Religion* (*Kitab al-radd wa al-dalil fi al-din al-dhalil*), or as it is better known, the *Kuzari*. The book takes the form of a fictional dialogue between the pagan king of the Khazars (a historical people who converted to Judaism in the ninth century) and a rabbi, with cameo appearances by a representative philosopher, a Christian and a Muslim. Through

the course of the conversation, the limitations and inadequacies of Aristotelian-Neoplatonic philosophy are made
clear. The **God** of the philosophers is a sterile, distant,
overly intellectualized being (the perfect and changeless
First Cause) who does not actively or freely will anything
(inasmuch as the world arises automatically and necessarily from His self-**knowledge**), experiences no emotions,
and has no knowledge or concern about the temporal particulars of human history. The world is not created – except
perhaps in a metaphorical sense – but rather is an eternal,
elaborate hierarchical system of emanated intellects and
spheres. **Prophecy** is explicable in essentially naturalistic
terms, as a conjunction of the human mind with the **active
intellect**. The philosophers recognize no noteworthy
distinction between the various monotheistic religions,
despite the fact that Christians and Muslims are constantly
at each others' throats; indeed, they view **religion** as a pop-
ularization of **philosophy** and a malleable tool in the hands
of the intellectual elite. Against this ostensibly reductive
picture, Halevi eloquently and persuasively defends the
God of Abraham, Isaac and Jacob – and by extension, the
value of a historically and geographically rooted tradition
informed by His presence via **revelation** and **miracles**. The
gist of Halevi's philosophy-critique is two-fold. First,
despite its claims to exhaustive theoretical knowledge, philosophy is ultimately incapable of providing any actual
praxis, and at the end of the day, practices are more important than beliefs. Contrasted with the rich, concrete particularities of Judaism's historical experience, the practical
counsels of philosophy are vacuous. Second, despite their
ostentatious claims to certitude, the philosophers' claims
concerning God and His relation to the world cannot in
fact be logically demonstrated; they are the product not of
reason, but of overzealous, undisciplined speculation
rooted in the specious intellectual inclinations of the

Greeks' own cultural particularism. Halevi on the other hand repeatedly shows the humane reasonableness of Judaism and celebrates its particularism without attempting to universalize it (particularly in his discussion of prophecy, which he confines to Jews and the land of Israel). The dialogue ends with the rabbi praising, and yearning to return to, his ancestral homeland, a sentiment shared by Halevi as well. Living at a time when the once peaceful Andalusia was increasingly becoming a place of interreligious warfare, he journeyed home to Palestine before he died.

See **Aristotle; God; Ibn Gabirol; Ibn Maymun; Levi ben Gerson; Neoplatonism; rationalism; traditionalism**

Further reading: Frank and Leaman 1997; Halevi 1964; Silman 1995; Sirat 1985

Hanbalites (*hanabila*): Founded by Ahmad ibn Hanbal (164–241/780–855), Hanbalism is a robustly **traditionalist** school of **jurisprudence** and **theology**. The most conservative of the four major **Sunni** schools of jurisprudence, it depends almost exclusively on the Qur'an and traditional reports (*hadith*, plural: *ahadith*) of the sayings and customary practice (*sunna*) of the Prophet **Muhammad** and his companions (*sahaba*). Hanbalites reject reliance upon personal opinion (*ra'y*), although tolerate the use of analogy (*qiyas*) to varying degrees. In the realm of theology, they are generally hostile towards any kind of figurative **interpretation** (*ta'wil*) or speculative reasoning (*'aql*) that departs from the literal sense of scripture and tradition. They are thus frequently at odds with more **rationalist** speculative theologians (e.g. the **Mu'tazilites** and later, the modern **Ash'arites**), as well as with the philosophers. In part because of this, the Hanbalites are often caricatured as intolerant fanatics and hide-bound anti-intellectual traditionalists, but their theological interventions could be subtle, resourceful and surprisingly moderate. For instance, Ibn Hanbal himself believed that **God** is as He describes Himself in the **Qur'an**, and that the ambiguous passages (which mention God's hand, face, throne, etc.) must be taken *bila kayf*, i.e. without asking why or specifying their modality. Through this exegetical strategy (which the Ash'arites appropriated) he sought to avoid falling into **anthropomorphism** (*tashbih*, lit. 'making [God] similar [to created things]') on the one hand and divesting (*ta'til*) God of His **attributes** on the other, as the negative theologies of the Mu'tazilites and philosophers seemed to do through their emphasis on divine **transcendence** (*tanzih*). He did maintain, however, that the divine names and attributes are eternal. One particular consequence of this was that the Qur'an (as the speech of God) must be eternal and uncreated, a doctrine which resulted in Ibn Hanbal's persecution and imprisonment during the Mu'tazilite inquisition under the 'Abbasid caliphs al-Ma'mun and al-Mu'tasim. On other theological fronts, he staked out a middle ground between the **Jabrites** and **Qadarite**-Mu'tazilites on the problem of **free will** and predestination. On the question of what makes someone a Muslim, he characterized **belief** as acceptance by the heart accompanied by outward expression and action, and maintained that the sinner is still a believer, although subject to punishment (making faith something relative and dynamic, which can increase or decrease depending on one's actions). Ibn Hanbal was a cautious and subtle jurist as well. He opposed any attempt to codify his juristic thought (thus insuring that the Qur'an and *sunna* themselves were never overshadowed) and insisted upon the indispensability of **independent judgement**, which the other Sunni *madhhab*s would soon set aside in favor of **obedience** (*taqlid*, lit. 'imitation'). Perhaps the greatest thinker in the Hanbalite tradition was **Ibn Taymiyya**, whose penetrating criticisms of the philosophers (as well as the modern **Ash'arites**, monistic **Sufis**, **Shi'ites**, etc.) are deservedly famous. Hanbalism had a formative effect on later modern revivalist movements in Sunni **Islam** such as the Wahhabis and the Salafis.

See **Ibn Taymiyya; interpretation; Islamism; law; theology; traditionalism; Zahirites**

Further reading: Hallaq 1997, 2005; Hurvitz 2002; Schacht 1964/83

happiness (*sa'ada*): see **ethics; political philosophy**

Hashawites (*hashwiyya*): A malleable but generally pejorative term applied by more **rationalist**-oriented theologians to extreme **traditionalists** who take a credulous and unduly literal approach to scripture, particularly regarding **anthropomorphic** accounts of **God**.

See **Hanbalites; traditionalism; Zahirites**

heresy (*zandaqa*): see **belief, freethinking**

hikma (wisdom): see **philosophy**

humanism: A tendency in Islamic thought that mostly flourished in the lively intellectual milieu of fourth/tenth-century Baghdad, under the Buyid dynasty. Generally **Aristotelian** in spirit, the humanist movement included thinkers such as Yahya **ibn 'Adi**, **al-Sijistani**, and **al-Tawhidi** (as well as lesser lights), and reached its apex with **Miskawayh**. Perhaps even more so than the earlier *falasifa*, the humanist thinkers were marked by a commitment to **reason** as the path to **knowledge**, salvation and **happiness**. For them, traditional religious concerns were generally peripheral, and their recognition of **Islam** is interpreted primarily as a practical concession to the dominant conventions of their particular community and culture. This is not to say that they disparaged **religion** (as, for example, **freethinkers** such as **Ibn al-Rawandi** and Abu Bakr **al-Razi** had); rather they saw it as one possible source of (partial) truth among many. Well-educated cosmopolitans with the collective insights of Arabic, Persian, Indian and Greek civilization at their disposal, the humanists sought theoretical and practical knowledge wherever they could find it. They were particularly committed to the project of reviving the so-called 'ancient sciences' (al-'ulum al-awa'il) of the Greeks. They crafted syncretic philosophies that drew from diverse schools and traditions, and produced volumes of **wisdom** literature, which compiled aphorisms, arguments and biographical anecdotes from their wisest and most admirable predecessors. This enthusiasm for collecting and synthesizing the insights of the past dovetailed with the humanists' ethical perfectionism and proximity to the *adab* tradition (which emphasized the cultivation of good manners, refinement and urbanity). The point of their scholarship and discussions was thus not to produce a watertight theoretical system, but rather to learn from exemplary individuals about the proper formation of character and the attainment of happiness, i.e. the good life for human beings.

See *adab*; Ibn 'Adi; Miskawayh; al-Sijistani (**Abu Sulayman Muhammad**); al-Tawhidi

Further reading: Goodman 2003; Kraemer 1986a/93; Netton 1992/99

I

Ibn 'Adi, Yahya (279–363/893–974): A student of Matta ibn Yunus and **al-Farabi**, the Syrian Monophysite Jacobite Christian Yahya ibn 'Adi was one of the most respected

logicians and influential intellectuals in the fourth/tenth
century. He founded the **Aristotelian** school in Baghdad,
translated numerous Greek philosophical texts from
Syriac to Arabic, and wrote a number of logical, philosophical and theological treatises. Among his more important works are *The Reformation of Character* (*Tadhib
al-akhlaq*), an ethical work on the cultivation of virtue
which takes as its starting point a Platonic model of the
soul (this would serve as a template for **Miskawayh**'s book
of the same title), and *Essay on Unity* (*Maqala fi al-
tawhid*), in which he applies his considerable logical skills
to defending the compatibility of God's **unity** with the
notion of the trinity (characterized as the three divine
attributes of goodness, power and wisdom). He addresses
al-Kindi on this point specifically in a separate work entitled *Exposition of the Error of Abu Yusuf Ya'qub ibn
Ishaq al-Kindi in his Treatise 'A Rebuttal of the Christians'*
(*Tabyin ghalat Abi Yusuf Ya'qub ibn Ishaq al-Kindi fi
maqalatiha fi al-Radd'ala al-nasara*). Yahya ibn 'Adi was
one of the few Christian philosophers who possessed an
intellectual authority even among Muslims. Though not
an influential figure in the long term, he was arguably the
preeminent thinker of his day and represents a crucial link
in the genealogy of classical Islamic **philosophy**. A number
of his students went on to become eminent intellectual
figures in their own right: **al-Sijistani, al-Tawhidi** and
Miskawayh, as well as the Nestorian Christian Ibn al-
Khammar and the Jacobite Christian Ibn Zur'a.

See ethics; **al-Farabi; God (unity of); Miskawayh; al-
Sijistani (Abu Sulayman Muhammad); al-Tawhidi**

Further reading: Ibn 'Adi 2002; Kraemer 1986a/93,
1986b; Netton 1992/99

Ibn al-'Arabi, Muhyi al-Din (560–638/1164–1240): Although
not a philosopher in the narrow, technical sense of the

word, Ibn al-'Arabi's significance within the Islamic philosophical tradition is considerable. Arguably the most
important of the Sufi mystics, 'the Greatest Master' (*al-
shaykh al-akbar*) and 'Reviver of Religion' (*muhyi al-din*)
had his first illumination at the unprecedented age of
fifteen, while growing up in Andalusia, prior to any formal
religious or spiritual training. So unusual was this event
that **Ibn Rushd** himself is said to have questioned the precocious youth about the content of his mystical experience, inquiring whether the insights it disclosed were the
same as those attained via reasoning. 'Yes and no,' was Ibn
al-'Arabi's disconcerting answer, 'and between the yes and
the no spirits take wing from their matter and necks are
separated from their bodies.' This formative experience
started him on his spiritual journey, and along the way he
produced an enormous body of writing that would leave
an indelible mark on Sufi theory and practice. His two
most important works are the voluminous *Meccan
Illuminations* (*al-Futuhat al-Makkiyya*), which was
prompted by another mystic vision he underwent near the
Ka'ba in Mecca, and the more concise *Bezels of Wisdom*
(*Fusus al-hikam*), which is generally seen as containing the
essential core of his insights. Countless commentaries have
been written on the latter.

Unlike most of the philosophers before him, Ibn al-
'Arabi places little stock in the power of **reason**. While it
plays an important role in enabling us to understand the
nature of the material world in all its multiplicity and diversity, it is severely limited in its ability to produce **knowledge**
of the highest realities. True knowledge is 'knowledge of
the mysteries' (*'ulum al-asrar*) or **gnosis** (*ma'rifa*), which
has as its practical prerequisite spiritual exercises that
prepare the heart to receive an influx of divinely bestowed
illumination. Mystic knowledge is ultimately made possible through the world of the **imagination** (*'alam al-khayal*),

a kind of intermediary realm or isthmus (*barzakh*) between the visible world of material bodies (*shahada*) and the invisible world of spirits (*ghayb*) which most people have access to only in dreams. This is the place, according to Ibn al-'Arabi's symbolic reading of the **Qur'an** and *hadith*, where **miracles**, **revelation** and the events of the **afterlife** take place. It is also the locus of unveiling (*kashf*), an event in which the gnostic experiences the divine **unity** behind the multiplicity and diversity of the cosmos. Imagination thus can be said to lie at the very center of Ibn al-'Arabi's mystic **epistemology**.

According to Ibn al-'Arabi's **metaphysics**, God is unknowable in his essence, but the entire cosmos is a self-revealing of God insofar as it is a manifestation of His names (*asma'*) or **attributes** (*sifat*). Indeed the divine names *require* the creation (or more accurately, the **emanation**) of the universe, without which they could not be given expression. This means that every creature, event and action in the universe is a divine act, and God is in a sense everywhere. This unity of all things with the divine is what later philosophical Sufis came to call the 'oneness of existence' (*wahdat al-wujud*). **Traditionalists** such as **Ibn Taymiyya** were appalled by the notion, which they interpreted as a kind of heretical monism or pantheism. Yet Ibn al-'Arabi's actual position is more subtle and nuanced than this. Although God comprises the totality of the cosmos (and can thus be said to be immanent), He also transcends it insofar as He is the essential unitary reality that gives rise to it. Accordingly, 'panentheism' might be a more accurate description of Ibn al-'Arabi's metaphysics. Further, the experience of 'annihilation' (*fana'*), i.e. the dissolution of the individuated, finite self in which one sees through the multiplicity of the manifest world and experiences its ontological unity, is followed by 'perpetuation' (*baqa'*), a state in which one sees the

world with 'two eyes', as it were – simultaneously recognizing one's creaturely uniqueness even as one also sees
one's unity with God. In this way, Ibn al-'Arabi's philosophical **Sufism** strikes a careful and subtle balance
between the traditional theological poles of **transcendence** (*tanzih*) and similarity (*tashbih*).

If the universe as a whole manifests the diversity of the
divine names, the individual human being can be understood as its microcosm. Somewhat as the *falasifa*
espoused the 'imitation (*tashabbuh*) of God', Ibn al-
'Arabi speaks of assuming the character traits of God (*al-
takhalluq bi akhlaq Allah*), all of which lie latent within
the human being as expressions of the divine names. The
'perfect human being' (*al-insan al-kamil*) is the person
who manifests God's attributes in balanced, harmonious
proportion, an ideal Ibn al-'Arabi associates first and
foremost with the Prophet **Muhammad** (who is the archetypal perfect human being), and by extension with the
other prophets and saints. Unperfected human beings
are, to a greater or lesser extent, merely microcosmic
fragments of the complete, original Muhammadan reality
(*al-haqiqa al-Muhammadiyya*). As with the older philosophical ideal of *tashabbuh*, Ibn al-Arabi's unique ethical
perfectionism is closely bound up with knowledge of
God as the Real (*al-haqq*), except that for him it is an intimate, experiential, mystic gnosis rather than a rational-
theoretical knowledge. He calls this stage of human
ethical-epistemological perfection the 'station of no
station' (*maqam la maqam*).

After his death, Ibn al-'Arabi's bold and original ideas
were denounced by the *soi-disant* defenders of tradition
within Islam, who saw little in them but heretical monism
and even antinomianism. On the other hand, his effect
upon Sufi **mysticism** is simply inestimable, and his impact
upon post-**Illuminationist** philosophers such as **al-Dawani**

and **Mulla Sadra** is considerable as well. Indeed, one might even say that despite his controversial status in the Islamic tradition, Ibn al-'Arabi is a towering figure whose overall widespread influence has few peers.

See **al-Ghazali**; **God (imitation of)**; **Ibn Masarra**; **Ibn Sab'in**; **mysticism**; **Neoplatonism**; **Sufism**; **al-Suhrawardi**

Further reading: Addas 1993; Chittick 1989, 1997; Chodkiewicz 1993; Corbin 1969/98; Ibn al-'Arabi 1980, 2002

Ibn Bajja, Abu Bakr al-Sa'igh (d. 533/1138): A polymath of sorts, Ibn Bajja (Latin: Avempace) was a physicist, physician, musician, poet and vizier, as well as the first great Andalusian philosopher of the Islamic West. Although his philosophical output was far less prolific than **al-Farabi**, **Ibn Sina** or **Ibn Rushd** (involvement in worldly affairs and an early death limited his productivity in this respect), Ibn Bajja is traditionally ranked with these giants as one of the great philosophers of **Islam**. His key philosophical writings are *Letter on the Conjunction of the **Intellect** with Human Beings* (*Risalat al-ittisal al-'aql bi al-insan*), *Governance of the Solitary* (*Tadbir al-mutawahhid*) and *Letter on Bidding Farewell* (*Risalat al-wada'*). At the heart of Ibn Bajja's thought is the idea of conjunction (*ittisal*), that is, the union of the **soul** with the **active intellect**, and through that, a kind of intellectual contact with the divine. This connection with the innermost, eternal reality of things is available neither to the ignorant multitude nor even to the **Sufis** (who misunderstand the nature of their mystic experiences), but only to philosophers, who grasp by means of their **reason** the true objects of **knowledge**: immaterial, timeless, universal and intelligible forms. In this act of knowledge, the souls of the knowing philosophers become indestructible and eternal, like their objects of knowledge. They also become numerically one with each other, since they all cognize the same intelligibles (Ibn Bajja subscribes to a form of **monopsychism**). But most importantly, through this knowledge they actualize and complete their rational nature, thereby realizing the highest end of life and attaining **happiness**. With this, we run up against the practical dimension of Ibn Bajja's thought. Like his predecessor al-Farabi, he agreed with **Plato** that the appropriate role of the philosopher involves not just theoretical contemplation of first principles, but also wise governance of the virtuous city. However, instead of focusing on the seemingly unrealizable ideal of the philosopher-king, Ibn Bajja grappled with the grim fact that few, if any, cities are actually virtuous, and that, unfortunately, the philosopher is most often a marginal, disenfranchised figure. He thus advocated a life of solitude and relative isolation for philosophers, so that they do not become corrupted by the ignorance and vice of the cities in which they must live. Ironically, in describing these ostensibly happy, self-sufficient knowers, he appropriates a term that al-Farabi had reserved for unreformed troublemakers in healthy cities: 'weeds'.

See **active intellect; al-Farabi; philosophy; political philosophy; psychology**

Further reading: Ibn Bajja 1963; Leaman 1985/2002; Rosenthal 1958/85

Ibn Gabirol, Solomon ben Judah (1021–58): Chiefly remembered as one of the greatest Sephardic poets, Ibn Gabirol was also one of the most original and resourceful of the medieval Jewish philosophers. As an inhabitant of Andalusia, he wrote in Arabic and was deeply influenced by the Islamic intellectual milieu in which he lived and worked. His key philosophical production is *The Fountain of Life* (*Yanbu' al-hayat*), which takes the form of a dialogue between a master and his pupil. By means of this literary device he lays out a complex and sophisticated Neoplatonic cosmology which nonetheless diverges from that of his Muslim brethren in important and interesting ways. Rejecting the demand that all creation be understood as a timeless, logical, involuntary **emanation** from God's self-knowledge, Ibn Gabirol identified divine will as the primary nexus between God and creation. In this way he attempted to preserve a robust, voluntaristic conception of divine and human freedom against the implicit necessitarianism of the *mashsha'i* philosophers. Further, he articulated a universal hylomorphism in which the **Aristotelian** distinction between form and matter became applicable to spiritual as well as corporeal substances ('intelligible matter' functioning here as the principle of individuation). Lastly, he conceived of corporeal substances as composed of a plurality of forms, a stance that raised difficult questions about the unity of the individual. Ironically, such innovations had little or no lasting effect within either the Islamic or Jewish intellectual traditions. In philosophical circles, Ibn Gabirol's **Neoplatonism** was quickly overshadowed by the Aristotelianism of thinkers such as **Ibn Maymun** and **Levi ben Gerson**, even as it was preserved figuratively through his Hebrew poetry (see particularly *The Kingly Crown* [*Keter Malkut*]). However, *The Fountain of Life*, which was translated into Latin as *Fons Vitae* and attributed to the 'Arab' Avicebron (also: Avicebrol or Avencebrol), did have a profound effect on Latin Christian philosophers such as Albertus Magnus, Thomas Aquinas, Bonaventure and Duns Scotus, provoking them to careful reflections on the nature of identity, individuation and personal **immortality**.

See **afterlife; causality; Neoplatonism; psychology**

Further reading: Frank and Leaman 1997; Goodman 1992b; Ibn Gabirol 1962; Sirat 1985

Ibn Hazm, Abu Muhammad 'Ali (384–456/994–1064): One of the towering figures of the Islamic West in al-Andalus, Ibn Hazm was indisputably the greatest and most original thinker of the **Zahirite** juridical-theological school. He was also a philosopher, poet and historian of religious ideas, and is said to have composed over 400 works in all these various areas, although only a relatively small number are still extant. Among these are numerous influential legal studies, as well as his most important theological work, *The Book on Religions and Schools of Thought* (*Kitab al-fisal fi al-milal wa al-ahwa' wa al-nihal*), his main work in **logic** and the **philosophy** of **language**, *The Approach to the Limits of Logic* (*al-Taqrib li hadd al-mantiq*), a treatise on **ethics**, *Character and Right Conduct in the Healing of Souls* (*al-Akhlaq wa al-siyar fi mudawat al-nufus*), and *The Dove's Neck Ring* (*Tawq al-hamama*), a treatment of love that blends **metaphysics**, **psychology**, social commentary and autobiographical anecdote. In keeping with the Zahirites' insistence on interpreting the **Qur'an** and *sunna* literally, Ibn Hazm generally held a dim view of **reason**, although did not reject it outright. Reason on his account plays an essential if subsidiary role in enabling us to grasp the relevant facts necessary for understanding an authoritative text, based on its actual language and context. It is not qualified to discover truths or legislate values on its own, independently of **revelation**, tradition or sense perception. When reason presumes to determine what revelation may or may not mean – and thus diverges from the apparent sense of the text towards some putative allegorical or esoteric meaning – it opens the door to arbitrariness, unproductive disputation and ultimately, deviation from the tradition of genuine **Islam**. Although Ibn Hazm does not subscribe to the grammarian Abu Sa'id al-Sirafi's criticism of **Aristotelian** logic (i.e. that it is intimately bound up with the concrete particularities of the Greek language, which it cannot presume to transcend), he still regards it as far more modest in its application than the philosophers thought it was, and balks at the assumption that logical-linguistic categories necessarily carve nature at the joints.

Although Ibn Hazm was scrupulous about offering fair, accurate presentations of his adversaries' positions, he often failed to recognize their real internal force, and his objections can thus sometimes seem like irrelevant intellectual sniping. But Ibn Hazm was a serious and perhaps overly sensitive man, with a profound appreciation for the important truths that language can reveal, if only it is used carefully and treated respectfully. He also had a keen sense for the ways in which language can be employed in the service of our passions, prejudices and individual preferences, thus obfuscating the truth and misleading human beings. It was this kind of abuse that he saw in the thought of his adversaries, and read in this context, Ibn Hazm's cautious **traditionalism** can serve as a valuable antidote to the potential excesses of **rationalism**.

See **interpretation**; **rationalism**; **traditionalism**; **Zahirites**
Further reading: Chejne 1982; Hourani 1985; Ibn Hazm 1953/97, 1990

Ibn Kammuna, Sa'd ibn Mansur (d. 682/1284): Ibn Kammuna was a Jewish physician and philosopher whose thought was profoundly influenced by – and whose thought in turn profoundly influenced – the Islamic philosophical tradition. Some have even claimed that he converted to **Islam**, although there is some dispute about this. His central intellectual endeavor was to synthesize and clarify the two great philosophical systems of his time: the **Peripatetic** school and the **Illuminationist** school. His chief philosophical works include *The New Philosophy* (*al-Jadid fi al-hikma*), *Commentary on [Ibn Sina's] Remarks and Admonitions* (*Sharh al-Isharat wa al-tanbihat*) and *The Refinement and Commentary on [al-Suhrawardi's] Intimations* (*al-Tanqihat fi sharh al-Talwihat*). The last of these is generally considered one of the clearest and most exhaustive treatments of the philosophy of Illumination, and historically played a pivotal role in the formation of the *ishraqi* school. Ibn Kammuna is representative of the more discursive, systematic and scientific strain of the Illuminationist tradition. His powerfully analytic mind brought an unparalleled clarity and precision to the variety of topics he examined, whether he was refining and supplementing **Aristotelian logic** with his notions of conception and assent (ostensibly neglected processes of explanation and proof necessary to ground demonstrative science), refuting the *mutakallimun*'s ontology of atoms and accidents (by considering the nature of spatial extension and divisibility), clarifying debates concerning the createdness or eternity of the world (by distinguishing between 'creation by essence', which involves real ontological dependence, and 'creation by time', which simply involves temporal priority and in any case presupposes matter and motion), shedding new light on Ibn Sina's distinction between **essence and existence** and al-Suhrawardi's insistence on the **primacy of essence** (showing how 'thingness' [*shay'iya*] is more general than existence [*wujud*] and analyzing being into the three categories of being by itself and for itself, being for itself and not by itself, and being not for itself and not by itself), or demonstrating that the **Necessary Existent** must be unitary. He is particularly famous for his use of various paradoxes that later came to be known as Ibn Kammuna's fallacies, and which earned him the title 'the devil of the philosophers'. Among these are the possibility of two necessary existents, the existence of non-existent things, and the self-referential liar's paradox, to which he proposed two possible solutions: rejecting the principle of bivalence and introducing a third truth value (neither true nor false) or classifying the sentence as false because the subject and object are not distinguished. He also composed a seminal work of comparative **religion**, *Inquiries into Three Faiths* (*Tanqih al-abhath li al-milal al-thalath*), which is still praised for its evenhanded, dispassionate and rigorous discussion of the creeds of the three monotheistic religions, focusing particularly on the phenomenon of **prophecy**. Unfortunately, the book was not well-received in its day. Its publication is said to have sparked a riot in Ibn Kammuna's hometown of Baghdad in 682/1284, prompting the prince to order that the author be burned at the stake. Luckily, he escaped with the help of friends, fleeing to another city. He died later that year.

See **creation vs. eternity of the world; epistemology; essence and existence; Ibn Sina; Illuminationism; al-Suhrawardi**

Further reading: Ibn Kammuna 1971, 2002; Pourjavady and Schmidtke 2006

Ibn Khaldun, 'Abd al-Rahman (732–808/1332–1406): Ibn Khaldun is something of a *sui generis* figure in the Islamic philosophical tradition. An enormously original and important thinker who stands out even more strikingly because of the age of intellectual decline in which he lived and thought, Ibn Khaldun eschewed the traditional concerns of most previous philosophers (**logic**, natural **science, psychology, metaphysics/theology** and **ethics**), devoting his energies instead to the formation of the human sciences and their philosophical foundations. He was born of Arab descent in Tunis and held numerous high government posts throughout Northern Africa and Andalusia before intermittently serving as a judge and teaching Malikite **jurisprudence** at several prestigious universities in Cairo. His controversial and troubled political career no doubt provided him with some of the hard-won empirical insights that would eventually be systematized in his groundbreaking *Prolegomena* (*Muqaddima*) to the *Book of Lessons* (*Kitab al-'ibar*). The latter work – a sprawling universal history of the Arabs and Berbers – constitutes a remarkable intellectual achievement in itself, but is dwarfed in importance by its multi-volume introduction, which sets forth the basic principles of the first genuinely scientific study of human society and history. Ibn Khaldun was well aware that he was forging a new discipline altogether, which he named the 'science of culture' (*'ilm al-'umran*). Previous scholars, he believed, had failed to understand the true significance of history, through their lack of distanced objectivity and their inability to grasp the larger, universal laws that govern the development of human society. What Ibn Khaldun found when he studied the data of past and present societies was a cyclical model of history driven by the interactions of two basic social groups: the nomads and the townspeople. The nomads are rural folk, essentially savage and uncivilized (*badawi*), but at the same time possessing kind of simple, natural virtue. Tough, self-reliant, fiercely independent, warlike and possessed of a strong sense of social solidarity (*'asabiyya*), they are the engine of conquest that leads to the establishment of empires. Yet the consequent shift to urban life and the arts, sciences and culture that come with being civilized (*hadari*) brings with it new luxuries and indulgences that gradually undermine the simple tribal virtues that made them a force to be reckoned with in the first place. Within a few generations, the nomads grow acclimated to their comfortable new way of life, losing their warlike virtues and relying increasingly upon foreign mercenaries for their military might. The new complex realities of governing an empire drive the rulers to consolidate their own power, which leads in turn to the development of an elaborate bureaucracy, often comprised of conquered foreigners. As they grow increasingly corrupt and decadent, it becomes harder to sustain their moral authority and support accordingly wanes. Expenditures rise, requiring ever higher taxes, which discourage production and result (paradoxically) in lower revenues. All these developments corrode social solidarity, leaving the townspeople ripe to be conquered by another uncultured but vital and cohesive nomadic society, much like they had once been. Although on Ibn Khaldun's account there appears to be an almost inexorable logic to the emergence, flourishing and decay of civilizations, religion functions as a bit of a wild card, reinforcing social solidarity and helping to found great empires. He does acknowledge as well that a radical change in overall conditions (due for example to disease, technology or invasion) might possibly give rise to a whole new arrangement. Indeed, Ibn Khaldun believed that he himself was witnessing the emergence of a new world (in Europe), even while his own society was decaying.

Ibn Khaldun did not consider himself a philosopher, nor was he viewed this way until relatively recently. Indeed, he was quite critical of philosophy, specifically the **Neoplatonic-Aristotelian** school, which seemed to view **reason** as a sufficient means for the attainment of comprehensive **knowledge**, virtue and **happiness**. However, his suspicion of **philosophy** was of a considerably higher caliber than the garden-variety anti-intellectual Neo-**Hanbalism** so prevalent during his era; his orientation is rather more like that of **al-Ghazali**, whose critique of the philosophers was based on a thorough understanding of their methods and an appreciation of their legitimate insights. Ibn Khaldun's objection to Neoplatonic-Aristotelian philosophy is two-fold. First, it fails to recognize the inescapably empirical character of all knowledge. In attempting to draw conclusions that go far beyond the limits of experience, its metaphysical-theological speculations exceed the legitimate bounds of reason. Second, it has a corrosive effect on **religion**, and by extension, on social solidarity, which according to Ibn Khaldun is the essential force that sustains society. Yet, while critical of the perceived transgressions of speculative philosophy, Ibn Khaldun by no means renounced reason altogether. He admitted that it provided valuable training for the mind, so long as one was inoculated against its excesses by a preliminary study of the traditional Islamic sciences. More importantly, his whole philosophy of history is itself a product of reason – not a hubristic reason that strives fruitlessly to grasp transcendent realities, but a reason that is always tethered to the concrete particularities of historical experience, in order to reveal the larger patterns and laws that govern human society. Ibn Khaldun's philosophy of history and science of culture are so novel and ambitious that it is difficult to identify any real intellectual predecessors. Nor did he have any true successors, at least not until the emergence of history and sociology as scientific disciplines in the modern period.

See **epistemology**; **al-Ghazali**; **Hanbalites**; **political philosophy**; **science**

Further reading: al-Azmeh 1981/2003; Ibn Khaldun 1950/87, 1958/67; Mahdi 1957/64; Zaid 2003

Ibn Masarra, Muhammad ibn 'Abd Allah (269–319/ 883–931): The earliest Andalusian philosopher in the Islamic West, Ibn Masarra was a charismatic figure who founded a Sufi hermitage in the mountains outside his birthplace in Cordoba. His followers – the *masariyya* – sought inward or **esoteric** (*batini*) knowledge, practised asceticism (*zuhd*), examined their consciences daily and cultivated virtues such as humility, patience, the forgiving of wrongs and love of one's enemies as a means to the purification of the **soul**. Few of Ibn Masarra's writings remain; most of what is known about him comes down to us from second-hand accounts by **Ibn Hazm, al-Shahrastani, al-Shahrazuri,** and **Ibn al-'Arabi,** among others. These accounts are generally unsympathetic, Ibn al-'Arabi's being the noteworthy exception. There are several reasons why more traditional thinkers were distrustful of Ibn Masarra's thought. First, although he believed that **reason** and **revelation** constituted two mutually confirming paths to the same goal (i.e. salvation through knowledge of **God's unity**), he boldly suggested that each approach was sufficient unto itself. Second, like his father, Ibn Masarra maintained strong **Mu'tazilite** commitments, at a time when that once-influential theological movement was coming under increasing attack. Thus, in an attempt to preserve God's absolute unity (as well as to protect human free will), he distinguished between the Creator's *eternal* **knowledge** and power on the one hand and His *created* knowledge and power on the other. To **traditionalists,** this denied divine omniscience and omnipotence, since it implied that God knows things only as universals and not as particulars. Third, whether fairly or not, Ibn Masarra's philosophy was typically affiliated with the ambitious – if rather speculative and mythical – Neoplatonism of Pseudo-Empedocles. This fact alienated traditionalists and **rationalists** alike. The former found the residual elements of pagan Greek thought too pronounced to tolerate (despite a heroic attempt to reconcile the atemporal, automatic and necessitarian process of **emanation** with God's free willed, deliberate, creative action in time). On the other hand, Islamic **Peripatetics** like **al-Farabi** and **Ibn Sina** found Ibn Masarra's unsystematic **Neoplatonism** to be intellectually undisciplined and wooly-headed. But in methodological terms, what set Ibn Masarra apart from both traditionalists and rationalists was his heavy reliance on symbolism, esoteric images and visionary language – in part a function of his initiatory **Sufism**, in part a clever protective measure against the increasing unacceptability of his ideas. The strategy proved relatively successful; although his followers would later come under persecution, the master lived and died peacefully. And in spite of such criticism and persecution, Ibn Masarra's philosophical mysticism would survive to have a considerable influence on subsequent generations of Sufis, most notably, Ibn al-'Arabi.

See **Ibn al-'Arabi**; **Mu'tazilites**; **Mysticism**; **Neoplatonism**; **Sufism**

Further reading: Asín Palacios 1972/97

Ibn Maymun, Musa (1138–1204): Known to his own people as Rabbi Moshe ben Maymon (i.e. Rambam) and to the Christian Latins as Moses Maimonides, Ibn Maymun is arguably the single most important thinker in the history of Jewish philosophy. Born in Cordoba, he and his family soon fled the rising wave of persecution initiated in Andalusia by the Almohad invasion, living first in the Maghrib (Fez) and ultimately in Egypt (Cairo), where he became a respected physician and ultimately the leader of its Jewish community. It is perhaps no surprise, then, that the Rambam's philosophical and theological writings were so deeply informed by the Islamic philosophers (particularly **Peripatetic** thinkers such as **al-Farabi**, **Ibn Bajja**, **Ibn Sina** and **Ibn Rushd**), and through them their Greek predecessors, in addition to the traditional Rabbinic-Talmudic sources. Ibn Maymun's intimate engagement with the Islamic *falasifa* can be seen particularly in his major philosophical work, the *Guide of the Perplexed* (*Dalalat al-ha'irin*), which was written in Arabic. Addressed to a particularly promising student, the stated purpose of this book was to help him (and others like him) reconcile the apparent tensions between Biblical and philosophical claims about **God**, the universe, and the meaning of religious **law**. He focuses first on the **anthropomorphic** language of the Torah, developing an elaborate hermeneutics to justify interpreting such passages figuratively, while showing how these concessions to human understanding (which, if taken literally, would lead to idolatry) effectively point the thoughtful towards a more sophisticated and adequate conception of God's oneness. Although he follows the philosophers in casting God as the unmoved First Mover and **Necessary Existent**, he formulates a more all-encompassing negative theology, according to which our conception of God is increasingly refined by negating not only deficiencies, but even positive attributes traditionally predicated of the divine. He then weighs in on the old controversy regarding the status of the world, considering the alleged 'proofs' for both Mosaic creation *ex nihilo* and Aristotelian eternity, and concluding that neither is really demonstrable, strictly speaking. Having reined in the overly ambitious nature of the debate, he goes on to defend the createdness of the world, on the modest grounds that it is both more plausible and more compatible with the conception of God disclosed through revealed law. Regarding the question of **prophecy**, he strikes a balance between popular views (which cast it purely as a function of divine will) and philosophical interpretations (which instead cast it as a function of the particular individual's nature and his efforts to perfect it). On Ibn Maymun's view, both conditions are necessary, but neither in and of itself is sufficient. His practical philosophy resourcefully blends Aristotelian virtue **ethics** (with its doctrine of the mean and its emphasis on the perfection of character) with Biblical law-based command ethics (which make possible the perfection of human nature) and the Platonic ideal of imitating God. The philosophical temperament that emerges from these (and other) discussions in the *Guide* is to most appearances one of moderate **rationalism**. Ibn Maymun exhibits a profound respect for Aristotelian philosophy but believes it is essentially harmonizable with the Mosaic tradition, which he sees as reasonable through and through. Yet a number of writers (both medieval and modern) have pointed out that his actual stance may have been more complex than this. For the *Guide* employs an esoteric strategy of writing that arguably masks, through its unnecessarily awkward organization and puzzling contradictions, considerably more radical, and potentially heretical, opinions (e.g. the eternity of the world, the identification of God with nature, the rejection of bodily resurrection and possibly even **monopsychism** à la **Ibn Rushd**). But while Ibn Maymun may very well have occasionally employed the art of dissimulation in his writing, it is far from clear as to whether his true views were that much at odds with the general positions mapped out in the *Guide*. Whether read as a moderate or extreme Aristotelian rationalist, his influence on the Jewish intellectual tradition is virtually inestimable, due not only to the *Guide*, but to his seminal *Mishneh Torah* (which systematized and codified the rabbinic law), as well as numerous other key legal works. He also had some influence on subsequent Islamic philosophers, although considerably more on Christian philosophers (most notably

Aquinas, who among other things adopted his nuanced stance regarding the createdness of the world), and modern European philosophers such as Spinoza and Leibniz.

See afterlife; creation vs. eternity of the world; ethics; God; interpretation; law; prophecy; psychology

Further reading: Buijs 1988; Leaman 1990; Frank and Leaman 1997; Maimonides 1963, 1976/84; Sirat 1985

Ibn al-Rawandi, Abu al-Husayn Ahmad ibn Yahya ibn Ishaq (d. c. 245/910): A protean freethinker who experimented with **Mu'tazilism** and **Shi'ism** before finally embracing atheism, Ibn al-Rawandi was condemned by most Muslims as a dangerous heretic. Of the 114 books he composed only a few fragments remain, preserved through the refutations of subsequent authors. Of these, the most important are *The Scandal of the Mu'tazilites* (*Fadihat al-mu'tazila*), which attempts to refute the major Mu'tazilite theologians, *The Refutation* (*al-Damigh*), which attacks the **Qur'an**, and *The Book of the Diamond* (*Kitab al-zumurrud*), which offers up a scathing critique of **prophecy**. In these works alone, he (1) rejects all religious dogmas as unacceptable to **reason**, (2) argues that prophets – **Muhammad** included – are like sorcerers and magicians, and that their **miracles** are entirely fictitious, (3) questions the necessity of prophecy and revelation if **God** is indeed all-powerful, (4) denies that the Qur'an is the revealed word of God and that it has any unique aesthetic value, (5) maintains that the God of the Qur'an is ultimately all-too-human and imperfect (i.e. lacking in knowledge and wisdom, easily angered, quick to punish, excessive, arbitrary and unjust), (6) argues that the world is eternal and we are by no means compelled to posit a first (divine) cause, and (7) points out that Paradise as described in the Qur'an does not seem particularly desirable. No surprise, then, that he was branded as a dangerous heretic, but Ibn al-Rawandi's bold and radical **freethinking** is nonetheless a testament to the striking diversity of ideas that emerged within the Islamicate context.

See **belief; freethinking; Mu'tazilites; prophecy; Qur'an; rationalism**

Further reading: Stroumsa 1999

Ibn Rushd, Abu al-Walid Muhammad (520–595/1126–98): The most important of the Andalusian philosophers, Ibn Rushd – or Averroës, as he was known to the Latins – was chief physician to, and favored intellectual companion of, the Almohad caliph Abu Ya'qub Yusuf. He was also a respected jurist, grand judge (*qadi*) of Cordoba and the last great figure in the classical period of Islamic **philosophy**, at least in the West. His philosophical works can be divided into two general categories: (1) his polemical or dialectical works, which are concerned primarily with establishing the legitimacy of philosophy within the context of **Islam** and defending it against the attacks of theologians like **al-Ghazali,** and (2) his magisterial three-tiered system of commentaries (short, middle and long) on **Aristotle**'s corpus, encouraged by his older friend **Ibn Tufayl** and commissioned by Abu Ya'qub Yusuf. Among the first group are texts such as the *Decisive Treatise Determining the Nature of the Connection Between Religious Law and Philosophy* (*Fasl al-maqal*), *Exposition of the Methods of Proof Relative to the Doctrines of Religion* (*Kashf 'an al-manahij*), and *The Incoherence of the Incoherence* (*Tahafut al-tahafut*). In the *Decisive Treatise*, Ibn Rushd argues that the **Qur'an** itself makes philosophical inquiry obligatory to those who are capable of it and that advocates of 'orthodoxy' who forbid such examination or accuse its earnest (if occasionally fallible) practitioners of **unbelief** (*kufr*) are acting contrary to religious law. **Interpretation** of unclear or ambiguous Qur'anic passages is unavoidable, as virtually all Muslims recognize, and when the apparent sense of scripture is at odds with the conclusions of strict, demonstrative reasoning, it must be interpreted figuratively. This is because 'Truth does not contradict truth, but rather is consistent with it and bears witness to it.' The overzealous theologians do more damage to religion than the philosophers, because they indulge in hasty and often groundless interpretations of scripture that violate its apparent sense as well as the dictates of reason. They also employ the same dialectical method of presentation indiscriminately to all believers, not realizing that the universal message of Islam requires different media for different audiences with different capacities. While the demonstrative, dialectical and rhetorical methods all are capable of arriving at essentially the same truth, the first is really only appropriate for a handful of intellectuals, the second for dogmatic but reasoning theologians, and the third for the common people. In short, abstruse metaphysical questions are best left in the hands of qualified experts. To broadcast the methods and conclusions of the philosophers or the theologians to simple believers (for whom the literal, apparent sense of scripture is sufficient) is to jeopardize their faith and do them harm.

The *Expositions of the Methods of Proof* and the *Incoherence of the Incoherence* fill in the specific details of Ibn Rushd's defense of philosophy and critique of the destructive overreachings of **theology**. The former examines the ways in which the methods and doctrines of the various theological sects fall short intellectually and create dissension, confusion and disbelief among the common people. The latter is a point-by-point rebuttal of al-Ghazali's *Incoherence of the Philosophers*, a book which had effectively turned the tide against the once-influential **Neoplatonic**-Aristotelian mode of philosophy, charging figures like **al-Farabi** and **Ibn Sina** with failing to meet the rigorous methodological standards that they themselves laid down and wandering into the realm of heretical innovation and even unbelief in twenty of their theses. Ibn Rushd defends the **eternity** of the universe against al-Ghazali's creationist critique, arguing that the creative action of an eternal agent such as God can have no beginning in time, and deftly deconstructing al-Ghazali's Philoponian argument against the possibility of an actually infinite temporal series. Regarding **God's knowledge** of temporal particulars, Ibn Rushd maintains that to conceive of **God** as knowing either particulars or universals in the way human beings know them is to reduce Him to inadequate, creaturely terms. For while originated, human **knowledge** is *caused by* objects of knowledge (which in turn are created by God), divine knowledge is the *cause* of its objects. That having been said, insofar as God's knowledge is actual rather than abstract or merely potential, it is closer to our knowledge of the particular than to the universal. As for al-Ghazali's famous critique of **necessity** in causal relations between natural events, Ibn Rushd argues that it rules out the possibility of scientific knowledge of the world, destroying God's wisdom and providence in a misguided attempt to valorize His omnipotence. Unsurprisingly, he is a bit cagey on the question of miracles. While acknowledging their religio-political importance, he rejects the idea that they actually constitute divine violations of natural law (a self-contradictory impossibility in his view), and casts them instead as rare and as yet unexplained natural occurrences.

Although Ibn Rushd is primarily concerned with rebutting al-Ghazali's criticisms of the **Peripatetic** philosophers, he takes great pains to distance himself from his predecessor Ibn Sina as well. He rejects **emanation** as a legitimate model for expressing the relation between God and the world, conceiving of the Creator both in more traditional Islamic terms as a willing agent and in more purely Aristotelian terms as first mover and final cause of an eternal universe. He reduces Ibn Sina's **essence/existence** distinction from a fundamental ontological fact to a mere mental abstraction, and replaces Ibn Sina's sometimes heavy-handed reliance on the modalities of necessary and possible existence with the more flexible explanatory categories of **actuality and potentiality**. In doing so, Ibn Rushd endeavors to extricate the true teaching of Aristotle from the numerous Neoplatonic accretions that had for so long obscured and hindered its vitality.

This is a task he continues in his voluminous Aristotelian commentaries, particularly the long versions that were the fruit of his later years. These works are generally considered to offer the definitive statement of Ibn Rushd's mature views in demonstrative form (rather than merely dialectical or persuasive form, as in his polemical works). Although the commentaries are recognized for their comprehensive scholarship, hermeneutic sensitivity and fidelity to Aristotle's actual philosophy, the most important and exciting moments are those in which he ventures a new, creative interpretation in order to render intelligible some notoriously ambiguous passage or doctrine. The most well-known example of this is his *Long Commentary on De Anima*, where he arrives at the conclusion that there is ultimately only one material **intellect** and thus that **immortality** (which he interprets as a conjunction with the universal **active intellect**) is not individual or personal. Although in his earlier dialectical works Ibn Rushd had entertained the possibility (if indemonstrability) of personal immortality and bodily resurrection,

such suggestions seem like more of a political sop thrown
to common believers, who need to envision individual
reward and punishment in order to be saved and attain
happiness. The doctrine of '**monopsychism**', as it is sometimes called, is generally believed to represent his mature,
demonstrated position on the subject.

Towards the end of Ibn Rushd's life the political mood
of al-Andalus turned against him and his unapologetic
rationalism. His books were banned and burned, and he
was exiled. However, the Almohad caliph soon changed
his mind and Ibn Rushd joined him in Marrakesh, only
to die of old age soon after. He left behind no real students or followers in the Islamic world; his real influence
was felt most forcefully within the Jewish and Christian
intellectual traditions, inspiring various forms of
'Averroism'. In the Jewish tradition, Ibn Rushd's deep
understanding of Aristotle earned him respect and
prompted a super-commentarial tradition. At the same
time, his nuanced treatment of the relation between religious law and philosophy helped Jewish thinkers reconcile the seemingly conflicting claims of faith and reason
in resourceful new ways. In the Christian tradition, 'The
Commentator's' writings were chiefly responsible for the
resurgence of interest in (and better understanding of)
Aristotle. However, several of Ibn Rushd's ideas were
officially condemned by the church (monopsychism, the
attainability of happiness in earthly life, and the eternity
of the world), along with at least one idea that was
wrongly but persistently associated with him: the notorious doctrine of 'double truth' (i.e. that which is true
according to religion can be false for philosophy), which
Ibn Rushd, as well as many Averroists, actually would
have rejected. Some scholars have argued that Ibn
Rushd's thought had a distant but formative effect on the
European Enlightenments. In the late nineteenth and

twentieth centuries, Arab modernists seized upon him as a kind of intellectual exemplar whose thought represented the true, rational spirit of Islam – a spirit that had for too long been stifled by an ossified, increasingly authoritarian tradition.

See active intellect; afterlife; Aristotle; causality; creation vs. eternity of the world; epistemology; al-Ghazali; God (also: God's knowledge); Ibn Sina; Ibn Tufayl; interpretation; logic; metaphysics; Neoplatonism; psychology

Further reading: Arnaldez 2000; Ibn Rushd 1954/78, 1974/2005, 1977, 1983/98, 1984, 1999, 2001a, 2001b, 2002, 2007; Kogan 1985; Leaman 1988/98; Urvoy 1991

Ibn Sab'in, Abu Muhammad ibn 'Abd al-Haqq (614–69/ 1217–70): Known in Europe through his philosophical correspondence with Emperor Frederick II and beloved by his followers, the *sab'iniyyun*, Ibn Sab'in's life was nevertheless a hard one. He led a rather nomadic existence, characterized by controversy, quarrel, persecution and exile, which ended in either poisoning or suicide. This is in part attributable to his thought, for Ibn Sab'in was perhaps the most radical proponent of philosophical **Sufism** and put forth a particularly controversial type of monistic pantheism. Building upon the theories of his predecessor **Ibn al-'Arabi**, he espoused the Sufi doctrine of the **oneness of existence** (*wahdat al-wujud*), albeit in a purer, more comprehensive form. According to Ibn Sab'in, existence is ultimately an undifferentiated spiritual **unity**, with **God** as the sole reality of all things. In his main work, *Escape of the Gnostic* (*Budd al-'arif*), Ibn Sab'in deals with the question of how an individual can attain this experiential insight. Examining the opinions of the philosophical schools, he maintains that knowledge of the ultimate unity of all things cannot be reached by way of logical analysis or demonstrative proof, because such tools inevitably reinscribe multiplicity. Although he had a deep familiarity with the thought of the Islamic Aristotelians (and was himself sometimes characterized as a **Peripatetic** Sufi), he was highly critical of Aristotelian **logic** as a means for knowing reality and offered in its stead an illuminative logic based on intuition. Ibn Sab'in ultimately holds out the possibility of a direct, unmediated access to God through our innermost selves, which are of divine origin. He speaks of the divine self as the 'secret God has entrusted to us'. It is by discovering this secret – by knowing ourselves – that God's intimate, immanent presence is revealed. In short, the path to God is not the way of discursive reasoning and demonstrative proof, but rather the direct, intuitive, experiential discovery of our unity with the divine.

See **Aristotle; Ibn al-'Arabi; mysticism; Sufism**
Further reading: Corbin 1993; Nasr and Leaman 1996

Ibn Sina, Abu 'Ali al-Husayn (370–428/980–1037): Born near Bukhara, Ibn Sina – or 'Avicenna', as he was known to the Latins – may very well be the most important and influential thinker, not just of the **Neoplatonic-Aristotelian** (*mashsha'i*) school of Islamic **philosophy** in particular, or of the classical period of Islamic philosophy more generally, but of the whole Islamic philosophical tradition. His life as well as his thought is the stuff of legend. A precocious youth who frequently outstripped his teachers in the course of an ambitious and comprehensive education, Ibn Sina is said to have mastered all the known sciences by the age of eighteen. As a physician and political advisor during an unstable time, his adult life was filled with practical and sometimes dangerous worldly endeavors that often made it difficult for him to record his own original thoughts. Yet in spite of this, he was a prolific writer, penning hundreds of works on medicine, mathematics, the natural sciences and philosophy, as well as in Islamic sciences such as Qur'anic exegesis. Among his medical writings, his foremost contribution was the magisterial *Canon of Medicine* (*Qanun fi al-tibb*), which for at least six centuries was considered the definitive text in the field throughout both the East and the West and is used even to this day. His two major philosophical works are the encyclopedic *Healing* (*al-Shifa'*) and *Directives and Remarks* (*Isharat wa al-tanbihat*), which range in subject from **logic** to physics to mathematics to **metaphysics** to **mysticism**. His *Deliverance* (*al-Najat*) provides, as it were, a 'Reader's Digest' condensed version of *The Healing*, while the *Book of Knowledge* (*Danish-nama-yi 'Ala'i*) offers yet another concise presentation of Ibn Sina's system – this time written in Persian – which **al-Ghazali** used as a template for his *Intentions of the Philosophers*.

Although Ibn Sina made major contributions to virtually all the areas of philosophy, he is particularly known for his insights in the field of metaphysics. His complex and original system might be said to revolve around two chief insights. The first is that we have a basic, pre-conceptual intuition of being, rooted in an a priori awareness of our own existence unmediated by sense experience. Ibn Sina's '**floating man**' thought experiment, which illustrates this idea nicely, is ultimately intended to illustrate the substantiality of the **soul** (since it can conceive of itself independently of any reference to the body). But it also points towards the centrality of intuition (*hads*) in Ibn Sina's **epistemology** (a power that makes demonstrative reasoning possible, inasmuch as it enables us to hit upon the middle term of a syllogism) and the fundamental unity of being and knowledge in his overall philosophy. Ibn Sina's second chief insight is that the mode of our own **existence** (and of every other existing thing in the universe) is not sufficient unto itself; that is, it requires a more fundamental being to actualize and sustain it. In Ibn Sina's terminology, human beings (and all such finite existents) are merely possible or contingent (*mumkin*) rather than necessary (*wajib*) in themselves, which means that although they *do* exist, they could just as easily *not* exist. Ibn Sina's point here is ontological rather then simply temporal. It's not simply that there was a time when a particular tree (for example) did not yet exist and that there will come a time when it no longer exists; the point is rather that even while the tree exists, its mode of existence is dependent, insofar as it is conditioned and determined by other causes. Put differently, we could say that no contradiction or absurdity is involved in conceiving of a merely possible being as non-existent (its existence is not 'hard-wired' into it, so to speak). Ibn Sina articulates this insight through his influential distinction between a thing's **essence** or quiddity (*mahiyya*, lit. 'whatness') and its existence (*wujud*). In worldly, contingent things, there is no necessary connection between these two aspects; existence is a kind of accident, something superadded to an essence, which actualizes it and grants it being. Ibn Sina's argument for the existence of **God** is essentially an attempt to explain the puzzling existence of composite, contingent beings. By their nature they must depend upon other beings for their very existence. Yet merely possible beings cannot ultimately be caused by other merely possible beings, for in and of themselves they do not possess existence. Such a causal chain could go on indefinitely without ever explaining the bare existence of even one contingent entity. The only way to render the fact of contingent being intelligible is to posit the existence of a First Being whose mode of existence is *not* merely contingent. That is, we must posit the existence of a **Necessary Existent** (*wajib al-wujud*), a being whose non-existence is by definition inconceivable, whose essence and existence are one and the same. This is Ibn Sina's conception of God.

Ibn Sina's novel way of understanding the relation between God and the world enabled him to navigate a middle path between the dilemma of the *falasifa*'s eternal universe and the theologians' temporally originated world. The former seemed to imply that the universe was necessary in and of itself (since it always had been and always would be), thus rendering God superfluous as an existential explanatory principle. For this reason it was often associated with materialism and atheism. The latter faced a multiplicity of serious conceptual problems in positing a beginning to time caused by an ostensibly eternal God. Ibn Sina's new conception of God – as the ontological ground of an eternal but contingent universe – seemed to preserve the best aspects of both eternalism and creationism without getting bogged down in their respective problems. Ibn Sina's cosmology retains an unmistakably Neoplatonic cast, however. For him, the event of being is not a function of God's free, creative will, but rather is an automatic product of God's self-knowledge, which generates a complex hierarchy of intellects (the tenth and last of these being the **active intellect**, which gives rise to the terrestrial world and serves as a link of sorts between human intellect and the divine). This process of **emanation** is not temporal, but logical: reality unfolds syllogistically. This insures its intelligibility, but it also means that the relation between **cause** and effect is necessary, much like the relation between premises and a conclusion is. Thus, while the universe and everything in it is merely possible or contingent *in itself*, it is also necessary *through another* (i.e. as an effect in relation to its cause). Which is to say that things cannot be other than they are. This seems to commit Ibn Sina to a deterministic model of the universe that constrains (or redefines) divine freedom just as much as it does human freedom.

Grasping the intelligible structure of reality – and achieving knowledge about the existence and nature of its First Cause, God – has a salvific effect on the soul, enabling it to purify or perfect itself, and ultimately re-ascend to its ontological source. Ibn Sina argued for the **immortality** of the rational part of the soul (a point on which **Aristotle** was at best vague), but, contra the **Neoplatonists**, he also rejected its pre-eternity. He retained the Qur'anic notion of the resurrection (*ma'ad*, lit. '**return**'), but interpreted it figuratively and intellectually, as he did the promise of reward and punishment. These views reflect Ibn Sina's concern, which was greater than that of his *mashsha'i* predecessors, with remaining true to the religious particularities of Islam (**prophecy**, **revelation**, the hereafter, mystical experience), while still interpreting them in a philosophically respectable manner.

There is in fact a hotly disputed question as to whether or not Ibn Sina himself was a mystic. A few of his books (most of which are now unfortunately lost) suggest that he formulated an alternative, indigenous system – an '**Eastern philosophy**' or 'Oriental wisdom' (*al-hikmat al-mashriqiyya*) – which emphasized intuition over demonstrative proof, admitted mystic forms of gnosis, and was intended to complement or even supersede his Neoplatonic-Aristotelian system. While the case for reading Ibn Sina as a kind of proto-**Illuminationist** thinker is by no means clear-cut, it is at least safe to say that Ibn Sina had a healthy respect for mystic ways of knowing, even if he looked in on them from the perspective of an outsider.

Ibn Sina's influence far exceeded his eminent status within the *mashsha'i* tradition of philosophy. He was the definitive thinker to target when the theologians mounted their decisive attack on philosophy. It is often said that **al-Ghazali** effectively brought an end to the style of philosophy that Ibn Sina exemplified, but the truth of the matter is more complex. There were of course subsequent philosophers who continued in the mold of Ibn Sina, such as **al-Tusi**. But perhaps even more importantly, the philosophical theology of later **Ash'arite** thinkers like al-Ghazali, **al-Shahrastani** and Fakhr al-Din **al-Razi** would – ironically – be virtually unthinkable without Ibn Sina, whose terminology and method of demonstrative proof they appropriated. The same could be said for the school of Illumination; despite its vocal opposition to the 'Aristotelian' style of reasoning, figures like al-Suhrawardi were deeply indebted to Ibn Sina's 'Eastern philosophy' and emphasis on intuition, as well as his analysis of the relation between essence and existence. Ibn Sina's impact outside the Islamic tradition is widely recognized, and can be seen clearly in the thought of crucial thinkers such as **Ibn Maymun** (Maimonides) and Aquinas.

See **active intellect; afterlife; Aristotle; causality; Eastern philosophy; epistemology; essence and existence; al-Farabi; floating man argument; free will and predestination; al-Ghazali; Ibn Rushd; Illuminationism; metaphysics; Mulla Sadra; mysticism; Neoplatonism; philosophy; prophecy; psychology; al-Suhrawardi**

Further reading: Goodman 1992a/2006; Gutas 1988; Ibn Sina 1952/81, 1973/2001, 1974, 1984, 1985, 1996, 2005; Janssens 2006; Marmura 2005; Nasr with Aminrazavi 1999; Wisnovsky 2003

Ibn Taymiyya, Taqi al-Din (661–728/1263–1328): Ibn Taymiyya was perhaps the most important and influential proponent of the **Hanbalite** school of **jurisprudence**

and **theology**, upholding its **literalist** approach to **Qur'an** and *sunna* against a multiple front of sophisticated **rationalist** critiques. After an unusually ambitious and wide-ranging education that included **philosophy** and theology as well as Qur'anic exegesis, *hadith*, and jurisprudence, Ibn Taymiyya embarked on a prestigious teaching career. However, his life was repeatedly plagued with political woes. Like the founder of his school, Ibn Hanbal, he was persecuted and imprisoned for his robustly **traditionalist** views. He eventually died in jail at the age of sixty-five after being prohibited from writing altogether.

Over the course of his controversial life he is said to have penned many hundreds of works, most of which took the form of critiques or refutations. He attacked the philosophical theology of the modern **Ash'arites** (who in turn charged him with **anthropomorphism**) as well as monistic and antinomian **Sufis**, most notably **Ibn al-'Arabi** (although it should be noted that Ibn Taymiyya himself was a Sufi of the Qadirite order, founded by al-Jilani). He was also very critical of the **Jabrites**, **Qadarites**, Jahmites, **Mu'tazilites**, **Shi'ites** and *mashsha'i* philosophers. Against the last, he wrote several devastating critiques, the most important of which is his *Refutation of the Logicians* (*Kitab al-radd 'ala al-mantiqiyyin*), which is considered one of the most powerful and ambitious assaults on Aristotelian **logic**. He attacked the philosophers' logical apparatus because he believed it was the true source of their opinions regarding the nature of **God**, the universe and prophetic **revelation** – erroneous opinions that he believed were plainly at odds with scripture and tradition. His critique strikes at the most basic presuppositions of Aristotelian logic, in order to take down the whole metaphysical construction of the philosophers. In particular, he focused on its theory of definition (*hadd*) and the categorical syllogism (*al-qiyas al-shumul*).

Definition presupposes the ability to distinguish between a thing's essence and its accidents in a fixed, stable, univocal way, but Ibn Taymiyya argues that all attempts to do so run up against irresolvable interpretative disagreements. Definitions are thus inescapably conventional and relative to any given individual or group. By extension, Ibn Taymiyya undermines the fundamental distinction between **essence and existence**, and with it the philosophers' realist theory of universals. Universals do not carve nature at the joints, as it were; they exist only in the mind as abstractions, rather than in the external world. The same could be said for the cherished notion of the '**Necessary Existent**', which philosophers had vainly substituted for the self-described God of the Qur'an.

The philosophers bragged that the categorical syllogism produced necessary, demonstrative knowledge. But Ibn Taymiyya argues that it cannot really live up to some of the most basic requirements stipulated by **Aristotle** himself, i.e. that it must have no less (and no more) than two premises and a conclusion, that one of its premises must be universal, and that it must produce new **knowledge** from old knowledge. The number of premises necessary to a syllogism cannot really be fixed, since that ultimately depends on the position and epistemological requirements of the individual person (see, for example, the validity of the enthymeme and sorites). Further, the so-called 'universal' premise of the syllogism is never really universal, since it is simply a generalization cobbled together out of observations of particular instances. Finally, even if we assume (for the sake of argument) that a premise can be universal in the strict sense, the syllogism is incapable of genuinely producing new knowledge, since its conclusion is always just a particular reiteration of that premise. The categorical syllogism is thus hardly

as impressive as its philosophical practitioners pretend.
Ibn Taymiyya suggests that it is essentially the same as,
albeit inferior to, the analogical reasoning (*qiyas*) of the
jurists, and ultimately the only real source of certainty
is prophetic revelation. Thus the arch traditionalist
employs the most extreme manifestations of reason –
nominalism, empiricism and skepticism – to defeat the
rationalism of the philosophers.

See **Hanbalites; Islamism; law; logic; theology**
Further reading: Hallaq 1993

Ibn Tufayl, Abu Bakr Muhammad (d. 581/1185): One of the
most influential philosophers of the Islamic West, Ibn
Tufayl was a close companion of Abu Ya'qub Yusuf, the
Alhomad caliph of Andalusia, serving him in various
capacities as a court physician, possibly as a judge, and
less probably as a vizier. He seems to have been something
of a cultural minister as well, engaging in lengthy philosophical conversations with the caliph and bringing
numerous scholars and thinkers to his court. One such
thinker was the philosopher **Ibn Rushd**, who through Ibn
Tufayl's connections and encouragement took up the
monumental task of writing his three-tiered commentary
on **Aristotle**'s corpus, a project initially proposed by Abu
Ya'qub Yusuf himself. Ibn Tufayl had no time for such
undertakings, and indeed his body of writings is relatively
small. His major work is *Hayy ibn Yaqzan* ('Living, Son
of Awake'), a philosophical fable about an individual who
grows from infancy to adulthood on an uninhabited equa-
torial island. In the absence of human society, language,
culture, tradition and revelation, relying only upon observation and his own optimal **intellect**, Hayy comes to learn
about the physical world, the **soul** and **God**, recapitulat-
ing as he does the whole developmental history of
human **reason**. Having achieved comprehensive theoretical

knowledge of physical and metaphysical realities, the philosophical autodidact goes on to model his ethical life on the imitation of God, take up Sufi-like practices, and finally experience intimate, mystical **knowledge** of God, thereby suggesting that **philosophy** and **mysticism** are two sides of the same coin. Hayy is eventually discovered by Absal, a resident of a neighboring island, who teaches him to speak and tells him about the revealed religion of his homeland (a thinly veiled version of **Islam**), which turns out to be a symbolic presentation of the truths that Hayy has independently attained through reason and experience. Hayy returns with Absal to the neighboring island but soon realizes (à la **al-Farabi**) that the vast majority of people are not equipped to approach the truth as he did, that **prophecy** is a beneficial necessity, and that it is better for the simple folk to be left with their **literalist** faith, so long as it does not become too worldly and corrupt. Hayy and Absal return to the uninhabited island and live out their lives as philosopher-mystics, in solitude from the rest of humankind. Ibn Tufayl claims that his *Hayy ibn Yaqzan* is a presentation of Ibn Sina's '**Eastern philosophy**' (*al-hikmat al-mashriqiyya*), although the narrative of book is quite unlike Ibn Sina's 'visionary recital' of the same name. Its philosophical import is not always Avicennan either: in Ibn Sina's tale, 'Hayy ibn Yaqzan' is a poetic name for the active intellect, which on his account is external to and independent of particular human beings. In Ibn Tufayl's tale, however, it becomes a proper name, suggesting that the active intellect is in fact something intrinsic to the individual thinker.

See **active intellect**; **Eastern philosophy**; **epistemology**; **floating man argument**; **God (imitation of)**; **Ibn Rushd**; **Ibn Sina**; **Islam**; **mysticism**; **philosophy**

Further reading: Conrad 1996; Hawi 1974/97; Ibn Tufayl 1972/2003

Ikhwan al-Safa': see **Brethren of Purity**

Illuminationism (*al-ishraq*): Illuminationist (*ishraqi*) **philosophy** sees itself as an advance on **Peripatetic** (*mashsha'i*) philosophy, in the sense that it involves thinking on a more advanced level. It also has some strong objections to key claims of the Peripatetics, which it seeks to replace with an entirely new approach to **logic** and **metaphysics**.

For **al-Suhrawardi, knowledge** is direct experience of something, and we do not need to use any abstract concepts to understand our experience. He created the notion of '**knowledge by presence**' (*al-'ilm al-huduri*), which is taken to be something we cannot doubt, and is like the sort of experience we have when something is lit up before us. He uses terms to describe this like illumination (*ishraq*), presence (*hudur*) and manifestation (*zuhur*), all of which suggest something immediate. This sort of direct knowledge is 'truthful witnessing' (*mushahada haqqiya*), and the best example of it is knowledge of the self. Although it is direct, most people cannot use this knowledge directly, and prefer to employ reasoning, which is slower and less demanding. Our basic sense experiences represent 'simple meanings' out of which concepts are constructed. We do not need to look at them from the viewpoint of abstract concepts. For the Peripatetics it is matter that is the cause of the diversity of things, but for al-Suhrawardi it is rather the degree of perfection (*kamal*) or completeness by which a particular 'universal meaning' is represented in the individual, and this can be outlined in terms of luminosity. 'Illumination' means the direct lighting up of the soul by what are ultimately higher metaphysical lights. The soul itself is a light that has descended from the realm of light into the world of darkness and is not able to return to its original home. Since the soul and the higher levels of being are originally on the same level it is not difficult to understand how light can be received and what impact it makes. Illumination reveals the truth (*haqq*) immediately and requires no assent or judgement (*tasdiq*). Our rationality which is so important a way of finding out normally is useless at this level of direct knowledge, and has to be restricted to the less important and more indirect forms of knowledge.

One of the most interesting defenses of the notion of *al-'ilm al-huduri* is that provided by Mehdi Ha'iri Yazdi, whose basic argument is that knowledge of ourselves is not to be classified as propositional knowledge, consisting of statements which could be true or false. If this knowledge was capable of being true or false then it would have to be assessable, yet any such assessment already presupposes the self that is doing the assessing. Experience of the self is so perfect that it is undeniable. The metaphor of light here is important, since once something is lit up, it is there in front of us and we are aware of it. On this basis Illuminationist thinkers construct an elaborate **metaphysics**, replacing the language of subject and object in terms of different degrees of luminosity. They also reject the **Aristotelian** notion of definition as the foundation of science, preferring instead to refer to our experience for the most certain principles in which we can believe.

See **Eastern philosophy; epistemology; floating man argument; Ibn Kammuna; logic; metaphysics; al-Shahrazuri; al-Shirazi; al-Suhrawardi**

Further reading: Aminrazavi 1997; Corbin 1998; Ha'iri Yazdi 1992; Nasr 1964; al-Suhrawardi 1982/99, 1998, 1999; Walbridge 1992, 2000b, 2001; Ziai 1990

imaginal realm (*'alam al-khayal*, *'alam al-mithal*): see **Ibn al-'Arabi; al-Suhrawardi**

imagination (*khayal, takhyil*): see **aesthetics; Ibn al-'Arabi**

imam (spiritual leader): see **Shi'ites**

immortality of soul: see **afterlife; psychology**

independent judgement (*ijtihad*): Etymologically related to the term *jihad* (effort, striving), *ijtihad* is a legal concept that has to do with exerting oneself or exercising independent judgement. The history of *ijtihad* (also sometimes referred to as *ra'y*, or 'considered opinion') is somewhat stormy in the Islamic tradition: by the early third/ninth century the legal scholar al-Shafi'i had restricted its legitimate application to reasoning by analogy (*qiyas*) and by the end of that century there was a growing consensus among the various legal schools that the gate of *ijtihad* was closed. That is, most scholars believed the big questions had essentially been settled and independent reasoning in **law** was either unnecessary or required more knowledge than contemporary jurists could reasonably be expected to amass. Thus its opposite, *taqlid* (**obedience**, following, imitation), became the norm in **jurisprudence** and the representative legal scholar was a *muqallid* (follower, imitator) rather than a *mujtahid* (independent thinker). However, this view has not gone unchallenged: a wide range of figures, from **Ibn Rushd** and the Arab modernists to the **Twelver Shi'ites** and **Isma'ilis**, to **Ibn Taymiyya** and the Salafis, have argued forcefully in defense of *ijtihad*.

See **law; obedience; rationalism; traditionalism**
Further reading: Hallaq 1997, 2005; Schacht 1964/83

innovation (*bid'a*): see **belief**

intellect (*'aql*): see **active intellect; psychology**

interpretation (*ta'wil*): A distinction is drawn early on in the Islamic tradition between two types of Qur'anic exegesis: interpretation based on what has been handed down from authoritative sources (*tafsir bi al ma'thur*) and interpretation based on **reason** and considered opinion (*tafsir bi al-ra'y*). The former type of interpretation (sometimes just referred to as *tafsir*) privileges the apparent or literal meaning of the text and is typically favored by **traditionalists**, who were mistrustful of the promptings of individual human reason (e.g. the **Hanbalites** and their progeny, although the most extreme school in this respect was the **Zahirites**). The latter type of interpretation (sometimes just referred to as *ta'wil*) often points in the direction of a more figurative, **esoteric** or spiritual understanding, and is generally favored by more **rationalist**-oriented theologians, philosophers and mystics. The **Mu'tazilites** and Greek-influenced philosophers, for instance, diverged in varying degrees from the apparent meaning of the **Qur'an** when it contradicted the conclusions of reason (e.g. anthropomorphic descriptions of the divine, **God**'s free creation of the world *ex nihilo*, etc.). The **Isma'ilis** similarly distinguished between the outer (*zahir*) and inner (*batin*) dimension of the Qur'an (hence their nickname, the *batiniyya*). For them *ta'wil* had to do with elucidating the esoteric meaning of the text, which could only be provided by the **imams**, who were believed to possess special, authoritative knowledge in such matters. For the **Sufis**, *ta'wil* involved a more profound, spiritual realization of the Qur'an's message, which might be illuminated or unveiled by first-hand experience, made possible through the practices established by Sufi masters.

See **Ash'arites**; **Batinites**; **Hanbalites**; **Isma'ilis**; **Mu'tazilites**; **Qur'an**; **rationalism**; **Sufism**; **traditionalism**; **Zahirites**

Iqbal, Muhammad (1289–1356/1873–1938): Sir Muhammad Iqbal was without a doubt the greatest Indo-Muslim philosopher-poet and possibly the most important and influential Islamic intellectual of the twentieth century. Encouraged by the eminent Orientalist Sir Thomas Arnold (who tutored him at the Government College in Lahore), Iqbal studied **philosophy** at Cambridge with the British Hegelian J. M. E. McTaggart and went on to write his dissertation at Munich University on the development of **metaphysics** in Persia. Upon his return to India, he first took up a position as Professor of Philosophy and English Literature, but soon decided to give up his teaching career and become a lawyer in order more effectively to propagate his political ideas and the broader philosophical conception of the human being upon which they were based. Iqbal's primary mode of expression was philosophical-didactic poetry, which he wrote in both Persian and Urdu. Of particular note are his *Secrets of the Self* (*Asrar-i khudi*), in which he first articulated his quasi-Nietzschean emphasis on the development of the self or ego (*khudi*) as opposed to mystical **annihilation** (*fana'*), and *The Mysteries of Selflessness* (*Rumuz-i bikhudi*), which stressed the development of the communal ego and the duties of the individual within the larger Muslim community. However, his magnum opus is the *Book of Eternity* (*Javid-nama*), which he dedicated to his son. The poem recounts a Dantian spiritual journey in which Iqbal travels through the spheres accompanied by the Sufi poet Rumi, engaging various leaders (both Muslim and non-Muslim) in dialogues about philosophical and political problems. Iqbal only published three prose works, two of which are in English: his dissertation, *The Development of Metaphysics in Persia*, and *The Reconstruction of Religious Thought in Islam*, which collected a series of lectures he had delivered at various universities in India.

Whereas the former is for the most part a work of historical scholarship, the latter articulates a new metaphysics by means of Iqbal's unique reconciliation of Muslim theology and European science and philosophy. It is generally considered one of the most important works of modern Islamic philosophy.

Iqbal's philosophy of the self envisions the trajectory of humanity in a dynamic, developmental and powerfully affirmative way. He rejects the myth of the Fall, or rather reinterprets it as a symbolic representation of the individual's development from 'a primitive state of instinctive appetite to the conscious possession of a free self, capable of doubt and disobedience'. Influenced by western 'vitalist' philosophers such as Friedrich Nietzsche and Henri Bergson, Iqbal adopts an evolutionary worldview, albeit with the full realization or perfection of the human self (*insani-i kamil*) – the ideal person – as its teleological apex. Interestingly, Iqbal thinks quite highly of Nietzsche, not only because of his dynamic conception of reality and his model of the *Übermensch* as the fully realized, striving human, but also because of his healthy anti-Platonism (Iqbal was of the opinion that Platonic mysticism had contributed to the decline of **Islam**). Nonetheless, in Iqbal's portrait, Nietzsche is like a man who has stopped at the *la ilah* ('there is no god') of the witnessing, before he has reached the final affirmation of *illa Allah* ('but God'). Iqbal's emphasis on the full realization or perfection of the self thus diverges from Nietzsche's insofar as it envisions God as the greatest self. It also diverges from monistic strains of **Sufism**, insofar as it rejects the **oneness of existence**, understood at least as strong identity with the divine. The perfection of the self results not in the vanquishing of God or the realization of one's unity with God, but rather with a fruitful, appropriate relationality to the divine. On Iqbal's account, the human being can perfect and fully actualize itself only in relation to God. Although the human being is the apex of creation, it is still the servant (*'abd*) of God.

The full development of the human self is never a *fait accompli*, but rather involves a ceaseless striving. Iqbal's concern is primarily with the journey rather than the destination, so to speak; one truly *is* only as long as one is moving. He even sees Satan (Iblis, al-Shaytan) as an ineliminable catalyst in the quest for the full realization of the self. For it is Iblis who gives humankind its taste for striving in the first place, provoking us to a perpetual struggle which makes possible our epistemological, ethical and spiritual development. Evil itself is thus redeemed by the necessary role it plays in actualizing human potential, and Iqbal envisions Satan's prostration before the self-perfected human being as a compensation for his earlier refusal to acknowledge the supremacy of Adam. One is reminded of Goethe's 'Faustian man' a bit here, except that Iqbal's optimal orientation towards the world is characterized by both **science** and **mysticism**, for without love (*'ishq*), **reason** (*'aql*) becomes demonic.

On Iqbal's account, even the **immortality** of the human soul is an achievement rather than a pre-given fact. This idea is ultimately bound up with Iqbal's understanding of **time**, which he conceives in a two-fold way, as created serial time on the one hand and uncreated time or pure duration on the other. The former is essentially clock time; the latter is the more fundamental constant and endless flow in which all creatures have their life and being. Through its own self-perfection, the human being has the ability to cast off the 'magician's girdle' (*zunnar*) of serial time and reach the 'eternal now' of the divine.

On the socio-political front, Iqbal's activism was an expression of his more fundamental spiritual and intellectual concerns. His energetic efforts to awaken the consciousness of Indian Muslims, his participation in organizations such as the All India Muslim League, and his idea of a separate Muslim homeland won him the title of 'spiritual father of Pakistan'. Yet Iqbal's concerns were by no means particularistic or merely nationalistic. He focused his efforts as well on the larger anti-colonialist pan-Islamist movement and ultimately the Muslim independence movement, which he saw as a vehicle, not for yet another kind of provincial exclusivity, but rather for the universal humanitarian ideal, which arguably had animated his thought and practice all along.

See 'Abduh (Muhammad); al-Afghani; Islamism; modern Islamic philosophy; Wali Allah (Shah)

Further reading: Hassan 1977; Iqbal 1908/64, 1930, 1950, 1953, 1966/2003; Schimmel 1963; Singh 1997; Vahid 1959

ishraq (Illumination): see **Illuminationism; al-Suhrawardi**

Islam: Literally, 'submission' to the will of God. The word *islam* is etymologically related to the Arabic word *salam* and so carries a connotation of 'peace' as well. As one of the great monotheistic religions, Islam recognizes an important continuity with the Judeo-Christian lineage, viewing its predecessors not so much as alternative religions, but rather as incomplete, misunderstood or corrupted versions of itself. Of the three, Islam is the most uncompromisingly monotheistic, insisting upon God's absolute unity and uniqueness. Like Judaism and Christianity, it holds that God is the all-knowing and all-powerful Creator of the universe, that He has created it for a purpose, that He is personally concerned with the particularities of human affairs, and that He intervenes in history at pivotal moments. For Muslims, the most important of these interventions occurred between 610 and 632

CE, when God chose **Muhammad** as His last and greatest prophet and disclosed a series of revelations to him through the angel Jibril. These revelations, known collectively as the **Qur'an**, provide human beings with a **law** that makes known God's will and specifies certain beliefs and practices. On the Last Day, or the Day of Resurrection (*yawm al-qiyama*), God will judge each person based on whether or not he or she lived in accordance with His will and accordingly reward them in Paradise (*al-janna*, lit. 'the Garden') or punish them in Hell (*al-nar*, lit. 'the Fire'). Like Judaism (but unlike Christianity), Islam has a pronounced legalistic dimension. The Qur'an's requirements and prohibitions, supplemented by reports of the deeds and sayings of Muhammad and his companions, were soon codified by various schools of **jurisprudence** as Islamic law (*shari'a*). The five 'pillars' of Islam (*arkan al-islam*) comprise the basic practices required of every Muslim: the *shahada* or profession of faith ('There is no god but God and Muhammad is His Messenger'), *salat* or the prayer ritual (performed five times daily), *zakat* or the giving of charity, *sawm* or fasting during the month of Ramadan, and *hajj* or making the pilgrimage to Mecca. These observances function as a kind of external sign of submission to the will of God, but Muslims generally agree that it must be accompanied by an interior faith or **belief** (*iman*) as well. It should be noted that Islam signifies not only the **religion** revealed to Muhammad by God and its codification as Islamic law, but also the community (*umma*, *milla*) of the faithful. In spite of this general sense of identity and solidarity, there are various tendencies, schools, movements and sects within Islam. The most fundamental of these differences is the division between the **Sunnis** and the **Shi'ites**, which primarily has to do with the theologico-political question of who should lead the Muslim community.

See **afterlife; belief; God; law; prophecy; Qur'an; Shi'ites; Sunnis**

Further reading: Esposito 1991/2004; Hodgson 1974; McAuliffe 2001–6; Rahman 1979

Islamism: Islamism, sometimes loosely referred to as Islamic 'fundamentalism', is a broad and contested term. It is typically seen as comprising a number of political movements in the Islamic world, which strive to recapture the putatively original, uncorrupted and undiluted reality of **Islam** through the establishment of an Islamic state based on the divine **law** (*shari'a*). A useful distinction can be drawn between three stages of this modern phenomenon. The first stage revolves around a series of revivalist efforts in the eighteenth and nineteenth centuries, the most notable of which is the Wahhabi movement of central Arabia, inspired by the thirteenth/fourteenth-century **Hanbalite** thinker **Ibn Taymiyya** and founded by Muhammad ibn 'Abd al-Wahhab. This early stage of Islamism is characterized by an attempt to return to the original form of Islam, purifying it of pagan customs, innovative traditions and foreign accretions. It generally calls for the exercise of **independent judgement** rather than blind **obedience**, the withdrawal or migration from areas dominated by unbelievers, the declaration of *jihad* or holy struggle (in the lesser, political sense) against the enemies of Islam, and the yearning for a single leader with the ability to renew the spirit of Islam (e.g. the Mahdi). This nascent, pre-colonial form of Islamism tends to involve little engagement with external systems of thought; it is mostly an internal dialogue of Muslims with themselves.

The second, 'reformist' stage revolves initially around a number of nineteenth- and twentieth-century public intellectuals such as al-Afghani, Muhammad 'Abduh and

Rashid Rida who also descried both the internal corruptions of Islam and the destructive external effects of western secularism and colonialism upon the Islamic world. The early reformists, however, had a more rationalist bent. They were engaged in an open dialogue with European culture and science and sought to establish the relevance of Islam to modernity even as they strove to establish an autonomous Islamic polity. Their ideas gave rise to influential organizations such as the Salafis and Hasan al-Banna's Muslim Brotherhood (*al-ikhwan al-muslimun*).

The Egyptian-based Muslim Brotherhood in particular became a powerful international mass movement which, along with the emergence of sovereign nation-states in the Islamic world, gave rise to a more radical form of Islamism. Two of the chief architects of radical Islamism, the Indian/Pakistani thinker Abu al-A'la al-Mawdudi and the Egyptian intellectual Sayyid Qutb, passed through the ranks of the Muslim Brotherhood before splintering off to espouse their own, more exclusivist agendas. Its third great theoretician was the Iranian Shi'ite philosopher-scholar Ayatollah Ruhollah Khumayni (Khomeini), who led the Iranian revolution. These three influential thinkers formulated a thorough-going critique of western modernism, i.e. the secular division between religion and state, democracy, nationalism, socialism, relativism, atheism, and the rationalist confidence in the capacity of **science** and technology to solve all of humanity's problems – all of which Qutb characterizes as pagan ignorance (*jahiliyya*). Human nature is taken to have remained the same for all time, so the divine revelation of the **Qur'an** remains relevant throughout history and the novelties and innovations of modernity are irrelevant to the fundamental, timeless truths disclosed by Islam. Finally, faith in the **unity** of God requires the reestablishment of a pan-Islamic polity in which all aspects of life are based purely on religious law. It is important to note that this theocratic state is more of a contemporary political ideology rather than an historical actuality in Islam. The Islamist 'return' to ostensibly pure origins involves a great deal of creative interpretation and indeed is unthinkable without its radical confrontation with modernity. For this reason, it is not strictly speaking a form of **traditionalism**, despite its historical roots in that phenomenon and its virulent opposition to **rationalism**.

See **'Abduh (Muhammad)**; **al-Afghani**; **Hanbalites**; **Ibn Taymiyya**; **political philosophy**; **traditionalism**; **Wali Allah (Shah)**; **Zahirites**

Further reading: Choueiri 1990/97; Esposito and Voll 2001; Euben 1999; al-Khumayni 1981; al-Mawdudi 1932/80; Qutb 1990

Isma'ilis (*isma'iliyya*): An important and influential division of **Shi'ite Islam**, the Isma'ilis branched off from the **Twelver Shi'ites** over the identity of the last **imam**. The Isma'ilis identify him as their seventh imam, Isma'il ibn Ja'far (who is rejected in Twelver genealogy), and believe he went into occultation and will return at the end of time as the Mahdi (hence the name 'Isma'ilis', or 'Seveners' [*sab'iyya*], as they have also sometimes been called). Unlike the Twelvers, who – as a general rule at least – historically have tended towards political quietism during the period of the imam's occultation, the Isma'ili movement has generally been characterized by different kinds of political activism, ranging from the founding of the Fatamid dynasty in Tunisia and Egypt, to the propagandist activities of their missionaries (*da'i*s) throughout the **Sunni** 'Abbasid provinces, to the more radical methods of Hasan-i Sabbah, who from his seemingly invulnerable mountain fortress of Alamut founded the Nizari Isma'ili state in Persia and Syria.

Isma'ilis are also noted for distinguishing between an external, apparent (*zahir*) meaning of revelation and a more fundamental and important inner (*batin*) meaning. It is believed that the hidden, **esoteric** truths of the **Qur'an** can only be disclosed through the complex, symbolic and allegorical interpretations of divinely guided imams, which are then selectively disseminated through their missionaries in a hierarchical and highly secretive manner. For this reason they are sometimes referred to as the *batiniyya* ('esotericists'), or alternatively the *ta'limiyya* (loosely, 'authoritarians') because of their emphasis on the authoritative teaching (*ta'lim*) of the imams. The inner teaching involved a messianic eschatology, a cyclical theory of history and an elaborate mythical cosmology, which by the fourth/tenth century was effectively replaced by a more intellectually sophisticated **Neoplatonic** system.

The Isma'ili conception of God as 'Originator' (*al-mubdi'*) places a great emphasis on His absolute **transcendence** and **unity** – and by extension, His fundamental difference from all created things. In order to do justice to this uniqueness, the Isma'ilis developed a negative **theology** that denied intellectual as well as corporeal **attributes** to the divine and employed a rigorous strategy of 'double negation' (God is not a thing, but also *not* not a thing, etc.). The effect of this was to render God altogether mysterious and unknowable.

This points up a certain ambivalence that the Isma'ilis felt with regard to the proper place of **reason** within their system. On the one hand, they insisted upon the authority of the divinely guided prophet and imams: universally distributed human reason is, on their account, not capable of uncovering the ultimate soteriological import of revelation, or grasping the true nature of reality on its own. However, the Isma'ilis' own **metaphysics** posited the ontological primacy of reason or **intellect** (*'aql*) within creation: intellect is the first and only being 'originated' by God, and that from which everything else in the universe ultimately proceeds. The prophets and imams are invested with authoritative **knowledge** precisely because of their privileged relation to intellect; even revelation itself is ultimately a manifestation or incarnation of intellect, and thus cannot be at odds with reason.

The Isma'ilis' ambivalence towards reason is reflected in their view of **philosophy**. In theory, they held it in rather low regard, characterizing it as fruitless, even contradictory speculation in the absence of the divinely guided authoritative teaching of the prophets and imams. Yet the Isma'ilis' own texts are often extremely philosophical in nature and their greatest intellectual achievements would have been unthinkable without the contributions of Neoplatonism. Some of the major Isma'ili thinkers are Muhammad al-Nasafi, Abu Hatim al-Razi, Abu Ya'qub **al-Sijistani**, Hamid al-Din **al-Kirmani** and **Nasir-i Khusraw**. The secretive intellectual circle known as the Ikhwan al-Safa' or '**Brethren of Purity**', the **Ash'arite** theologian **al-Shahrastani** and the Twelver Shi'ite philosopher **al-Tusi** have been identified by some scholars as potential, or at least partial, Isma'ilis as well.

See **Batinites; interpretation; al-Kirmani; Nasir-i Khusraw; Neoplatonism; Shi'ites; al-Sijistani (Abu Ya'qub); Twelver Shi'ites**

Further reading: Corbin 1993; Daftary 1990; Walker 1993

J

al-Jabiri, Muhammad 'Abid (1936–): see **modern Islamic philosophy**

Jabrites (*jabriyya*, *mujbira*): An early theological movement that upheld the doctrine of *jabr*, or divine compulsion. The Jabrites maintained that it is not humans but **God** alone who acts, that human beings have no real power over their choices and actions, and that all events are ultimately determined by God's will. Accordingly, they argued in defense of *qadar*, or **predestination**. The Jabrites drew primarily upon traditional sources such as the **Qur'an** and *hadith* in support of their position, pointing to numerous fatalistic-sounding passages, e.g. where **Muhammad** speaks of God's 'primordial pen' (which sets forth everything that will happen until the Day of Judgement) and asserts that a person's place in Paradise or Hell is predetermined. The **Ash'arites**, who subsequently put forth a more qualified version of the predestination doctrine, supplemented this kind of exegetical defense with rational arguments that emphasized God's absolute omnipotence, a premise that left little room for the power or freedom of the individual will. Although the Ash'arites presented their own doctrine of 'acquisition' (*kasb*) as a happy mean between the Jabrites' fixation on divine compulsion and the **Qadarites'** privileging of **free will**, the **Mu'tazilites** (who were also staunch defenders of free will) simply lumped them in with the other *jabriyya*. Obvious similarities notwithstanding, one can differentiate between different degrees of Jabrism. While more extreme versions of the doctrine would seem to suggest that *everything* is predetermined (i.e. not only what happens to an individual, but how he or she reacts), more moderate and subtle versions of the doctrine attempted to leave a little room for some kind of individual moral responsibility. This qualified version of Jabrism won out over the Qadarites' and Mu'tazilites' free will **theology** and effectively became a mainstream **Sunni** position.

See **Ash'arites**; **causality**; **free will and predestination**; **God**; **Mu'tazilites**; **occasionalism**; **Qadarites**; **Qur'an**; **theology**; **traditionalism**
Further reading: Watt 1948, 1962/85

jurisprudence (*fiqh*): see **law**

al-Juwayni, Abu al Ma'ali (419–478/1028–85): The Persian al-Juwayni is a Janus figure of sorts in the history of **Ash'arite** *kalam*, occupying an intermediate position between its old (*mutaqaddimun*) and new or 'modern' (*muta'akhkhirun*) theologians. On the one hand, he espoused many traditional Ash'arite views: e.g. the idea of **God** as omnipotent **cause** of everything that occurs, the doctrine of 'acquisition', the derivation of **ethics** from revealed scripture rather than **reason**, and the insistence that God's actions cannot be understood or evaluated in terms of human conceptions of justice. On the other, he introduced innovations that would come to characterize the more sophisticated modern school of Ash'arite philosophical theology, laying the groundwork for thinkers such as **al-Ghazali**, **al-Shahrastani** and Fakhr al-Din **al-Razi**. His protracted skirmishes with the philosophers pushed him to adopt more rigorous methods of reasoning and argumentation (i.e. **Aristotle**'s demonstrative syllogism), and even to cast rational inquiry as a religious duty. He learned from the **rationalist Mu'tazilite** theologians as well, appropriating Abu Hashim's theory of modes (*ahwal*) and applying it to his theory of **knowledge** and conception of the divine **attributes**. Other innovations that would have an important bearing on modern Ash'arite philosophical theology are al-Juwayni's emphasis on the absolute, unqualified freedom of God (whose actions are undetermined by anything but God Himself), his rejection of necessary causal relations in nature (and thus determinism), and his move away from the **tradi-tionalist** *bila kayf* strategy of scriptural hermeneutics (towards a recognition of the necessity of **interpretation** [*ta'wil*] when confronted with concealed or obscure passages). Al-Juwayni's greatest work of **theology** was the now-incomplete and unpublished *Book of the Summa* (*Kitab al-shamil*); his chief extant work is *The Guide to the Cogent Proofs of the Principles of Faith* (*Kitab al-irshad ila qawati' al-adilla fi usul al-i'tiqad*). Known as the 'Imam of the Two Holy Cities' (*imam al-haramayn*) because of his teaching at both Mecca and Medina, he later held an appointment at the Nizamiyya *madrasa* in Nishapur, where he taught his most famous student, al-Ghazali.

See **Ash'arites; al-Ghazali; theology**
Further reading: Hourani 1985; Saflo 1974

kalam: see **theology**

Kharijites (*khawarij*): The Kharijites were an early theologico-political movement that emerged out of controversies surrounding the status of the third and fourth caliphs, 'Uthman and 'Ali. The first members of this school were initially partisans of 'Ali (*shi'at 'Ali*), but 'went out' or 'seceded' (*kharaja*) because of his ambivalent response to the murder of his predecessor 'Uthman, which they believed was justified because of 'Uthman's wrongful actions. The first main issue that concerned the Kharijites was the question of the caliphate: who can legitimately claim to lead the Muslim community? They maintained, contra the **Shi'ites**, that any believer who is morally and religiously beyond reproach and endorsed by the community is qualified to be caliph regardless of origin, but that any caliph who diverges from the right path is no longer a legitimate ruler and should be deposed. On these grounds they opposed 'Ali's caliphate while also condemning 'Uthman and justifying his murder. A second – and closely related – issue with which they were concerned was the legal and eschatological status of Muslims who commit grave sins. On this question they argued that Muslims who sin are in effect unbelievers and accordingly forfeit all their rights and protections under Islamic **law**. Those who disagreed with them were, perhaps unsurprisingly, branded as unbelievers and treated as such. The Kharijites were notorious for their fanaticism and violent activism, and ultimately their ideas were rejected in favor of a more moderate position that acknowledged the legitimacy of both 'Uthman and 'Ali (as well as a broader, more nuanced conception of belief). Yet despite the extremism of their views, the Kharijites played a crucial role in the emergence and early development of Islamic **theology**.

See **belief; Islam; Murji'ites; Shi'ites; theology**

Further reading: van Ess 2006; Watt 1973, 1962/85

al-Kindi, Abu Yusuf Ya'qub ibn Ishaq (d. c. 252/866): Dubbed the 'philosopher of the Arabs', al-Kindi is the first major figure in the Islamic philosophical tradition. A polymath who wrote extensively on medicine, mathematics, music, astrology and optics as well as **philosophy**, al-Kindi lived in Baghdad during the great cultural and intellectual expansion of the 'Abbasid caliphate and played a notable role in the Greco-Islamic translation movement that it sponsored through the 'House of Wisdom' (*bayt al-hikma*). He is believed to have encouraged and corrected the translation of Pseudo-Aristotle's *Theology*, which was enormously influential among the *falasifa* and led many thinkers to interpret **Aristotle** in the light of **Neoplatonic metaphysics**.

Of the 260 works al-Kindi is believed to have authored, only a small percentage survive. His key extant work is *On First Philosophy* (*Fi al-falsafa al-ula*), which appropriates numerous Aristotelian concepts, translating, refining and supplementing them to accommodate the new concerns of a world shaped by **Islam**. Particularly noteworthy is his defense of philosophy against those who attack it in the name of **religion**. Al-Kindi legitimizes the retrieval of Greek insights by arguing that we must pursue **knowledge** regardless of the source, and seize upon the truth wherever we find it. He goes on famously to argue for the compatibility of philosophy and religion. When the two do occasionally diverge, al-Kindi appears to privilege the latter over the former: for instance, he rejects Aristotle's claims about the eternity of the world in favor of the Qur'anic **creation** *ex nihilo* model. However, his concerns are ultimately more explicitly philosophical than those of the theologians with whom he is sometimes affiliated (due to his **rationalism**, his conception of **God** as having no **attributes**, and his political affiliations, some scholars have cast him as a **Mu'tazilite**).

The aim of the philosopher, according to al-Kindi, is not only to attain the truth insofar as it is possible, but also to act in accordance with it. Accordingly, his philosophy has a strong practical dimension, and he espouses a form of ethical perfectionism that draws from **Socrates** and the Stoics, emphasizing control of the passions and the sufficiency of virtue for **happiness**.

Al-Kindi's importance in the Islamic philosophical tradition consists first and foremost in his ambitious retrieval of Greek learning, his defense of reason, and the formative role he played in forging a philosophical vocabulary in Arabic.

See **Aristotle; creation vs. eternity of the world; ethics; metaphysics; Neoplatonism; philosophy; Socrates**

Further reading: Adamson 2006; Atiyeh 1966/77; Druart 1993; al-Kindi 1974, 2002

al-Kirmani, Hamid al-Din (d. c. 412/1021): One of the greatest **Isma'ili** philosophers from the time of the Fatimid caliphate, al-Kirmani built upon the **Neoplatonic** cosmological systems of his missionary forebears (e.g. al-Nasafi, Abu Hatim al-Razi and **al-Sijistani**), but influenced by the **Peripatetic** philosophers, introduced a more **Aristotelian** element. His principal work is the *Peace of the Intellect* (*Rahat al-'aql*). Like his Isma'ili predecessors, al-Kirmani was concerned with preserving **God**'s absolute **unity** and **transcendence** from even the most intellectually sophisticated and well-meaning but inadvertently destructive theological and philosophical assays. Towards this end he adopted **al-Sijistani**'s rigorous negative **theology**, which, not content with merely negating traditional creaturely attributes, negated their negations as well. Contrary to philosophers like **al-Farabi** and **Ibn Sina,** he argued that God cannot even be characterized as the First Being, First Cause or **Necessary Existent,** for the divine is ultimately beyond the reach of **intellect** and rational discourse. Previous attempts at divine characterization in fact apply not to God, but rather to what al-Kirmani calls the 'first intellect', i.e. the first and only thing that God directly originates (*abda'a*). Their primary error consists in identifying the first intellect with God; al-Kirmani's project is in a sense to divest it of its 'divinity'.

As in al-Sijistani's system, the ontological emergence of all subsequent beings is a matter of temporal procession (*inba'atha*) rather than origination (*ibda'*). Here, however, al-Kirmani abandons the traditional Neoplatonic dyad of intellect (*'aql*) and **soul** (*nafs*), replacing it with a Farabian hierarchy of successive intellects. The first intellect, having been brought into being by God the 'Originator' (*mubdi'*), is overjoyed with its own existence (it 'blushes', in al-Kirmani's metaphor), and through this radiating joy gives rise to the second intellect, which is essentially a kind of reflection or representation of the first. Because of its relational status in the emerging hierarchy of being, the second intellect has a two-fold nature: it is both **cause** and effect, actual and potential being, form and matter (which al-Kirmani associates with the Qur'anic symbols of pen and tablet). It in turn gives rise to eight further intellects, along with their respective material spheres. The tenth and final intellect plays a central role in the governance of terrestrial affairs and provides human beings with the revealed religious **law**, which has unfolded and developed through its procession down the hierarchy of intellects.

Interestingly, for al-Kirmani the individual human soul does not share a direct kinship with the intellects. Indeed, he maintains, as al-Farabi arguably had, that the soul does not exist prior to the material body and that, at least in its original state, it cannot exist independently of it. However, the soul is capable of attaining perfection and thus becoming immortal and self-sufficient. It achieves this through **knowledge** and right action, which is made possible only by a teacher (a prophet or **imam**, who represents the perfection of intellect) and the soteriological teaching provided by the tenth intellect. Al-Kirmani's ambitious, syncretic cosmology ultimately proved less influential than that of his predecessor, al-Sijistani. However, his thought represents the most sophisticated version of Isma'ili philosophy that emerged in the Fatimid period.

See **al-Farabi**; **God (anthropomorphic descriptions of)**; **Isma'ilis**; **Neoplatonism**; **psychology**; **al-Sijistani (Abu Ya'qub)**; **theology**

Further reading: Nasr with Aminrazavi 2001; Walker 1993, 1999

knowledge (*'ilm*): see **epistemology**

knowledge by presence (*al-'ilm al-huduri*): see **Illuminationism; al-Suhrawardi**

L

language: In **religion**, issues of language and meaning are highly significant. A religion based on a text has to determine what the text means, and although this might have been clear to those who were present when the revelation of the **Qur'an** was given in the seventh century CE, it certainly is not after that date. It may not have been entirely clear to the early Muslims either, since they came to **Muhammad** for help on interpretive difficulties frequently. An early controversy in **Islam** took place between those who thought that the grammar (*nahw*) of Arabic is what is needed to resolve issues of meaning, and those who thought that something stronger such as **logic** should be invoked. This is an argument about whether the best people to resolve issues of meaning are grammarians, those who understood the *alfaz* or literary aspects of the text, or those who were best able to assess the *ma'ani* or meanings, the philosophers. The latter argued that they were the best people for the job since they understood not just one language, but all languages, in the sense that their conceptual machinery could deal with issues in any and every language.

This was not just an abstract argument, of course, since its outcome had implications for who was going to have the main hermeneutical role in **religion**, those trained in the religious sciences or the philosophers. There were strong arguments on both sides, and the opponents of the philosophers had at their disposal a wide range of theoretical techniques, including not only grammar, but law, the determination of when the revelations in the Qur'an were given (in Mecca or Medina, and when), the context of the **revelation**, how one passage contrasts with others, and so on.

Another controversy that continued for some time was between those who thought that language brings with it an ontology, in the sense that it is linked with what actually exists, and those who argue that language is independent of existence. **Al-Ghazali** and **Ibn Sina** both argued that language is independent of ontology, in that our use of language is a matter only of employing concepts, and the actual existence of what those concepts refer to is an entirely different issue. **Essence and existence** are then entirely separate from each other. Al-Ghazali used this to suggest that anything can happen since only **God** can make things happen, and so we could imagine observing someone writing a book without a head. God could make someone write without a head if he wanted to, despite our normal experiences. We would still mean the same thing by the concepts 'head', 'human being' and 'writes'. **Ibn Rushd** accepted the logical distinction between essence and existence here, but argued on the contrary that our ordinary experience of the world is part and parcel of what we mean when we use words, and if someone said that a headless person wrote a book, we would not understand what he meant. What is behind this disagreement is a difference in how to link God with the world. For Ibn Sina and al-Ghazali, the world is only as it is because of divine action, and something is needed to get it going, and keep it going. For Ibn Rushd, by contrast, the constitution of the world is something that has to exist in the way that it does, and although God is no doubt responsible for it distantly, what comes about has to come about in that way. So meanings are strongly linked with the nature of reality and our experience of the world, and the use of **imagination** to suggest otherwise breaks down because it produces ideas that have no meaning.

An important issue is the acceptability of using language to describe God. Given the Islamic ban on *shirk*, associating partners with God or idolatry, there are good grounds for sharply distinguishing between God and His creation, to the extent perhaps even that the ordinary language we use to describe the world cannot be used to describe the Deity. Yet the Qur'an does use ordinary language to describe both Him and His creation. Al-Ghazali suggested that there is no problem in applying predicates or qualities to God, and they are taken to mean what they mean when we apply them to ourselves, but they differ in their scope. Ibn Rushd did not accept this approach, especially since he agreed with **Aristotle** that there can be no priority or posteriority within the same genus or kind of thing, which God certainly is. Trying to apply a predicate to God makes Him too much like His creatures. But it is important that we can say something about God, and Ibn Rushd advocates treating Him as like us equivocally, so that there is no direct line from us to Him. His possession of qualities are seen as paradigmatic, and our possession of them is merely a weaker version of something perfect.

See **assimilation; Batinites; essence and existence; God (anthropomorphic descriptions of); Ibn Hazm; Ibn Taymiyya; interpretation; logic**

Further reading: Black 1990; Kennedy-Day 2003; Leaman 1997, 2000; Mahdi 1970; Margoliouth 1905; McAuliffe 2001; Walbridge 2000a

law: Islam consists of two significant sources of law. First there is the revelation of the **Qur'an**, the word of **God**, and secondly the *hadith*, short stories and reports of the Prophet's life and sayings, and of those close to him, which illustrate his and the early community's ideal practice (*sunna*). The doctrines and rules of behavior that can be linked with these sources are divine law or *shari'a*. In the Qur'an itself there are quite a few indications of legal doctrine, but this is enormously expanded in the *hadith* literature, and then later on in the various legal texts that came to be written to codify and determine different versions of Islamic law. Particularly interesting debates took place on the role of *ijtihad* or **independent judgement**, on *qiyas* or analogy, and on the significance of *maslaha* or considerations of welfare in determining law. Different schools of jurisprudence (*fiqh*) arose and argued not only about what the Islamic law is on a particular issue, but also on how to produce legal judgements. The **interpretation** of the Qur'an was a particularly controversial issue, especially given the doctrine of abrogation or *naskh*, by which later verses can abrogate earlier ones, a doctrine that is capable of introducing a good deal of independence in legal judgement. Some philosophers during the classical period were also jurists and employed legal examples in their work; for example, Ibn Rushd, who in his *Decisive Treatise* argues that Islamic law makes the study of philosophy not only permissible, but obligatory.

See **Hanbalites; independent judgement; interpretation; Islam; Qur'an**

Further reading: Calder et al. 2003; Hallaq 1997, 2005; Ibn Rushd 2001a; Schacht 1964/83

Levi ben Gerson (1288–1344): Perhaps the most important of the radical Aristotelian thinkers in the Jewish philosophical tradition was Rabbi Levi ben Gerson (alternatively, Gershon or Gershom; Latin: Gersonides). While he did not live in an Islamicate milieu – his home was in southern France – and did not write in Arabic like many of his predecessors (e.g. **Saadia Gaon**, Judah **Halevi**, **Ibn Gabirol**, **Ibn Maymun**, etc.), he was nonetheless profoundly influenced by Islamic **philosophy**. His indebtedness can be traced back through Ibn Maymun (who himself had an intimate familiarity with the doctrines and methods of the classical Islamic philosophers, particularly the *mashsha'un*) and **Ibn Rushd** (on whose Aristotelian commentaries he wrote numerous super-commentaries). In many ways his thought can be seen as an attempt to strike a balance between the harmonizing Aristotelianism of the former and the more radical, unadulterated Aristotelianism of the latter. In addition to the afore-mentioned super-commentaries, he produced works in the areas of astronomy, mathematics and Biblical exegesis.

His great original contribution in the field of philosophy is the *Book of the Wars of the Lord* (*Sefer Milhamot ha-Shem*), which argued resourcefully for a number of bold and controversial theses. A substantial portion of the book is dedicated to the question of whether the world is created or eternal. Levi ben Gerson rejects the traditional **creation** *ex nihilo* position on Aristotelian grounds, arguing that all generation must be from something, that pure form alone couldn't bring corporeal things into being without preexisting matter, and that the creationist model inescapably implies the existence of a vacuum, which is an impossibility. However, he also rejects the eternalist position, on the grounds that it entails the existence of an actual infinite, also an impossibility. Yet surprisingly, he rejects Ibn Maymun's contention that no position on this question is demonstrable, and formulates his own quasi-Platonic *formatio mundi* model according to which the universe is created by **God** out of preexisting, eternal matter. Further, he argues (again, apparently contra **Aristotle**) that, although the universe is generated, it is by its very nature indestructible.

Another topic on which Levi ben Gerson takes a fairly radical position is the hoary question regarding **God's knowledge** of spatio-temporal particulars. He defends the much-maligned claim that God has no real knowledge of future contingents. Although it seems as though Levi ben Gerson has sacrificed divine omniscience in order to preserve human freedom, he denies this is the case, since omniscience implies that one knows only what is actually knowable, and future contingents are not knowable because they have not yet been determined. In any case, 'ignorance' of spatio-temporal particulars is in fact not really a deficiency, since true **knowledge** is always of the universal, not of the particular.

In his **psychology**, Levi ben Gerson argues on behalf of the **immortality** of the **soul**, while limiting it to the rational part. However, he rejects the standard position of the *falasifa* that the soul becomes immortal through conjunction with the **active intellect**, and by extension, the Averroist doctrine of **monopsychism**, which ultimately rules out the possibility of individual or personal immortality. In doing so, he defends a philosophical conception of immortality that nevertheless preserves the uniqueness of the individual soul. What makes this compromise position possible is his particular conception of the active intellect as a kind of blueprint for the rational order of the cosmos. On his account, the active intellect grounds and preserves the distinctions created between individual souls by differing degrees of acquired knowledge, even after the destruction of our material aspect. It also justifies the great premium he places on human **reason** and the confidence he has in our ability to achieve extensive knowledge of God and the world (the objects of human thought are essentially the same as those of God's thought; the only difference is that God's knowledge is more perfect). It is perhaps no surprise, then, that Levi ben Gerson sees **revelation** as in some sense answerable to the claims of reason and interprets scripture figuratively when necessary in order to show its reconcilability with his own philosophical conclusions.

See **creation vs. eternity of the world; epistemology; Ibn Maymun; Ibn Rushd; psychology**

Further reading: Frank and Leaman 1997; Gersonides 1984, 1992; Sirat 1985

literalism: see **interpretation**

logic (*mantiq*): Logic first came of interest in the Islamic world through the need to argue with members of other religions in the Middle East who had a good grasp of how to argue. The **Qur'an** advises that people should be introduced to **Islam** with 'beautiful preaching' (16.125; 29.46). To a certain extent this involves argument, and the Qur'an does constantly call on its hearers and readers to consider the strength of the points made in the text. The encounter with Greek texts led to a good deal of translation into Arabic of Greek logic, but this was not uncontroversial. There was a celebrated debate in front of the court in Baghdad on the merits of a logic that originates outside the Islamic world and becomes the judge of Arabic culture. Those who defended logic said it was just a tool or instrument and had nothing to do with any particular subject matter, since it applied to every subject matter. This was met by the counter-argument that in fact logic brings a lot of theoretical baggage along with it, and is not appropriate as a technique to be used by Muslims.

They have their own theoretical sciences, such as grammar, Qur'anic exegesis, **jurisprudence, theology** and so on, disciplines that arose in the Islamic world and are specifically designed to deal with Islamic texts. The best-known debate took place between the Muslim al-Sirafi, opposing logic, and Abu Bishr Matta, a Christian, defending it. Al-Sirafi wonders why people think that Greek logic applies to Arabic texts, and the reply is that logic applies to statements in any **language**. **Al-Farabi** expressed this best later on, arguing that logic is the deep grammar of language itself, and has to be utilized if we are to analyze language.

There were three major attacks on Greek logic within the Islamic world, one from the perspective of **Sufism**, one from the **traditionalists** and finally the *ishraqi* or **Illuminationist** thinkers. The Iberian thinker **Ibn Sab'in** accused logicians of analyzing things by breaking them down into their parts, thus violating the basic **unity** (*tawhid*) of everything in **God**. Logic implies that it is the parts that are real, whereas from the Sufi point of view it is the whole. **Ibn Taymiyya** directly attacked the Aristotelian notion of definition (*hadd*) for its assumption that there is a basic distinction between the essential and accidental properties of a thing. He is a nominalist, and argues that universals or general terms should be analyzed in terms of the individuals that constitute them. We can think in terms of universals, but they are merely a way of bringing together particulars in our minds, and possess no independent existence of their own. Another problem with the notion of definition is that we never know whether or not we really distinguish between its essential and its accidental properties, since our experience will not provide us with this sort of information. We can experience the existence of objects, but what features they must possess and which they could do without, and yet stay the same sort of object, is not something we get from experience. So we cannot really have the confidence that logic says we can about how to define things. Only God can enlighten us on these topics, and for that we need not Greek logic but the Qur'an and other Islamic texts.

Aristotle's *Organon* is an account of the whole variety of deductive techniques that apply to concepts, so that there is a hierarchy of argumentative or deductive power, with demonstration (*burhan*) at the summit, where we operate with true premises and use them to arrive at valid and entirely general conclusions. The **Peripatetic** philosophers used the organon of Aristotle to argue that every human enterprise is characterized by some reasoning process or other. After demonstration comes dialectic (*jadal*), where the premises we use are those supplied by the side with which we are debating, and so we have no reason to think they are true. They might be, but they might not, and we might not be able to find out. Then we descend in logical strength, reaching rhetoric (*khitaba*) and poetry (*shi'r*), for example, where the point is to affect emotions by the use of **imagination**, and where the validity of the conclusion may be restricted, limited to a particular audience within a certain context on a unique occasion. Religions are replete with such examples of logic, since their purpose is to persuade and warn, and for that the emotions need to be affected through some attempt at explaining why the audience should have those feelings.

See **Aristotle; al-Farabi; al-Ghazali; Ibn Rushd; Ibn Sina; Ibn Taymiyya; al-Suhrawardi**

Further reading: Abed 1991; Black 1990; Gwynne 2004; Hallaq 1993; Ibn Sina 1984; Lameer 1994; Leaman 1997, 2000; Mahdi 1970; Margoliouth 1905; McAuliffe 2001; Walbridge 2000a

Maimonides, Moses: see **Ibn Maymun**

mashsha'un ('Walkers', Peripatetics, Aristotelians): see **Aristotle; philosophy**

metaphysics (*ma ba'd al-tabi'a; ilahiyyat*): After a brief initial engagement with political issues, the *kalam* theologians quickly turned their focus upon the nature of **God** and His relation to creation. In order to address this issue properly, they were forced to grapple, at least in a preliminary way, with questions concerning the basic structure of reality and the ultimate **causes** and constituents of things. But it is not until the discovery and translation of philosophical texts by **Plato**, **Aristotle** and the **Neoplatonists** that metaphysics emerges within the Islamic context as a subject in its own right.

It should not be surprising, then, that most of the different Arabic characterizations of the science of metaphysics are derived from Aristotle, the so-called 'First Teacher'. As early as **al-Kindi**, metaphysics is described as 'first **philosophy**' (*al-falsafa al-ula*), because it is 'the science of the first reality (*haqq*), which is the cause of all reality, and knowing a thing requires knowing its cause'. **Al-Farabi** (the 'Second Teacher') fixes upon another well-known Aristotelian formula for metaphysics: the science of 'being qua being' (*al-mawjud bi ma huwa mawjud*), that is, the study of all things insofar as they exist. It is thus the broadest and most fundamental of all disciplines. Of course, Aristotle had also described the subject matter of his *Metaphysics* as a **theology**, or 'science of the divine' (*'ilm al-ilahi*), but al-Farabi insists that this is only a particular subset of being qua being rather than the subject as such. Indeed, for the careful Muslim reader, the apparent universality or homogeneity of Aristotle's description belied the bewildering multiplicity of its actual subject matter. Aristotle recognized that being (*wujud*, *anniyya*) is said in many ways and immediately identified ten different categories, including substance (*jawhar*) and its various accidents (sing: *'arad*), e.g. quantity, quality, relation, etc. But his *Metaphysics* traffics in additional important distinctions, for example that between the universal (*kulli*) and the particular (*juz'i*), the four causes (sing: *'illa*), **actuality** (*fi'l*) vs. potentiality (*quwwa*), and necessary (*wajib*) vs. possible (*mumkin*) existence, not to mention the implicit but crucial distinction between **essence** (*mahiyya*) and **existence** (*wujud*) that the Muslim **Peripatetics** teased out. All this, in addition to offering a rational account of **God**!

Ibn Sina, who claims he read Aristotle's *Metaphysics* 'forty times' without comprehending it and attributes his eventual success to al-Farabi's commentary on the work, accepts the Second Teacher's stance to some extent, even arguing that God is not the subject matter of metaphysics per se, but rather its goal. Nonetheless, Ibn Sina and his followers typically refer to metaphysics as the science of 'divine things' (*ilahiyyat*), insofar as it involves the study of God and other separate, immaterial causes of the physical universe that are not themselves subject to generation and destruction.

To complicate matters further, Aristotle never actually used the term metaphysics himself. It is the title given to his book by a later commentator, who simply identified it based on its traditional position in his overall corpus: it is the book that comes after the *Physics* (Gr: *ta meta ta phusika*, Ar: *ma ba'd al-tabi'a*). With the gradual reification of this name, philosophers began to see it as defining the actual subject matter of Aristotle's strange science rather than simply describing its literal position in

Aristotle's oeuvre. The ambiguity inherent in the description has generated different conceptions of the main task of metaphysics, depending on whether one reads the 'after' (*ba'd*) in 'after the physics' literally (i.e. 'following', 'succeeding') or figuratively (i.e. 'above' [*fawq*], 'beyond' [*wara'*]).

Neoplatonic metaphysicians in the Islamic tradition (e.g. Ibn Sina, **al-Kirmani**, **al-Suhrawardi**, **Ibn al-'Arabi**, **Mulla Sadra**, etc.) tend to privilege the latter sense. Accordingly, they conceive of metaphysics as a kind of foundational first science that begins with the ultimate principle of existence – God as the One, the **Necessary Existent**, the first metaphysical 'efficient' cause (understood as an ontological ground that continually bestows existence upon beings rather than initiating temporal movement), the Originator, the Light of Lights, Truth/Reality, etc. – and in effect *derives* or *deduces* the world from this principle, via the process of **emanation** (*fayd*, lit. 'overflowing'). For instance, on the Neoplatonic-Aristotelian model, God necessarily gives rise to the universe through His archetypal self-knowledge, which emanates a hierarchical procession of intellects and corresponding celestial spheres. The last of these intellects (the '**active intellect**') gives rise to, and governs, the sublunary world of generation and destruction. This is the realm of nature (*tabi'a*) and thus the appropriate domain of the other, specific rational sciences, which study its phenomena, from minerals to plants to animals to the human being. The study of the human **soul** (*nafs*) and **intellect** (*'aql*) is thus part of the natural sciences, but in studying such things we are directed back to the immaterial, separate, absolutely unitary and simple source of all existents.

On the other hand, pure or 'radical' Aristotelians like **Ibn Rushd** tend to understand *ma ba'd al-tabi'a* ('the things which come after the physical things') more modestly and literally. On his view, metaphysics studies the principles of beings which (in their specific rather than generic sense) are the objects of the other sciences. In other words, the subject matter of metaphysics is not something transcendent of nature or known first and foremost, but rather something arrived at via induction, from investigation into its effects in the natural world. It functions not as the foundation of the natural sciences, but as their completion. Ibn Sina (in accordance with his Neoplatonic sympathies) had claimed that there is no apodictic demonstration of God; rather, God is the apodictic demonstration of everything else. Ibn Rushd rejects this a priori approach as senseless, just as he rejects Ibn Sina's Neoplatonic emanationist cosmology and his concept of God as the Necessary Existent and bestower, not just of motion, but of existence itself. The only way to prove the existence of God is to begin with physics – specifically, the phenomenon of motion. In short, then, Neoplatonic Aristotelians typically see the subject matter of metaphysics as being *above* and *beyond* nature. The movement of their thought is thus a kind of descent, whereby the natural world is deduced, only to return to the source from which they originally proceeded. Pure Aristotelians on the other hand see the subject matter of metaphysics as coming *after* nature. For them, the path of metaphysics is an ascent that begins with the empirical data of a dynamic material world and works its way up to the final explanatory principle of God.

One big controversy in Islamic metaphysics is the precise relation between God and the world. The Ash'arite theologians had envisioned a radically contingent world of insubstantial atoms (sing: *juz'*) and accidents (sing: *'arad*), which has an origin in time. God is not only the absolutely free Creator of the world *ex nihilo*, but the perpetual, omnipotent and direct cause of all things, without which nothing would have any efficacy, let alone existence. The Neoplatonic Aristotelians cast God as the Necessary Existent, which automatically and necessarily generates the eternal universe through its own self-knowledge, but which seems to have little or no awareness of (or concern for) the multiple, changeable, particular creatures that inhabit the material realm of nature. The *sui generis* freethinker Abu Bakr **al-Razi** defended an interesting *formatio mundi* model that posited the eternally enduring, independent existence of five principles: God, soul, time, space and matter. On his account, the **creation** of the universe is initiated by the pre-rational, impulsive desire of the soul to be embodied, followed by the beneficent intervention of God, who imposes order and regularity on its initially chaotic movements, giving it the rational means eventually to extricate itself from its unfortunate mistake. The **Isma'ilis** posited God as the absolutely transcendent, unitary and mysterious Originator, who creates only one being, the intellect, through His timeless command. An entire spiritual and material universe, saturated with symbolism, then proceeds from this first created entity, and can return to it (but not to the transcendent, mysterious Originator Himself) through the reason or intellect embedded in the Prophet's message and the **imam**'s authoritative teaching. The **Illuminationists** presented a model of reality as a hierarchy of pure lights, which ultimately derive their varying degrees of intensity from the Light of Lights, God. The philosophical **Sufis** envisioned the world – and on a microcosmic scale the human being – as an expression or manifestation of God's **attributes**, which belie the fundamental **oneness of existence**.

It is worth noting the diversity of methods as well that these various schools employ in fashioning their metaphysics. The **Ash'arite** theologians begin with the data of **revelation**, rationally reconstructing and defending the

Qur'anic picture by means of indirect, dialectical proofs (*jadal*). The Neoplatonic-Aristotelians construct their worldview by means of logical demonstration (*burhan*), which was supposed to produce necessary and certain conclusions based on self-evident first principles, much as the universe unfolds syllogistically and necessarily from the first principle of God. The Isma'ilis arrive at their cosmology through an **esoteric** (*batin*) allegorical **interpretation** (*ta'wil*) of scripture, vouchsafed by the authoritative teaching (*ta'lim*) of the infallible imam. The radical Aristotelians begin with the data of the natural world and undertake an inferential ascent to the ultimate realities necessary to explain that world. The Illuminationists discover their world of lights through a direct, unmediated, reflexive self-luminescence that they describe as '**knowledge by presence**' (*al-'ilm al-huduri*), and which can be cultivated through spiritual practice to disclose greater metaphysical insights. The Sufis' theophantic model of reality is rooted in mystical experiences ('taste' [*dhawq*], 'unveiling' [*khashf*], **gnosis** [*'irfan*]) made possible by rigorous spiritual training. Later metaphysical constructions of the **School of Isfahan** and their progeny constitute creative combinations of these multiple approaches. Given the rich synthetic legacy of metaphysics in the Islamic tradition, it is appropriate to employ a more indigenous Qur'anic term, which even the early *mashsha'i* thinkers sometimes used: *hikma*, or **wisdom**.

See **active intellect; Aristotle; causality; creation vs. eternity of the world; essence and existence; al-Farabi; free will and predestination; al-Ghazali; Ibn Rushd; Ibn Sina; Mulla Sadra; Neoplatonism; occasionalism; psychology; al-Razi (Abu Bakr); al-Sijistani (Abu Ya'qub)**

Further reading: Iqbal 1908/64; Kogan 1985; Marmura 2005; Nasr 1964/93; Netton 1989/95; Pines 1997; Shehadi 1982; Wisnovsky 2003 miracles (*ayat*, lit. 'signs'): see **al-Ghazali**

Mir Damad (950–1041/1543–1631): Nicknamed 'Son-in-Law' (*damad*) because of his relation to the famed **Shi'ite** theologian al-Karaki, Mir Muhammad Baqir Astarabadi was the founder of the enormously influential School of Isfahan, and was accordingly also given the honorific title of 'Third Teacher' (*al-mu'allim al-thalith*), after **Aristotle** and **al-Farabi**. The School of Isfahan formulated a **philosophy** that blended **Peripateticism**, **Illuminationism**, **Sufi** gnosis (*'irfan*), and Shi'ite (esp. Imami) **theology**. It is an eclectic synthesis that has dominated modern Islamic thought throughout Iran, Iraq and Muslim parts of South Asia. Apart from his advantageous historical situation and his creative ability to synthesize and build upon the insights of these diverse intellectual movements, one thing that sets Mir Damad apart from previous Islamic philosophers is his deep, extensive learning in the traditional (*naqliyya*) as well as rational sciences (*al-'ulum al-'aqliyya*), for example Qur'anic exegesis (*tafsir*), **jurisprudence** (*fiqh*), the sayings of the Prophet and Shi'ite **imams** (*hadith*), and more loosely, theology (*kalam*). Although he composed a number of important works in these areas of **knowledge** (not to mention poetry, mystical treatises, and commentaries on Peripatetic thinkers such as al-Farabi, **Ibn Sina** and **al-Tusi**), his reputation stands primarily on his original philosophical works, the most important of which is *The Fiery Embers* (*al-Qabasat*). The central issue of this book is the interface between time and eternity, and by extension, the much-disputed question of the originatedness (*huduth*) or **eternity** (*qidam*) of the world. In order to finesse the respective conceptual problems of both creationism and eternalism, Mir Damad articulates a complex cosmology predicated upon a subtle three-fold distinction between eternity (*sarmand*), atemporal pre-eternity (*dahr*) and time (*zaman*). These three states of being are perhaps most clearly understood in relational terms: eternity (or the 'everlasting') is a state in which there is a relationship only between the changeless and the changeless, atemporal pre-eternity (which S. H. **Nasr** suggestively translates as 'aeveternity' or metatime) involves a relation between the changeless and the changing, and time has to do with the relation between the changing and the changing. By introducing *dahr* as a kind of mediating buffer between *sarmand* and *zaman*, Mir Damad defuses the dilemma of either eternalizing (and thus deifying) the world or infecting **God** with change (and thus in effect de-deifying Him). On his account, the existence of our temporal world is preceded, not by nothingness (as the traditional creation *ex nihilo* model would have it), but rather by what exists in atemporal pre-eternity (i.e. pure archetypes). Thus the world is neither eternal nor originated in time; it is originated in atemporal pre-eternity (*huduth-i dahri*). Mir Damad's synthetic but original cosmology had a considerable influence on subsequent thinkers. He is known for a number of other related contributions, for example his treatment of the problem of change in the divine will (as implied by **revelation**), his resourceful new approach to the problem of **free will** and predestination, and his nuanced codification of the question of the **primacy of essence** vs. **existence**. Mir Damad's greatest student was **Mulla Sadra** – undoubtedly the single most important and influential modern Islamic philosopher. As is the case with every great thinker, he was not content merely to reiterate his teacher's views, and eventually came to reject a number of Mir Damad's key doctrines, among them the theory of metatemporal origination and the primacy of essence. Mulla Sadra differed quite strikingly from his teacher in his manner of presentation as well. Whereas Mir Damad's style is often dense, unwieldy and rather difficult to navigate, Mulla Sadra mastered the art of writing in a clear and elegant style. The disadvantage of this literary prowess was that it made his philosophical doctrines more accessible to religious authorities (*'ulama'*), who viewed them as blasphemous and accordingly persecuted him. Mir Damad, on the other hand, encountered no such religio-political harassment. Whether his intellectual freedom was a function of the great esteem in which he was held by the Safavid Shahs 'Abbas I and Safi I or due to the impenetrable nature of his writing is something of an open question. If it was a function of his inaccessible style (as Mir Damad allegedly confessed to Mulla Sadra in a dream), the question remains whether that itself was due to politically prudent **dissimulation** (*taqiyya*) or just the seemingly irreducible complexity, subtlety and originality of his philosophical insights.

See **creation vs. eternity of the world; essence and existence; Ibn Sina; Mulla Sadra; Sufism; al-Suhrawardi**

Further reading: Corbin 1993; Nasr 2006

Miskawayh, Ahmad ibn Muhammad (320–421/932–1030): Philosopher, historian, physician, chemist and librarian, the Persian-born Miskawayh was one of the most learned and cultured courtiers of the cosmopolitan Buyid dynasty. Like many of the great Islamic **humanists** of his age, Miskawayh's forte lay not in his metaphysical speculations (a somewhat unsystematic mélange of **Aristotelian**, **Neoplatonic** and **Islamic** ideas), but rather in his engagement with the imminently practical question of how to live a good life and achieve **happiness** (*sa'ada*). His principal work, *The Refinement of Character* (*Tahdhib al-akhlaq*), artfully blends a **Platonic** conception of the **soul** (as immortal, ontologically distinct and separable from the body) with Aristotelian virtue **ethics** (casting virtue as a 'mean' between two vicious extremes) and Cynic-Stoic therapies for irrational passions (in order to restore and preserve the 'health' of the soul), as well as the Arabic *adab* tradition (focusing on the education and cultivation of well-mannered and urbane individuals). The single thread that winds its way through this generous synthesis is a commitment to human **reason**; indeed Miskawayh conceives of virtue itself as the perfection of the rational aspect of our soul, which is what makes us uniquely human. The tone of the book is practical rather than theoretical. Miskawayh discusses various traditional Greek and Arabic virtues, but focuses in particular on justice, love and friendship. He thus makes much of the fact that we are necessary to each other's perfection, even if the highest form of happiness ultimately transcends such social requirements (and indeed, physical conditions altogether), culminating in proximity to the divine, which he describes as 'God's friendship and love'. In keeping with Miskawayh's humanistic orientation, **Islam** (and religion as such) is recognized as important, practically useful and essentially reasonable, but is relegated to an instrumental role in the pursuit of human virtue and happiness. *The Refinement of Character* has remained an important didactic text in the Islamic philosophical tradition, as much for its serene, elegant, rigorous, yet popularly accessible style as for its learned and tolerant synthesis of moral insights. Its lasting influence can be seen in the ethical thought of **al-Ghazali, al-Tusi, al-Dawani** and Muhammad **'Abduh**, among others.

See *adab*; ethics; humanism; Ibn 'Adi

Further reading: Fakhry 1991; Goodman 2003; Kraemer 1986a/93, 1986b; Miskawayh 1968/2002

modern Islamic philosophy: There has been for the last couple of centuries a lively philosophical atmosphere in the Islamic world, and every variety of **philosophy** has found supporters somewhere. The place to start when thinking about modern Islamic philosophy is the Rebirth or Renaissance (*nahda*) movement which started in Syria, became established in Egypt, and from there spread out through the Arab world, and beyond. The *nahda* movement tried to defend **Islam**'s continuing relevance in the modern world, and encourage the Islamic world to embrace modernity. The major thinkers were al-Tahtawi, **al-Afghani** and Muhammad 'Abduh, who in different ways set out to institutionalize modernity in the Islamic world by giving it a religious rationale.

There have been some recurrent themes in modern Arab philosophy. One is the relationship Islamic philosophy should have with western philosophy. Also, some Arab thinkers use philosophy to try to make sense of what they see as the leading intellectual issues of the time. Muhammad 'Abid al-Jabiri, a Moroccan philosopher, is critical of much traditional Islamic thought, arguing that we need to form a clear view of the reasons for the decline of the Arab world, something of a theme in much Arab philosophy. He criticizes the *nahda* for reintroducing the **Peripatetic** thinkers into philosophy, since they were nothing more than employers of foreign ideas in their work. We should not use traditional Islamic ideas either, he argues, but rather deconstruct that heritage. He attacks in particular what he takes to be wrong with Arab culture – the worship of words, the desire for authority, both human and divine, and the idea that anything can happen. The result is that **language** comes to replace reality, power replaces freedom and there is a lack of confidence in the causal nature of the world in favor of a reliance on arbitrary action. Al-Jabiri makes the perceptive remark that the failure of Islamic philosophy in the sense of *falsafa* to continue for long is due to its failure to reflect on its own, i.e. Arab, history, since it is so Greek-orientated that it can only reflect on Greek culture, something of which it is not a part. Western philosophy, by contrast, has constantly meditated on its own history and has not been frightened to challenge and discard what it did not like. The way forward involves trying to recapture the spirit of **Ibn Rushd** in particular, and incorporate his thought into the practical organization of society.

Other thinkers are far more critical of Ibn Rushd in particular and take an entirely different view of the past. **Islamism**, for example, argues that we need to return to the original period of the Prophet and the early Islamic state if we are to construct an appropriate **political philosophy**.

Philosophy has continued very vigorously in the Persian cultural world, and has moved out of the theological school, the *madrasa*, into the university. Compared to the Arab world, where philosophy for a long time came under some suspicion from the religious authorities, it has had a much more constant presence in Iran, perhaps reflecting the much more favorable attitude that **Shi'ism** tended to adopt towards philosophy as compared with **Sunni** culture. Mehdi Ḥa'iri Yazdi develops a theory of **knowledge by presence**, a form of knowledge which is incorrigible and which grounds our other knowledge claims, using ideas from both *ishraqi* thinkers like **al-Suhrawardi**, and the modern philosopher Wittgenstein. Another Iranian thinker, 'Ali Shariati, develops a view of the human being as having **God** at its **essence** while maintaining the scope to determine its own form of existence. The notion of **unity** (*tawhid*) he regards as therapeutic, to establish both personal and political justice and harmony. He interprets the main figures of Shi'ite Islam as models for us not only morally but also to bring about progressive social and political ideals. Seyyed Hossein **Nasr** uses **Sufism** to argue for a new attitude to the natural world, one that regards it as exemplifying the divine and for which we are put in charge by God. We then have a responsibility not to abuse it, and **science** is not an amoral activity, but something that involves unlocking the secrets of a world created by God and for which we have responsibility.

It is worth pointing out also that within the Islamic world today philosophy is pursued as it is everywhere else, often with no reference to religion at all. However, there are many interesting attempts to combine Islam with philosophical thought in order to throw light on both areas of thought and life.

See 'Abduh (Muhammad); al-Afghani; Iqbal (Muhammad); Islamism; Nasr (Seyyed Hossein)

Further reading: Cooper et al. 2000; Hahn et al. 2001; Ha'iri Yazdi 1992; Hourani 1983; al-Jabiri 1999; Rahman 1982

monopsychism: see **afterlife; Ibn Rushd; psychology**

Muhammad, the Prophet (570–11/632): see **Islam**

Mulla Sadra (c. 979–1050/1571–1640): Sadr al-Din Muhammad al-Shirazi, more commonly known by his honorific title Mulla ('Master') Sadra, is without doubt the most important and influential of the modern Islamic philosophers. He studied with the great formative thinkers of the School of Isfahan (**Mir Damad**, Shaykh-i Baha'i and possibly Mir Abu al-Kasim Findiriski), building upon their insights to formulate his own 'transcendent wisdom' (*al-hikma al-muta'aliya*). Mulla Sadra's original **philosophy** blended and transformed **Ibn Sina's Neoplatonic Aristotelianism**, **al-Suhrawardi's Illuminative** wisdom, **Ibn al-'Arabi's Sufism**, and the **theology** of the **Ash'arite Sunnis**

and **Twelver Shi'ites** in an even more ambitious and resourceful way than his teachers had imagined possible. Like Mir Damad, he placed great importance upon the traditional sciences (e.g. grammar, Qur'anic exegesis, **jurisprudence**, reports of **Muhammad** and the **imam**s) as a source of **knowledge** as well. Thus his transcendent wisdom can be seen as a synthesis of revealed knowledge (**Qur'an**), demonstrative knowledge (*burhan*) and mystic **gnosis** (*'irfan*).

One of the things for which Mulla Sadra is most immediately known is his rejection of al-Suhrawardi's claim about the **primacy of essence**, which Mir Damad himself had defended. The debate about the primacy of essence or existence is traceable to Ibn Sina's distinction between **existence** (*wujud*) and existent (*mawjud*), and his idea that existence is an 'accident' (*'arad*) superadded to an essence (a position held before him by the *kalam* theologians). Mulla Sadra adopts (albeit reinterprets) the first doctrine and rejects the second. Al-Suhrawardi had claimed that existence (as a universal over and above particular existing things) is simply a mental abstraction or secondary intelligible that possesses no reality prior to or independent of the human mind. Mulla Sadra drives a wedge into al-Suhrawardi's essentialist position by distinguishing between existence as concept (*mafhum*) and existence as reality (*haqiqa*). Insofar as the latter constitutes the existential or ontological ground of everything, it cannot simply be a mental abstraction. If anything can be said to be an abstraction lacking in extra-mental reality, it is essence. Further, existence cannot be an accident or attribute because it can be neither described nor logically defined. Description presupposes that we move from what is known to what is less known, yet what is more immediately known and self-evident than existence? Logical definition, on the other hand, presupposes the identification of genus and specific differentia, which by necessity excludes certain entities. But as Ibn Sina (following Aristotle) recognized, existence is so general and fundamental that there can be nothing outside of it. Indeed, in accordance with Ibn Sina, Mulla Sadra maintains that existence can only be known through intuition (*hads*), a kind of direct, non-discursive apprehension which he also sometimes characterizes in Illuminationist and Sufi terms (e.g. illuminative presence [*al-hudur al-ishraqi*] and unveiling [*kashf*]).

Al-Suhrawardi had conceived reality as a hierarchy of lights of varying degrees of intensity or luminosity. Mulla Sadra takes up this notion of intensity and radicalizes it by applying it to existence itself. According to Mulla Sadra's **metaphysics**, things possess a greater or lesser degree of existence. Since existence is not only the ground of all entities, but the source of their reality or truth (*haqiqa*) and thus their meaning, the more existence a thing possesses, the more it is saturated with reality-truth and meaning. Al-Suhrawardi's hierarchy of lights thus gives way to an ontological hierarchy of existence-reality-truth-meaning, with **God** at the apex and inanimate material objects at the bottom. On the one hand, this entails that existence is not homogeneous; things exist in qualitatively different ways, with widely varying degrees of intensity, richness and complexity. On the other hand, Mulla Sadra rejects the idea that there is a hard and fast distinction between fixed, essentially different types of being. For him, all things are on a kind of continuum, which he describes as the graduation or 'systematic ambiguity' of existence (*tashkik al-wujud*).

This insight is closely connected with two other important ideas in Mulla Sadra's metaphysics. The first is that all things are the manifestation of, and exist only as a part of, one great unitary reality. In other words, Mulla Sadra sees his metaphysics of graduated existence as disclosing the same essential insight as Ibn al-'Arabi's mystical experience of the **oneness of existence**. Second, Mulla Sadra's cosmos is a profoundly dynamic one, characterized by deep change and constant flux. Rejecting Aristotle's metaphysics, in which change applies only to qualities but not to the fundamental underlying substances, Mulla Sadra introduces the idea of substantial motion (*al-harakat al-jawhariyya*), according to which entities are not essentially stable things, but rather more like processes through and through. Although al-Suhrawardi's metaphysics of illumination (and before it, the Neoplatonic model of **emanation**) had already begun to move away from Aristotle's substance metaphysics by emphasizing continuity and permeability over mutually exclusive, substantial combinations of form and matter, its ontological hierarchy of lights was still essentially static. For Mulla Sadra, existence is a systematically ambiguous continuity not only because all beings are (in ontological terms) more or less intense manifestations of the one true reality-existence, but because (in temporal terms) their identities are fluid and not ultimately stable. Only the oneness of existence retains an essential identity in the midst of its teleological development, as all things move towards greater intensity and perfection.

This dynamic, anti-essentialist model has significant implications for a number of other traditional concerns, one of which is the question of the originatedness or **eternity** of the world. While Mulla Sadra understands the overall process of the unfolding of the universe as eternal, his metaphysics of deep change effectively suggests that the universe is repeatedly and continuously created in time. In this way, he bridges the seemingly insuperable chasm between the creationist theologians and eternalist philosophers.

His notion of the systematic ambiguity of existence has significant implications as well for the conception of the **soul**. On Mulla Sadra's account, the soul is 'bodily in origination but spiritual in subsistence', which means it becomes increasingly spiritual or intellectual as it grows richer and denser and more intense in existence-reality-truth-meaning. By articulating a dynamic, developmental and ultimately monistic ontology in which there is no hard and fast distinction between the material and the spiritual, he bypasses the kind of mind-body dualism that was being codified in Europe during his own lifetime, and which would create so many problems for modern western philosophers.

Mulla Sadra's **epistemology** is closely bound up with his metaphysics as well, and produces a number of important insights that enable him to move beyond the impasses of previous philosophers. One of these is his retrieval of the Avicennan notion of intuition, and his corresponding critique of the **Peripatetics**' emphasis on abstraction (*tajarrud*), that is, the act of grasping intelligibles by mentally extricating or disentangling them from the concrete particulars in which they are embedded. On Mulla Sadra's view, this is a rather paltry, anemic kind of knowing, which by its very nature cannot capture the true reality of the object of knowledge. Instead, he conceives of true objects of knowledge as something more akin to self-intellecting Platonic Forms. The more the human intellect comes to know these intellgibles, the more intense and perfect it becomes, until it unifies with the **active intellect** itself. On this point, Mulla Sadra differs from both Ibn Sina and al-Suhrawardi in positing the unification of the **intellect** and the intelligibles (*ittihad al-'aqil wa al-ma'qul*), whereas the most his *mashsha'i* and *ishraqi* predecessors would have admitted is their conjunction (*ittisal*). This leads him to privilege the

Illuminationist idea of **knowledge by presence** (*al-'ilm al-huduri*) over the kind of propositional knowledge typically valorized by the Peripatetics (i.e. 'knowledge by representation' [*al-'ilm al-irtisami*]). Building upon Ibn Sina's **'floating man'** argument, al-Suhrawardi's idea of self-luminosity or immediate non-discursive reflexive awareness of one's own existence as the paradigmatic case of knowledge, and the general sense of existence (*wujud*) as comprising both 'being' and 'finding', Mulla Sadra argues for the ultimate unity of knowledge and existence.

Mulla Sadra's single most important work is the multivolume *Transcendent Wisdom Concerning the Four Intellectual Journeys* (*al-Hikma al-muta'aliya fi al-asfar al-'aqliyya al-arba'a*), usually just referred to as *The Journeys* (*al-Asfar*). He also wrote a sprawling (albeit incomplete) philosophical commentary on the Qur'an which synthesizes Ibn al-'Arabi's Sufi symbolic-esoteric reading, the Shi'ite Imam Ja'far al-Sadiq's interpretations of Qur'an and *hadith*, insights from Fakhr al-Din **al-Razi**'s Sunni Ash'arite theology and **al-Tusi**'s Twelver Shi'ite theology, and al-Farabi and Ibn Sina's Peripatetic interpretation of scripture. Among Mulla Sadra's influential shorter philosophical works, three have been translated into English: *The Wisdom of the Throne* (*Hikmat al-'arshiyya*), *The Book of [Metaphysical] Penetrations* (*Kitab al-Masha'ir*) and *The Elixir of the Gnostics* (*Iksir al-'arifin*). Mulla Sadra's works are particularly remarkable for the clarity and eloquence of expression, much more so, say, than those of his teacher Mir Damad. Unfortunately, this caused him problems with some of the religious authorities of seventeenth-century Safavid Persia. He was harassed, persecuted and forced into exile for his allegedly blasphemous conclusions by the Akhbaris, **literalists** who might be thought of as the

Shi'ite version of the Sunni **Hanbalites**. Indeed, despite the recognition and support Mulla Sadra garnered from less anti-intellectual quarters and the considerable number of students he attracted, his influence was relatively minor, at least initially. It was only in the nineteenth century that the Master's 'transcendent wisdom' was fully appreciated and codified. Among his intellectual progeny may be counted Mulla 'Abdullah Zunuzi, **al-Sabzawari**, Muhammad Rida Qumsha'i, Mirza Mahdi Ashtiyani and the twentieth-century thinker, Muhammad Husayn Tabataba'i.

See **Aristotle; epistemology; Ibn al-'Arabi; Ibn Sina; metaphysics; Mir Damad; al-Sabzawari; Sufism; al-Suhrawardi; Twelver Shi'ites**

Further reading: Kamal 2006; Mulla Sadra 1982, 1992, 2002; Nasr 1978, 1996, 2006; Rahman 1975

Murji'ites (*murji'a*): Like the **Kharijites** and **Shi'ites**, the Murji'ites were a theological-political movement that arose in response to the formative controversy surrounding the third and fourth caliphs, 'Uthman and 'Ali. They were vexed by the same questions that occupied the Kharijites – the question of the legitimization of political authority and the status of Muslims who commit grave sins – but took a considerably more moderate stance on both. First, the Murji'ites endeavored to restore unity to the Muslim community by advocating a kind of agnosticism with regard to 'Uthman and 'Ali. They maintained that any judgement about that matter must be deferred to **God**, and believers accordingly should neither affiliate themselves with nor dissociate themselves from either caliph. This was referred to as the doctrine of 'deferral' or 'postponement' (*irja'*) – hence the name *murji'a*, which means those who defer or postpone judgement. Second, they believed – contra the Kharijites – that consistently right action is not a necessary condition of being a believer, and that Muslims who commit grievous sins should not be legally excluded from the community of believers. They can be qualifiedly condemned as sinful believers, but whether they are ultimately to be punished or forgiven is a function of God's will, which human beings cannot pretend to know. This ushered in a broader, more inclusive conception of faith as knowledge in the heart (specifically, submission to and love of God) and affirmation by the tongue. Although later rejected by **Mu'tazilites** as well as many **Ash'arites** and **traditionalists**, the Murji'ite doctrine of the primacy of belief initially won support from a broad array of heterogeneous scholars (perhaps most notably Abu Hanifa, the founder of the legal school of Hanifism), helping to usher in more equitable treatment for recently converted non-Arab believers. Once Muslims had come to a consensus regarding the first four 'rightly guided' caliphs, Murji'ism in many ways lost its political *raison d'être*, and subsequent theological schools focused increasingly on more speculative matters. However, unlike the extremist ideology of the Kharijites, the Murji'ites' ideas were for the most part taken up into mainstream Islamic thought.

See **Ash'arites**; **belief**; **Islam**; **Kharijites**; **Mu'tazilites**; **Shi'ites**; **theology**

Further reading: Watt 1962/85, 1973

mutakallimun (theologians): see **theology**

Mu'tazilites (*mu'tazila*): The Mu'tazilites were one of the two most influential schools of *kalam*, or **theology**. Founded in the early second/eighth century by Wasil ibn 'Ata' (according to traditional accounts), they placed great stock in the power and autonomy of **reason** for guiding the **interpretation** of **revelation** and the determination of proper **belief**. The exact source of their name, which means 'those who withdraw or separate themselves', has been disputed, but most likely has to do with their doctrinal position vis-à-vis the intermediate eschatological status of sinning Muslims (somewhere between true believer and infidel). The Mu'tazilites adhered to five principal theses: (1) **God's unity**, (2) God's justice, (3) 'the promise and the threat' (of Paradise and Hell), (4) the aforementioned 'intermediate position,' and (5) the enjoining of what is good and the forbidding of what is bad. The first two principles are typically seen as foundational, and the Mu'tazilites accordingly often characterized themselves as 'the people of justice and unity' (*ahl al-'adl wa al-tawhid*). Emphasizing God's unqualified unity, they sought to purge their conception of God of all multiplicity: they argued that the various divine **attributes** mentioned throughout the **Qur'an** (e.g. **God's knowledge**, power, life, will, perception, etc.) are not in fact realities separate from the divine essence, but rather are identical with it. For the Mu'tazilites, God is absolutely unique and transcendent, and for this reason they refused to take the Qur'an's sometimes rather **anthropomorphic** descriptions of God at face value, insisting upon a more figurative interpretation, and stressing the necessity of rational argumentation for arriving at an adequate conception of God's unity and **transcendence**. In proclaiming God's justice, the Mu'tazilites were in effect taking up their **Qadarite** predecessors' emphasis upon the freedom of the human will. They argued that God could justifiably condemn people to Hell if and only if they were free to choose (and thus ultimately responsible for) their own actions. Because of the Mu'tazilites' emphasis on the centrality of reason and interpretation, their selective appropriation of Greek philosophical methods, their intellectualized conception of God, and their commitment to human **free will** and responsibility, they have sometimes been cast as **rationalists**, liberals, and even **freethinkers** within the Islamic tradition. This, however, is somewhat inaccurate: notwithstanding their commitment to reason, they were sometimes guilty of their own dogmatic intolerance, especially once they were backed by the political muscle of the 'Abbasid caliphate. Indeed, in accordance with their fifth principle, which effectively justified the exercise of compulsion and violence in defense of the faith, they zealously persecuted their intellectual enemies (specifically those who disagreed with them about the createdness of the Qur'an), having them silenced, imprisoned, and in some cases, killed. In part because of these political excesses, in part because they were outmaneuvered by the doctrinal compromises and syntheses of the relatively more moderate **Ash'arite** school, the Mu'tazilites' intellectual and political influence started to wane in the second half of the third/ninth century and they gradually ceased to be a vital force in the **Sunni** world. However, despite the Mu'tazilites' eventually marginal status, their historical importance and influence cannot be overestimated.

See **Ash'arites**; **God** (anthropomorphic descriptions of); **interpretation**; **Qadarites**; **rationalism**; **theology**; **traditionalism**

Further reading: Abrahamov 1998; Arberry 1957; van Ess 2006; Frank 1978; Martin et al. 1997; Watt 1948, 1962/85

mysticism: It is impossible to overemphasize the significance of mysticism in Islamic **philosophy**. Most of the classical thinkers regarded themselves as mystics, and some strains of Islamic philosophy were entirely mystical. **Isma'ili** thought, for example, is based on the idea that the meaning of scripture can only be derived from the teachings of the **imam**, someone who can expand the horizons of the **intellect** and come into contact with higher levels of reality. Within the **Sunni** world mysticism tended to take a **Sufi** direction, and two of the most radical thinkers were **Ibn Sab'in** and **Ibn al-'Arabi** in the Maghrib. Both put enormous emphasis on the **oneness of existence** as a result of the **unity** of the Deity, and called for a revaluation of **metaphysics** as a result to take account of this very basic fact. In the Persian world mysticism really took off and became a standard part of the philosophical curriculum, from the School of Isfahan of **Mir Damad** and **Mulla Sadra** right up to today. **Illuminationist** thought also uses mystical features in its structure, although in some ways it is also committed to aspects of **Peripateticism**. Persian thought became adept at combining the ideas of Persian thinkers with earlier philosophers linked with Sufism such as Ibn al-'Arabi and **al-Ghazali**.

See **Eastern philosophy; al-Ghazali; Ibn al-'Arabi; Ibn Masarra; Ibn Sab'in; Illuminationism; Mir Damad; Mulla Sadra; Sufism; al-Suhrawardi**

Further reading: Arberry 1950/90; Nasr 1981, 2006; Schimmel 1975; Sells 1994, 1996

nahda (Rebirth, Renaissance): see **'Abduh (Muhammad); al-Afghani, modern Islamic philosophy**

Nasir-i Khusraw (394–c. 465/1004–c. 1072): One of the great **Isma'ili** philosopher-missionaries of fifth/eleventh-century Persia and an exemplar for subsequent thinkers in that tradition, Nasir-i Khusraw is remembered also for his prized collection of poetry (*Diwan*) and his famous travelogue, the *Book of Travels* (*Safar-nama*). The seven-year journey recorded in the latter was apparently prompted by a spiritual crisis and consequent vision which Nasir-i Khusraw experienced in his fortieth year, and which ultimately led him to become an Isma'ili. His travels took him to Cairo (the capital of the Fatimid caliphate, a stronghold of Isma'ilism), where he became a missionary and propagandist for the movement. In his twilight years, he consigned himself to Yumgan, a politically safe but rather lonely place in what would now be Afghanistan, where he composed the majority of his philosophical works. Among these, the most important is *The Sum [or Harmonization] of the Two Wisdoms* (*Kitab jami' al-hikmatayn*), which attempts to reconcile revealed **religion** with Greek **philosophy**. His *Face of Religion* (*Wajh-i din*) provides a clear and forceful presentation of Isma'ili philosophy, particularly its **esoteric** hermeneutic method of interpreting symbols. His dialogically structured *Unfettering and Setting Free* (*Gushayish wa rahayish*) deals with key Islamic doctrines of the **soul** and eschatology within a philosophical framework. Throughout these works, Nasir-i Khusraw presents a **Neoplatonic** cosmology that eschews his predecessor **al-Kirmani**'s innovations (i.e. a Farabian hierarchy of ten intellects) in favor of the more economical emanationist model originally presented by thinkers such as al-Nasafi and Abu Ya'qub **al-Sijistani** (**God**'s command originates universal intellect, which gives rise to soul, which gives rise to nature, which gives rise to terrestrial beings). In order for each individual embodied soul to re-ascend and return to its spiritual origin, it must (like the universal soul) strive for perfection. This requires that we learn to read the apparent or external (*zahir*) text of the physical universe as so many symbols pointing toward its more fundamental inner or spiritual (*batin*) reality. Like al-Sijistani and other Isma'ili thinkers, Nasir-i Khusraw sees the intellect as playing an indispensable role in the attainment of salvific **knowledge**, yet insists upon the necessity of a divinely inspired guide or **imam** who alone can interpret the true, inner meaning of the revelation that will ultimately liberate us.

See **Batinites; God; Isma'ilis; al-Kirmani; Neoplatonism; psychology; al-Sijistani (Abu Ya'qub); Shi'ites**

Further reading: Daftary 1990; Hunsberger 2000; Nasir-i Khusraw 1993/2001, 1998; Nasr with Aminrazavi 2001

Nasr, Seyyed Hossein (1933–): Seyyed Hossein Nasr is very much a Persian thinker, although obliged to leave Iran in 1979 after the Islamic Revolution and the overthrow of the Shah. Educated both in Iran and the United States, he made important contributions to areas such as Islamic **science, mysticism** and more recently to the links between **religion** and ecology. A constant theme in his work is the need to revive the study of what he calls perennial philosophy, a system of thought where spiritual and moral values are regarded as part of the basic principles of the system. According to Nasr, perennial philosophy is shared by many different traditions and although it differs in particulars, certain ideas are always found, and these include the sacred nature of the world as **God**'s creation, the idea that the meaning of the world is something hidden, the significance of the distinction between the exoteric and the **esoteric,** and other aspects of what he calls *hikma* or **wisdom.** He contrasts this with what he takes to be the narrow approach of the **Peripatetic** thinkers, concerned as they were, according to him, only with rationality. This produces a one-dimensional attitude to the world, Nasr suggests, and should be replaced with a much more open attitude to different sorts of knowledge and experience.

See **modern Islamic philosophy; mysticism**

Further reading: Hahn et al. 2001; Nasr 1964/93, 1968/97, 1968, 1981, 1993, 1996, 1997, 2006 nature (*tabi'a*): see **metaphysics; science**

Necessary Existent (*wajib al-wujud*): see **God; Ibn Sina**

necessity and possibility: see **causality; Ibn Sina; metaphysics**

Neoplatonism (*al-aflatuniyat al-muhdatha*): A creative synthesis of Pythagorian, Platonic, Aristotelian and Stoic **philosophy** – infused with a religio-mystic spirit – Neoplatonism
was the final flowering of ancient Greek thought (c. third –
sixth century CE). As a result of early Islamic expansionism
and the ambitious scholarly translation project beginning
in the third/ninth century under the 'Abbasid caliphate in
Baghdad, a considerable number of Neoplatonic texts
were made available in Arabic. Two of the key works were
mistakenly attributed to **Aristotle**: *Aristotle's Theology*
(actually a selective paraphrase of Books 4–6 of Plotinus'
Enneads) and *The Book of the Pure Good*, or *Liber de
causis* as it was known to the Latins (actually chapters
from Proclus' *Elements of Theology*). But whether associated with Aristotle or their true Neoplatonic authors, the
contents of these texts resonated powerfully with the
emerging worldviews of Islamic philosophers. The most
influential aspect of Neoplatonism was its hierarchical
model of reality, in which existence 'emanates', light-like,
from the divine One or Good (the First **Cause**, which itself
is beyond being) through the **intellect** (which encompasses
the intelligible forms and is being itself), to the **soul** (a kind
of amphibious entity, rooted in the intelligible world but
enmeshed in, and providing rational order to, the physical
world), to the material world of generation and destruction. This 'cascade of causality' is not a temporal event,
nor is it a result of **God**'s volition. Each hypostasis automatically gives rise to the next, through a kind of logical
entailment in which God's existentially overrich nature

necessarily and eternally manifests itself. Numerous Islamic philosophers in the classical period appropriated and elaborated extensively upon this model, most notably the early **Peripatetics** and **Isma'ilis**. However, while it proved an invaluable resource for articulating an Islamic **metaphysics** and rational **theology**, it also generated some serious conceptual problems. Perhaps most importantly, its necessitarian metaphysics of emanation seemed flatly to contradict the Qur'anic notion of God's free creation, His active, deliberate intervention in history, and the possibility of **miracles**. The Neoplatonic dimension of Islamic philosophy eventually came under devastating attack with **al-Ghazali**'s pivotal *Incoherence of the Philosophers* and never entirely recovered. Even the definitive philosophical reply, **Ibn Rushd**'s *Incoherence of the Incoherence*, distanced itself from Neoplatonism and hewed to a more purely Aristotelian line. However, significant elements of Neoplatonic metaphysics can still be found in subsequent Isma'ili thought, as well as **Illuminationism** and **Sufism**.

See **active intellect; Aristotle; Brethren of Purity; causality; al-Farabi; Ibn al-'Arabi; Ibn Masarra; Ibn Sina; Isma'ilis; al-Kindi; al-Kirmani; metaphysics; Nasir-i Khusraw; Plato; psychology; al-Razi (Abu Bakr); al-Sijistani (Abu Ya'qub); al-Suhrawardi**

Further reading: Adamson 2003; Dillon and Gerson 2004; Morewedge 1992; Netton 1989/95

obedience (*taqlid*): In the context of legal, theological and philosophical disputation, *taqlid* denotes unquestioning acceptance of authority without proofs or reasons, that is; blind submission to, or imitation of, a master or school. Although western Orientalists and modernist

Muslim thinkers have sometimes characterized the Islamic tradition as having an immature and counterproductive dependence upon authority, this term typically has a negative connotation within the tradition itself and is applied by a wide range of diverse thinkers to their adversaries. Although it might be applied to a **traditionalist** by one who valorized **independent judgement** (*ijtihad*) or considered opinion (*ra'y*) or **reason** (*'aql*), traditionalists themselves (e.g. **Zahirites, Hanbalites, Ash'arites**, etc.) commonly used it as a disparaging term in describing and attacking more **rationalist** opponents (e.g. **al-Ghazali**'s critique of the philosophers). In theological matters at least, one is hard pressed to find figures that explicitly advocate *taqlid*. In the realm of **jurisprudence**, the case is somewhat different, especially regarding the question of independent judgement. There *taqlid* has found many advocates, albeit in the context of generally nuanced debates about when and why and to what extent it is acceptable and even necessary for the less learned or experienced to accept the authoritative opinions of specialists and predecessors.

See **independent judgement; law; traditionalism**

Further reading: Hallaq 1997, 2005; Schacht 1964/83

occasionalism: The theory that **God**, because He is omnipotent, must be the only real agent and thus the single, proximal **cause** of all events in the world. It is closely associated in Islamic **theology** with the doctrine of **atomism**, according to which God creates, orders and recreates the world at every instant since the constituent building blocks of creation (atoms [sing: *juz'*] and qualities [sing: *'arad*]) have no intrinsic duration or efficacy. As formulated by the **Ash'arite** theologians, occasionalism raises problems for both natural causality and human **free will**, since all acts are directly traceable to God's will. However, **al-Ghazali**, in his *Incoherence of the Philosophers*, employs Ash'arite occasionalism to chisel away at **Ibn Sina**'s ostensibly deterministic metaphysics, arguing that there is no real necessary connection between cause and effect in nature. All events are connected at most by mere possibility, meaning that, in principle, they could always be other than they are, depending on God's will. The apparent order and regularity of nature is typically interpreted on the occasionalist model as a matter of divine custom. As is often pointed out, al-Ghazali's critique of Ibn Sina anticipates a similar analysis by the eighteenth-century empiricist, David Hume, although his aim – that is, the rational defense of God's omnipotence and absolute freedom, the createdness of the world, and the possibility of **miracles** – was quite different.

See **Ash'arites; causality; free will and predestination; al-Ghazali; Ibn Rushd; metaphysics; theology**

Further reading: Fakhry 1958; van Ess 2006; al-Ghazali 1997/2000; Pines 1997; Wolfson 1976

oneness of existence (*wahdat al-wujud*): see **Ibn al-'Arabi**

oneness of witnessing (*wahdat al-shuhud*): see **Wali Allah (Shah)**

Oriental wisdom (*al-hikmat al-mashriqiyya*): see **Eastern philosophy**

origination (*ibda'*): see **Isma'ilis**

P

perfect human being (*al-insan al-kamil*): see **Ibn al-'Arabi; Iqbal (Muhammad)**

Peripatetic philosophers (*mashsha'un*): see **Aristotle; philosophy**

philosophy (*falsafa*; *hikma*): *Falsafa* is an Arabic neologism for the Greek word *philosophia*, meaning 'love of wisdom'. The derivation of this term points to the profound initial influence of Greek thought upon Islamic philosophy, due to the eastern expansion of the Islamic empire and the subsequent translation of key Greek medical, scientific and philosophical texts into Syriac and Arabic. The 'classical' period of Islamic philosophy begins in the third/ninth century with **al-Kindi** and comes to a close with the death of **Ibn Rushd** at the end of the sixth/twelfth century. During this phase, thinkers drew liberally from the writings of **Aristotle** (whom they dubbed 'The Philosopher' and 'The First Teacher'), the **Neoplatonists** and, to a lesser extent, **Plato**, building upon their insights and reinterpreting them to address the concerns of a world shaped by **Islam**. One of the most prominent schools at this time was the *mashsha'un* (i.e. the 'Walkers' or **Peripatetics**), named after Aristotle himself – although they were equally indebted to Neoplatonism. Thinkers in this lineage (e.g. **al-Farabi**, **Ibn Sina** and Ibn Rushd) had an enormous impact on subsequent Jewish and Christian thinkers, passing on not only the accomplishments of Greek learning, but their own conceptual clarifications and innovations as well. Another major movement was the **Isma'ilis**, who creatively appropriated Neoplatonic cosmology in formulating their **esoteric** (*batin*) interpretations of scripture.

However, western scholars have sometimes overestimated the formative Greek influence upon Islamic philosophy. For philosophical inquiry and argumentation had already begun to emerge within the Islamic milieu via the science of **theology** (*'ilm al-kalam*), which was forced to grapple with difficult metaphysical questions quite early on in its development (e.g. the tension between predestination and **free will**, the problem of **anthropomorphic** conceptions of **God**, and the relation between God's various attributes and His essential **unity**). One might say that in the third/ninth century, philosophy first began to stand apart from – and sometimes over against – theology. Like their theological brethren, the philosophers (*falasifa*; sing. *faylasuf*) were committed to the demands of rational disputation. They typically insisted upon demonstrative proofs and rationally self-evident first principles, though, rather than dialectical argumentation and faith-based premises, and their inquiries were less wedded to the proper understanding and defense of revelation.

This is not to say that classical Islamic philosophy was antagonistic towards revealed **religion**. The *falasifa* often went out of their way to stress the compatibility and underlying conceptual unity of Islam and philosophy. Indeed, almost all *falasifa* were committed to the project of knowing God as the First **Cause** and ultimate Reality and perfecting themselves through a demanding ethical regimen (both of which were understood as having therapeutic and soteriological implications for the fate of the **soul**). However, because they granted primacy to **reason** and oftentimes reached conclusions that appeared to conflict with revealed truths, they came under increasingly intense scrutiny and critique from more orthodox elements.

Despite minor periodic resurgences, by the close of the sixth/twelfth century Peripatetic philosophy was more or less overtaken by theology, at least in the **Sunni** world. Yet philosophy in the broader, more inclusive sense – the sense captured by the indigenous Arabic term *hikma* (**'wisdom'**) – continued to flourish, now wedded to more explicitly Islamic concerns and paths to **knowledge**. It lived on in **Twelver Shi'ite** and Isma'ili philosophy, the later **Ash'arite** theologians (now schooled in philosophical insights and methods through their destructive engagement with the *falasifa*), the mystical thought and practice of the **Sufis**, and the school of **Illumination** (*hikmat al-ishraq*), which offered a bold new synthesis of philosophy and **mysticism**, the great **School of Isfahan**, which forged a more vigorous hybrid from the previously competing philosophies of *mashsha'i* and *ishraqi* thought, and the transcendent wisdom of **Mulla Sadra**, a bold, original synthesis that drew upon the combined insights of all these aforementioned schools and movements, and that would have a considerable influence on modern Islamic philosophy.

See **Aristotle**; **Illuminationism**; **Isma'ilis**; **mysticism**; **Eastern philosophy**; **Neoplatonism**; **rationalism**; **Sufism**; **theology**; **traditionalism**; **Twelver Shi'ites**

Further reading: Adamson and Taylor 2005; Corbin 1993; Fakhry 1970/2004; Leaman 1985/2002; Nasr and Leaman 1996; Nasr 2006

Plato (Aflatun) (429–347 BCE): Although Greek philosophy had a profound formative effect upon classical Islamic **philosophy**, Plato's particular influence was considerably less distinct here than it was in the West. There are at least two reasons for this. First, apart from the various epitomes and commentaries, only a few of Plato's actual texts – the *Laws*, *Sophist*, *Timaeus* and *Republic* – were available in Arabic translation. Second, Muslim thinkers tended not to differentiate Plato's ideas sharply from those of his progeny. Like the earlier Greek **Neoplatonists**, they saw the philosophies of Plato and **Aristotle** as essentially in agreement. Thus, when aspects of Plato's **metaphysics**, **psychology** and **epistemology** were appropriated by Islamic philosophers – that is, the intelligible forms as a changeless reality above and beyond the natural world of generation and destruction, the immateriality and immortality of the **soul,** the superiority of **reason** or **intellect** over sense experience – they often took on a distinctly Aristotelian or Neoplatonic cast. Plato's **ethics** and **political philosophy** had a clearer and more direct influence: his emphasis on the rule of reason over the passions or appetites, the notion of virtue as the health of the soul, and the definition of philosophy as 'the imitation of God insofar as it is possible for a human being' appealed to a number of the early ethical thinkers such as **al-Kindi,** Abu Bakr **al-Razi** and **Miskawayh,** while his notion of the ideal coincidence of knowledge and political power (i.e. the philosopher-ruler) was adopted in various ways by thinkers such as **al-Farabi, Ibn Bajja** and **Ibn Rushd. Al-Suhrawardi** and his followers singled Plato out, seeing his supposed **mysticism** as more amenable to their philosophy of **Illumination** than were Aristotle's syllogistic reasoning and substance metaphysics. In general, however, it could be said that 'the sublime and divine Plato' ultimately functioned as more of a malleable symbol of pre-Qur'anic wisdom than as a substantive intellectual influence in Islamic philosophy.

See **Aristotle; ethics; al-Farabi; God (imitation of); Illuminationism; Neoplatonism; political philosophy; al-Razi (Abu Bakr); Socrates; al-Suhrawardi**

Further reading: Plato 1997; Rosenthal 1975/94, 1990; Walzer 1962

poetry (*shi'r*): see **aesthetics; logic**

political philosophy: Political philosophy in **Islam** is very much built around Islam itself, and in particular the **Qur'an** and what it has to say about how people ought to live together. The translation of Greek texts, but not

Aristotle's *Politics*, led to a model based on **Plato**'s *Republic* in which the ruler is both the supreme intellectual and also religious authority in the state. The prophet receives from on high inspiration and uses it to advertise a perfect way of life for the individual and the community. **Al-Farabi** produced a well-developed theory according to which the prophet becomes supreme ruler and directs the state in such a way as to bring about the very best type of organization. **Religion** has the role of explaining to the people as a whole why they should obey the authorities and submit to the **law**. Later on, **Ibn Bajja** and **Ibn Tufayl** produce accounts of what solitary life would be like, if personal or political circumstances make it necessary, and this allows them to contrast the individual with the group. Whereas living in a community is the best form of life for everyone, they make clear that sometimes the individual has to establish an appropriate lifestyle outside of society. **Ibn Rushd** returns to discussing society, and the role of **philosophy** in it as its guide, but a guide that does not impose itself on the community as a whole in the sense of making everyone participate in it. Only a limited group of people can do philosophy, and for the rest religion will have to suffice as their guide to how to act. Religion plays a vital role in the state by linking everyone together within the community, while philosophy is restricted to those who can benefit from it. In a rather aggressive way Ibn Rushd demotes the theologians in the state by arguing that it is only the philosophers who can, with their skills in demonstration, interpret scripture in such a way as to fix its meaning precisely and once and for all.

See **al-Farabi**; **Ibn Bajja**; **Ibn Khaldun**; **Ibn Rushd**; **Islamism**; **law**; **prophecy**

Further reading: Butterworth 1992; Lerner and Mahdi 1963; Mahdi 2001; Rosenthal 1958/85

possible/contingent existence (*mumkin al-wujud*): see **Ibn Sina**

predestination/destiny (*qadar*): see **free will and predestination**

primacy of essence (*asalat al-mahiyya*): see **essence and existence; al-Suhrawardi**

primacy of existence (*asalat al-wujud*): see **essence and existence; Mulla Sadra**

prophecy (*nubuwwa*): The **Qur'an** is full of stories of prophets, and **Muhammad** is the last prophet, so the notion of prophecy is not surprisingly much discussed in Islamic **philosophy**. The criteria of prophecy are more an issue for **theology**, but the nature of prophecy is philosophical and deals particularly with the connections between philosophy and prophecy. They are regarded as being particularly close. Within the **Peripatetic** tradition the traditional religious account of the prophet as someone chosen by God needs to be refined to include the detail that the prophet has to be an appropriate sort of person to be chosen. The prophet is in contact with the **active intellect**, the repository of abstract and creative thought, because he has the right sort of mind and upbringing to connect with it. On the **Neoplatonic** model so popular within the tradition, and adopted in one form or another by **al-Farabi, Ibn Sina** and **Ibn Rushd,** there is a continuing flow coming from the higher levels of reality downwards, and those whose minds are attuned to it can receive the emanations and use them to change what they think and do. The philosophers use it to develop their thinking, and in addition to this the prophets use it to develop their talking. They can as a result embody their theoretical insights into imaginative political **language**. That means that they can then broadcast abstract truths to the widest possible audience, something essential if most people are to grasp those truths. Naturally they will use the appropriate language and imagery for their audience, and talk to them in ways that will resonate with them, thus moving them in the right direction insofar as their behavior and thinking goes.

Prophetic knowledge starts with abstract ideas and then illustrates those ideas in the appropriate imaginative and sensory language of the community addressed for them to be generally understood. That is why the Qur'an and other religious books are full of different kinds of language, designed to fit different kinds of audience. The idea is that the same truth is going to be identified in different ways for those who require such a mode of address in order to understand what they are told. Prophets have a fully developed intellect, since they can grasp how to present information in suitable ways by thinking abstractly, while for most of us the process goes the other way—we start with sensory experience and if all goes well eventually make our ideas more abstract. Ibn Sina describes a form of thought where a thinker has a good grasp of the universal principles by which the world works, and then can take a particular piece of information from his experience and predict the future. The principles are like the major premises in a syllogism, and the piece of information the minor premise, and the conclusion follows logically as in any valid syllogism. This explains how a prophet can predict what is going to happen. He does not have access to secret information but rather to the principles that direct the world, and can use that **knowledge** to discover precisely what the future will be. Philosophers and prophets know similar things, although they have different abilities to communicate their message. Prophets are designed to do this since they can express abstract truths in symbolic language. Philosophers can understand the abstract truths that lie behind symbolic language, but are not necessarily good at the process of using that language to move an audience. In either case the abstract truth is the same for both groups, of course, the only thing that differs being the type of delivery. It is worth noting how well this model of prophecy fits in with the Qur'anic account, and yet how far it is from its literal sense.

See **active intellect; al-Farabi; Ibn Rushd; Ibn Sina; Islam; psychology; Qur'an**

Further reading: Leaman 2006a; Rahman 1958

providence (*'inaya*): see **God's knowledge**

Pseudo-Aristotle: see **Aristotle; Neoplatonism**

psychology: The understanding and proper care or development of the human soul (*nafs*) is a matter of great concern within the Islamic philosophical tradition. It is a topic on which Qur'anic **revelation** and Greek **philosophy** intersect in provocative but productive ways. Many philosophers – most notably the **Peripatetics** – accepted in one way or another **Aristotle**'s account of the soul as put forth in *De anima*. They appropriated the notion of the soul as the 'form' or 'actuality' of the body, which in itself is only potentially alive. They also took up Aristotle's three-fold model of the soul (vegetative, appetitive and rational), according to which the human being possesses nonrational powers of nutrition, growth, reproduction, locomotion and sensation that it shares with plants and animals, as well as an additional intellective part. The intellective part of the soul has two aspects: the practical, whose function is to manage ethical, social and political affairs in accordance with the good, and the theoretical, whose even higher function is to understand the intelligible, eternal aspects of the universe. While the *mashsha'i* philosophers focused a great deal on Aristotle's psychology of the external and internal senses (producing a number of new insights into the nature of sense perception, common sense, imagination, memory, etc.), their chief concern was with the proper self-understanding and cultivation of the rational part of the soul, which they considered a necessary condition for the full actualization or perfection of our nature, and thus the attainment of **happiness**.

Taking as their starting point Aristotle's brief but suggestive distinction between the 'agent' and 'potential' intellect in Book III of *De anima*, the *mashsha'i* philosophers identified four developmental stages of the **intellect** (*'aql*). The first is the 'potential' or 'material' intellect (*al-'aql bi al-quwwa*; *al-'aql al-hayulani*). This is the human being's innate capacity for receiving intelligible, universal forms. It is not literally corporeal, as the name might suggest, but rather simply a kind of unactualized potentiality (one might think of this analogously as a person's raw capacity to learn how to ride a bike). The second stage is the 'habitual' intellect (*al-'aql bi al-malaka*). This is potential intellect that has now developed the ability to grasp and employ universals in thought, yet is not perpetually doing so (cf. someone who has actualized their initial potential to learn how to ride a bike, but is not at present riding it). This is sometimes associated with the acquisition of primary intelligibles or axiomatic truths, such as the principle of non-contradiction. The third stage is the 'actual' intellect (*al-'aql bi al-fi'l*). Here the intellect has acquired secondary intelligibles from primary intelligibles, and is ready to employ them all at any time. One might think of this as rather like stage two, but more so (i.e.

someone who has completely mastered the art of riding a bike, and in effect has nothing left to perfect there, but who is not actually riding at the moment). The fourth and final stage in the development of the intellect is referred to as the 'acquired' intellect (*al-'aql al-mustafad*). Although there is some controversy among the philosophers as to how precisely this should be understood, the general idea is that it consists in the perfection of the intellect through the acquisition of all intelligibles. In this state, the human intellect is fully actualized, having achieved stable contact with the 'active' intellect (*al-'aql al-fa''al*).

The **active intellect** is the efficient **cause** that actualizes the movement of all human thought. Aristotle himself had little to say about this mysterious power. Some of his Hellenistic commentators understood it as simply part of the make-up of each individual's psychology; others associated it with **God**. The Islamic philosophers conceived of the active intellect as the last of a **Neoplatonic** chain of celestial intellects emanated from God's self-knowledge. Its function is to give rise to and govern the sublunary sphere, by imparting order and intelligibility to it while also actualizing human thought. When we fully and actively grasp the intelligible structure of reality, we achieve a conjunction (*ittisal*) with the active intellect and assimilate ourselves to it. For some thinkers (e.g. **al-Farabi**), this conjunction is what makes **immortality** possible; for others (e.g. **Ibn Sina**), it is simply the condition of real happiness.

The **Qur'an** envisions the human soul as temporally created by God, yet subsequently eternal. It is separable from the human body, but will ultimately be joined to it again on the Day of Resurrection. Aristotle, on the other hand, viewed the soul as the animating and organizing principle of the body. He seems to have seen the two as inseparable (in the way that form and matter are inseparable), so it would appear that the soul is subject to generation and destruction just as the body is. However, he does hold out the possibility that something about the nature of the intellect in particular (specifically, its eternal objects of **knowledge**) makes it conceivably separable from the rest of the soul, and thus possibly immortal. The vast majority of Islamic philosophers took up some version of this position. Some thinkers retained a more robust conception of immortality that extended to the entire soul, for example Abu Bakr **al-Razi**, who was generally more sympathetic to **Plato** than to Aristotle (he even defended a version of the pre-eternity of the soul and metempsychosis), and Ibn Sina, who argued for the substantiality of the soul as such in a way that seemed more reconcilable with Qur'anic revelation. Most philosophers, however, viewed the intellect alone as immaterial and incorruptible, and thus eternal. They also typically conceived of eschatological notions such as Paradise and Hell in purely spiritual-intellectual terms, rejecting the Qur'anic doctrine of bodily resurrection as a crude but necessary figurative sop thrown to the uncomprehending vulgar multitude. This position was famously attacked by **al-Ghazali**, who nonetheless accepted the philosophers' general notion of the soul's incorporeality, making it less unpalatable to more orthodox, **traditionalist** tastes.

Two *mashsha'i* positions deserve separate mention because of their controversial nature. Al-Farabi argued that the intellective part of the soul is not immortal by its very nature, but rather *becomes* immortal only by being actualized in the manner described above. The unperfected intellect remains merely potential, that is, bound up with matter and thus subject to generation and destruction along with the rest of material nature. The precise character of achieved intellectual immortality in al-Farabi's texts is never entirely clear, but insofar as it involves a union with the active intellect, it seems not to be personal or individual, at least in any substantive sense. Indeed, al-Farabi may very well have ultimately rejected the notion of the immortality of the soul altogether, for he is reported to have said in his commentary on Aristotle's *Nicomachean Ethics* that human happiness exists only in this life (via conjunction with the active intellect) and that the idea of the soul, or even the intellect itself, surviving the death of the body is senseless mumbo-jumbo.

Ibn Rushd reaches a somewhat different conclusion, although one arguably anticipated by both al-Farabi and **Ibn Bajja**. According to Ibn Rushd's newly purified, hardline Aristotelianism, the 'material' intellect (*al-'aql al-hayulani*) cannot be mixed with matter, because if it were, it would not be potentially able to receive intelligible universals. But if it is by necessity immaterial, then the body cannot function as its principle of individuation. And in the absence of any principle of individuation, there can be only one material intellect. Thus, immortality is not personal or individual but rather collective, or perhaps better, universal. This doctrine, often referred to as '**monopsychism**' or the 'unicity of the soul', was quite controversial in Jewish and Christian intellectual circles, although it was virtually ignored by subsequent Islamic thinkers, who had already turned their attention to new, more philosophically sophisticated forms of **Ash'arite** and **Shi'ite theology, Sufism,** and **Illuminationism,** along with the good old unpurified Neoplatonic Aristotelianism of Ibn Sina. Yet insofar as such movements and their offshoots adopted some version of Neoplatonic emanationist **metaphysics**, they too frequently envisioned the **afterlife** as a kind of conjunction – if not identity – with the divine.

See **afterlife; al-'Amiri; epistemology; al-Farabi; floating man argument; al-Ghazali; Ibn Bajja; Ibn Rushd; Ibn Sina; Mulla Sadra; al-Razi (Abu Bakr)**

Further reading: Davidson 1992; al-Farabi 1963, 1973, 1985; Goodman 1969; Ibn Rushd 2007; Ibn Sina 1952/81; Smith and Haddad 1981

Q

Qadarites (*qadariyya*): An early theological movement that upheld the centrality of human **free will**. The rubric *qadariyya* is notoriously misleading: it actually derives from the Arabic word *qadar* – 'destiny' or 'divine pre-destination' – and was generally applied in a derogatory fashion to defenders of free will by advocates of predestination (i.e. **Jabrites**) and vice versa. However, historically it has been associated with the former rather than the latter. Politically, the Qadarites shared some of the **Kharijites**' views, most notably the doctrine that any good Muslim can in principle qualify as the caliph but that the caliph must hew to the path of righteousness or risk being justifiably deposed. However, they are primarily remembered for their theological defense of free will. The early Qadarites were adamant that evil not be ascribed to **God**: only good comes from God, evil being traceable to either human beings or Satan. According to the more moderate version of this position, human beings have the capacity to choose between good and evil. God, it was allowed, knows from all eternity what we will do, but does not preordain or cause it. The more extreme forms of Qadarism rejected even God's foreknowledge of human choices. Both versions, however, seem committed to the premise that 'ought implies can': that is, God would not require human beings to act righteously and avoid evil if it were not within the power of our will. The free will doctrine was taken up by the **Mu'tazilites**, albeit in slightly altered form. It would be a grievous injustice, they argued, if God were to reward or punish people for matters they have no real power over, since moral accountability presupposes that one could have chosen otherwise. Thus, if we want to affirm God's justice we must also affirm human free will. The Qadarites faced staunch opposition from more **traditionalist** advocates of predestination and divine compulsion, and were ultimately outflanked by the **Ash'arites**, who attempted to stake out a 'middle ground' between free will and divine compulsion (which often seems closer to the latter than to the former).

See **Ash'arites; free will and predestination; Jabrites; Kharijites; Mu'tazilites; theology**

Further reading: van Ess 2006; Watt 1948, 1962/85

quiddity (*mahiyya*, lit. 'whatness'): see **essence and existence**

Qur'an ('Recitation'): The Qur'an, or Koran as it is sometimes spelled, is the foundational text of **Islam**. Muslims believe it is the revealed word of **God**, disclosed gradually (over a period of twenty-two years) to the Prophet **Muhammad** via the angel Jibril. In the establishment of Islam as the final great monotheistic religion, the revelations were committed to memory by Muslims, and after Muhammad's death they were recorded and organized into the text as we know it today. The text comprises 114 chapters (*sura*s), which in turn are divided into verses (*ayat*, lit, 'signs'). Each *sura* is identified as having been revealed to Muhammad either while he was in Mecca or Medina, although they are organized by length rather than by place or time of revelation. With the exception of one, they all begin with the famous invocation, 'In the name of God, the Merciful, the Compassionate' (*Bismillah al-rahman al-rahim*). The Qur'an is believed to be stylistically perfect and inimitable – a fact that is often taken as evidence of its divine source – and has spawned countless commentaries and translations (or more accurately, 'interpretations').

The revelations of the Qur'an represent the culmination of all previous revelations, beginning with Adam. In some cases, it reconfirms previous revelations, in some cases it fine-tunes them, and in some cases it supersedes them. It provides human beings with a **law** (*shari'a*) which makes known God's will and specifies certain beliefs and practices in the form of legal commandments and prohibitions. It is believed that on the Last Day God will judge each person based on whether he or she lived in accordance with this law and accordingly reward them in Paradise or punish them in Hell.

There are numerous theological and philosophical debates surrounding the nature of the Qur'an and its revealed law. One regards the ontological status of the Qur'an as the speech (*kalam*) of God. Insofar as this is considered one of God's multiple **attributes** (*sifat*), there is a question of how it ultimately relates to His unitary essence. By extension, *kalam* theologians disputed whether the Qur'an is created or not. **Mu'tazilites** and **Shi'ites**, who rejected the idea of a multiplicity of divine attributes over and above God's **unity**, tended to conceive of such things as a function of God's relation to the world. They thus viewed the speech of God as contingent and created. **Traditionalists** like Ibn Hanbal and his followers on the other hand argued that it must be uncreated and eternal, since it is a part of God. The issue was so controversial and so freighted with political significance that those who fell on the 'wrong' side of the issue (e.g. Ibn Hanbal) were sometimes imprisoned and punished. In the wake of such political excesses, the **Ash'arites** attempted a rapprochement between these two extremes, by distinguishing between the uncreated nature of God's speech as divine attribute and its 'created' expression, that is the Qur'an itself and its recitation by human beings.

Another issue that concerned both theologians and philosophers was the question of **interpretation** (*ta'wil*). **Literalists** and traditionalists (ranging from garden-variety **Hashawites** to **Zahirites** and **Hanbalites** to Ash'arites) tended to adhere closely to the apparent, external sense of scripture with greater or lesser degrees of subtlety. More **rationalist** thinkers such as the Mu'tazilites and *falasifa* felt the need to devise metaphorical interpretations of the Qur'an's ambiguous passages (*mutashabihat*), in order to defuse **anthropomorphic** portrayals of God and other conceptual problems. Sometimes rather strained figurative readings of scripture were put forth in order to harmonize revelation with philosophical doctrines, which were taken to be the necessary conclusions of universal **reason**. Although such thinkers were generally concerned with reconciling the apparent tension between reason and revelation, they could not help but re-raise the question of which took primacy ultimately and trumped the other. The **Isma'ilis** pushed the envelope of interpretation further than the Mu'tazilites and *falasifa*; they insisted on an **esoteric** (*batin*), symbolic import to the Qur'an, which could only be excavated by means of the authoritative, infallible **imam**. The **Sufis** also offered rather speculative symbolic-allegorical readings of scripture, informed by the unveilings they experienced in mystical states.

A final philosophical question raised by the Qur'an is whether the theoretical and practical **wisdom** that it discloses is otherwise unavailable to human beings by their own devices, or whether it can in principle be discovered by reason and experience. Either alternative has important implications for the role and status of revelation. If it discloses otherwise unattainable insights, then revelation is necessary for all people. For without its insights, they will not be able to lead good, happy lives, perfecting their natures and ultimately achieving salvation. On the other hand, if revelation is simply a short cut to insights accessible through reason and experience, then it takes on a more modest, political function. For philosophers like **al-Farabi** and **Ibn Rushd**, it disclosed a valuable but ultimately surrogate salvific wisdom to those unequipped by nature to discover the real thing on their own.

See **God** (also: **anthropomorphic descriptions of; attributes of**); **interpretation; Islam; political philosophy; prophecy**

Further reading: Ali 1993; Arberry 1955/96; Leaman 2006a; McAuliffe 2001–6; Rahman 1980/94

Qutb, Sayyid (1324–86/1906–66): see **Islamism**

rationalism: A general tendency in Islamic thought that emphasizes the primacy of reason or **intellect** (*'aql*) over tradition (*naql*). Rationalist theologians and philosophers believe that **God**'s existence, His **unity** and **attributes**, the origin and order of the world and the purpose of human life can all be known via rational means, independently of **revelation** (*wahy*). This is because God and the world proceed according to – and in some sense are constrained by – rational laws, which can be grasped by the human intellect. Traditional sources of knowledge such as the **Qur'an**, *sunna* (customary practice) and consensus are still considered legitimate, but only insofar as they are confirmed by reason; if a contradiction arises between reason and revelation (or tradition in general), it must be resolved according to the demands of reason. Accordingly, **anthropomorphic** characterizations of God in the Qur'an must be interpreted figuratively, lest believers end up with an incoherent, all-too-human, insufficiently transcendent conception of God. Traditional reports of the Prophet **Muhammad**'s sayings and actions are sometimes rejected as unreliable due to methodological questions about their collection and transmission, particularly when they appear to be at odds with reason or experience. As a general tendency, rationalism can manifest itself in different degrees. Moderate rationalists (e.g. the **Ash'arites**) maintain that our obligation to employ reason comes from revelation (i.e. reason is a principal source of knowledge, but one that is ultimately vouchsafed by tradition), while relatively more robust rationalists (e.g. the **Mu'tazilites**, some later Ash'arite theologians, and *a fortiori* the Greek-influenced *falasifa*) believe that our God-given reason is self-legitimating and requires no traditional justification. The **Isma'ili** stance on reason is complex and ambivalent: they valorize intellect, but limit its domain to the **imams** and their authoritative teachings. Pure rationalism, according to which reason is the human being's *sole* authority and need not be reconciled with revelation, is relatively rare in the Islamic tradition and typically equated with **freethinking** and even **unbelief**. Although one finds numerous examples of rather robust rationalism in the classical period of Islamic philosophy, within the larger context of the Islamic tradition, pure rationalism (e.g. **Ibn al-Rawandi** and Abu Bakr **al-Razi**) is perceived as extreme and peripheral.

See **Ash'arites; Isma'ilis; Mu'tazilites; philosophy; theology; traditionalism**

Further reading: Abrahamov 1998; Bello 1989; Hourani 1985; Martin et al. 1997; Stroumsa 1999

al-Razi, Abu Bakr Muhammad ibn Zakariyya' (250–313 or 323/864–925 or 935): One of the most respected and influential physicians in the medieval period, al-Razi (Latin: Rhazes) wrote extensively on the subject of **philosophy** as well as medicine, viewing it as a 'medicine of the **soul**'. His philosophical contributions, however, generally elicited criticism and hostility within the Islamic tradition, and were often branded as heretical. Only a handful of his philosophical texts are extant today. In one of them, the *Spiritual Medicine* (*al-Tibb al-ruhani*), al-Razi draws upon his reading of Greek philosophy, as well as his own considerable experience as a physician, to elaborate a Platonic-Epicurean account of pleasure as the return to a natural state of harmony from a prior dislocation, which he defines as pain. He goes on to espouse a prudential, hedonistic **ethics** which aims at minimizing pain through the guidance of **reason,** as well as the strategic use of mildly ascetic practices. In his *Book of the Philosophical Life* (*Kitab al-sira al-falsafiyya*), he defends philosophy as a way of life (focusing particularly on the paradigmatic figure of **Socrates**) and assumes a more critical stance towards asceticism, as potentially excessive and unproductive.

Al-Razi's rather naturalistic hedonism is, however, only one of the doctrines that earned him his reputation as a bold and potentially dangerous freethinker. Elsewhere, he argues that all human beings have the same fundamental capacity for reason and that the apparent inequality of people in this respect is ultimately a function of opportunity, interest and effort. Accordingly, al-Razi takes a rather dim view of **prophecy,** which in his view is both unnecessary and delusional, and indeed he criticizes all revealed religions as provincial and divisive. No one individual or group can legitimately claim a monopoly on the truth; each succeeding generation has the ability to improve upon and even transcend its predecessors' insights through rational argumentation and empirical inquiry.

Al-Razi thus holds out the possibility of progress not only in medicine and science, but in ethics and **metaphysics** as well. He sees his own unique metaphysics as an example of this: in an attempt to avoid the conceptual problems generated by both Islamic creationism and Greek eternalism, he posits the existence of five eternal, uncreated principles: **God**, soul, **time**, space and matter. From these building blocks he fashions a philosophical myth of the 'fall of the soul', in which the world comes to be out of pre-existing matter, within a framework of absolute time and space, as a result of the pre-rational, spontaneous urge of an immaterial life-force (the soul) and the compensating design of a divine, benevolent intelligence (God). The aim of the soul, according to al-Razi, is eventually to escape from its embodiment through the exercise of our God-given reason and return to its original state.

Yet despite his claims about the **immortality** and ontological independence of the soul, he retains an element of agnosticism about our ultimate fate. At the end of the *Spiritual Medicine*, while attempting to dispel the painful fear of death, he employs two very different kinds of therapeutic argument: a Platonic argument for the deathlessness of the soul and – in case that is unpersuasive – an Epicurean argument that death is nothing to us, since the soul dies with the body. Although, like Socrates, al-Razi believes the former, he is too much of a pragmatist and falliblist to reject the latter out of hand, especially when it too can help us lead a more rational – and less painful – life.

See **creation vs. eternity of the world; ethics; freethinking; metaphysics; philosophy; Plato; prophecy; psychology; rationalism**

Further reading: Goodman 1999a; Pines 1997; al-Razi 1950, 1993; Stroumsa 1999

al-Razi, Fakhr al-Din (543–606/1149–1209): Fakhr al-Din al-Razi in many ways represents the apex of 'modern' **Ash'arite** theology. Like his eminent predecessors, **al-Juwayni**, **al-Ghazali**, and **al-Shahrastani**, al-Razi strove to justify rational **theology**, even casting it as an obligation. He shared his predecessors' love-hate relationship with the philosophers as well, gleefully attacking their alleged errors wherever he found them but also appropriating their methods and sometimes even their conclusions. However, unlike al-Ghazali, al-Razi never accuses the philosophers of **unbelief**. Further, one could say that he is more forthright, explicit and confident about the extent to which he can legitimately incorporate the contributions of philosophy, perhaps most strikingly, **Ibn Sina**'s notion of **God** as the **Necessary Existent**. Of course, he takes Ibn Sina to task on many points as well, for example refuting the **Neoplatonic** emanationist principle that 'only one can come from one' and showing how God's knowledge of particulars would not necessarily entail any change in His unitary essence. But perhaps al-Razi's most interesting philosophical contributions arise as a result of his ability to internalize Ibn Sina's insights while ultimately moving beyond them. For instance, al-Razi takes up Ibn Sina's crucial distinctions between **essence and existence** (as well as necessary and possible existence), thus departing from the traditional framework of Ash'arite **metaphysics**. However, he argues that existence is distinct from – and superadded to – essence both with regard to created things and God Himself. Further, he casts pure existence as a mere concept or abstraction. With regard to the question of **free will**, he formulates a firmly deterministic position which sometimes seems to conflict with the Ash'arite notion of God's absolute freedom and even arguably goes beyond Ibn Sina's necessitarian model of God and the world. In short, al-Razi's critical-creative engagement with Ibn Sina radically transforms his Ash'arism (he even rejects their traditional doctrine of **atomism** in his early works). Al-Razi produced an enormous body of writings. His magnum opus is *The Keys to the Unknown* (*Mafatih al-ghayb*, also known as *al-Tafsir al-kabir*), a sprawling, multi-volume commentary on the **Qur'an** that shows al-Razi at the top of his theological and philosophical prowess. While this contains much of philosophical interest, his most important philosophical productions are his *Commentary on the Directives and Remarks* (*Sharh al-Isharat wa al-tanbihat*), which explicates and engages critically with Ibn Sina's encyclopedic work of the same name, his *Eastern Studies in Metaphysics and Physics* (*al-Mabahith al-mashriqiyya fi 'ilm al-ilahiyyat wa al-tabi'iyyat*), which again draws upon Ibn Sina's *Isharat*, as well as his *al-Shifa'* and *al-Najat*, and *The Harvest of Thought of the Ancients and Moderns* [or *Earlier and Later Scholars*] (*Muhassal afkar al-mutaqaddimin wa al-muta'akhkhirin min al-'ulama' wa al-hukama' wa al-mutakallimin*), which examines a series of theologico-metaphysical questions while surveying the views of scholars, philosophers and theologians.

Born in Rayy, Iran, al-Razi was initially quite poor but traveled widely, teaching and debating throughout the eastern parts of the Islamic world, where his combative personality and sometimes rather pugilistic approach to disputation earned him many enemies among the **Mu'tazilites**, Karramites, **Isma'ilis**, **Hanbalites** and philosophers. In spite of this, though, he was generally honored and supported generously by the reigning powers wherever he went, and eventually became quite a wealthy and prestigious figure. He was without a doubt the most important **Sunni** theologian of the twelfth century, and remains one of the most respected, admired and influential thinkers within the Islamic tradition.

See **Ash'arites; Ibn Sina; metaphysics; theology**

Further reading: Burrell and McGinn 1990; Kholeif 1966; Nasr 1996

reality/truth (*haqq, haqiqa*): see **God; metaphysics**

reason (*'aql*): see **epistemology; psychology; rationalism**

religion (*din*): see **Islam**

return, resurrection (*ma'ad*): see **afterlife; psychology**

revelation (*wahy, tanzil*): see **prophecy; Qur'an**

rhetoric (*khitaba*): see **logic; prophecy**

S

Saadia Gaon (882–942): One of the first great medieval Jewish philosophers, the thought of Saadia Gaon (Sa'adya Ben Yosef al-Fayyumi) was deeply informed by the Islamic context within which he worked. He produced the first and most widely used translation-interpretation of the Hebrew Bible (the Torah) into Arabic, the language in which his other many books were written as well. As a Rabbanite Jew, he was concerned with providing a reasoned defense of his tradition against the growing challenge of the Karaites, who recognized only the legitimacy of the Torah, rejecting the authority of the Talmud and subsequent rabbinic texts. Towards this end he found the methods – and in many cases, the doctrines – of the rationalist **Mu'tazilite** theologians to be a useful resource. Saadia's chief philosophical work, *The Book of Critically Chosen Beliefs and Opinions* (*Kitab al-mukhtar fi al-amanat wa al-i'tiqadat*), shows a pronounced Mu'tazilite influence, even with regard to its topical focus and organization. The book ranges from arguments for the createdness of the world, to a defense of **God's unity** (along with the obligatory critique of **anthropomorphism**), an influential discussion of the religious **law** (which analyzes the distinction between rational and revealed commands), human **free will** and responsibility, good and bad actions, the nature of the **soul** and its relation to the body, **resurrection**, the redemption of Israel, divine reward and punishment, and ultimately a Eudaimonistic consideration of the good life, which embraces a plurality of complementary goods taken in proper measure. Despite Saadia's affinity for Islamic **theology** and Greek **philosophy**, he was a bold and independent thinker and his conclusions are never simply derivative. He departs from his Muslim brethren on a number of key points, for example eschewing **atomism** (which traditionally served as the basis of the *kalam* theologians' arguments for the contingency and createdness of the world) and rejecting the alleged abrogation of the Mosaic **revelation**. He is also highly critical of the **Neoplatonists'** emanation model, which had a great influence within his own tradition as well as the Islamic philosophical tradition (in his youth he initiated a correspondence with the Jewish Neoplatonist Isaac Israeli, which was not well received). Although the Egyptian-born Saadia encountered some resistance and political setbacks throughout the course of his life, he was recognized as an authoritative thinker and indeed was nominated as *ga'on* (lit. 'eminence' or 'chief scholar') of the prestigious Talmudic academy of Sura' in Baghdad. His considerable impact on the Jewish intellectual tradition was not eclipsed until the advent of **Ibn Maymun**, better known in the West as Maimonides.

See **Mu'tazilites; rationalism; theology**

Further reading: Frank and Leaman 1997; Katz 1980; Saadia Gaon 1948, 1988

al-Sabzawari, al-Hajj Mulla Hadi (1212–95 or 1298/1797–1878 or 1881): The most important Iranian philosopher of the nineteenth century, al-Sabzawari revived **Mulla Sadra**'s transcendent wisdom and set the stage for the dominant trends of twentieth-century Iranian philosophy. He is best known for two complementary works: a didactic poem entitled *The Blaze of Gems* (*Ghurar al-fara'id*) and his *Commentary on the Didactic Poem* (*Shahr al-manzuma*). These two works taken together provided an elegant, comprehensive and carefully organized exposition of Mulla Sadra's system. The latter in particular, with its blend of rational argumentation and mystical intuition, became a standard text for philosophy students in Shi'ite *madrasa*s throughout the twentieth century and produced countless super-commentaries and textbook summaries. Al-Sabzawari is also famous for his influential commentary on Mulla Sadra's magnum opus, *The Journeys* (*al-Asfar*), as well as Jalal al-Din al-Rumi's key work of **Sufi** poetry, *Mathnavi*. Al-Sabzawari himself was an ascetic of saintly stature, whose piety led him to reject royal patronage. Several miracles are attributed to him.

See **Mulla Sadra**

Further reading: Nasr 1996; al-Sabzawari 1983; Toshihiko 1971

School of Isfahan: see **Mir Damad**

science (*'ilm*): During earlier periods, the Islamic world was very highly developed scientifically, and the translation project from Greek to Arabic that took place in Baghdad was primarily to translate scientific, not philosophical, texts. This led to a rich discussion of the classification of the sciences and different kinds of **knowledge**. One of the main tasks of the **Peripatetics** was determining the nature of knowledge and how it could be organized in such a way as to make science possible. They opposed **occasionalism**, the idea that causal links were arbitrary and depended entirely on the decisions of **God**. **Ibn Rushd** argued that this doctrine would make science impossible and our awareness of the world chaotic. **Ibn Sina** identified causal laws with necessary propositions, and saw the operation of the world as like a system of logical syllogisms, where everything has to take the course it does since it is necessitated by something prior to it. By contrast, **al-Ghazali** questioned the belief in science as ignoring the primary responsibility of God for everything, a responsibility that must not be ignored in our account of apparent scientific regularity.

There is a modern discussion of whether or not there is anything unique about the Islamic approach to science, very much taken up by those committed to **Sufism**. After all, if Muslims look at the world differently from other people, they should view science differently, since science is the study of how the world works. Western science is atomized and manipulative in its relationship to nature, since it does not see it as having any spiritual meaning. It is just there to be used and observed. By contrast, **Islam** encourages the view that the world is the product of God, so a deeper reality lies behind it, and its structure reveals to those who approach it in the right way an inner meaning. One aspect of this is to refer to the unity of the world as reflecting the **unity** of God, something it is difficult to understand but vital if we are to understand something vital about the world, how it all hangs together esoterically. Once we grasp this we will find it less easy to exploit or mistreat it, since it is in fact representative of its divine Creator, and we are entrusted with looking after it. The modern thinker Seyyed Hossein Nasr has argued in this way, and he certainly manages to differentiate sharply between western approaches to science and what he argues the Islamic approach ought to be.

See al-Biruni; epistemology; Ibn Rushd; Ibn Sina; metaphysics; psychology; rationalism; al-Razi (Abu Bakr); al-Tusi

Further reading: Bakar 1991, 1992; Hahn et al. 2001; Nasr 1968, 1976

al-Shahrastani, Abu al-Fath (c. 479–548/1087–1153): Al-Shahrastani is something of a contested figure in the history of Islamic philosophical theology. He has often been cast as an Ash'arite of the 'modern' variety and accordingly lumped together with figures such as al-Juwayni (many of whose students he studied under), al-Ghazali and Fakhr al-Din al-Razi. Indeed, like these thinkers, his theological commitments were informed and tempered by his careful engagement with the arguments of the philosophers. However, a growing number of scholars have made the argument that al-Shahrastani is in fact an Isma'ili, and indeed, many ideas of this sort can be found throughout his writings: the impeccability (*'isma*) of the prophet by virtue of his nature, the need for a divine guide (imam), the notion of God as unknowable Originator (*mubdi'*) who transcends all attributes and conceptual oppositions, the graduated/hierarchical picture of creation, the cyclical model of time, etc. Either way, it is safe to say that al-Shahrastani was a man of unusually broad learning and eclectic inclinations who did his best to understand, learn from and in some cases integrate choice insights from the various schools and thinkers he engaged with. It may thus be asking too much to expect him to have adhered strictly and univocally to only one movement's doctrines. The work for which he is perhaps best known, *The Book of Religions and Sects* (*Kitab al-milal wa al-nihal*), is still regarded as a remarkably objective and even-handed exposition of the religious and philosophical views of people throughout the world (i.e. Muslims, Christians, Jews, Mazdeans, Sabeans, the ancient Greeks, Islamic philosophers, Arab cults and Hindu sects). His *Furthest Steps in the Science of Theology* (*Nihayat al-aqdam fi 'ilm al-kalam*) sets out to demonstrate the limitations of theology, from the standpoint of a retooled, philosophically sophisticated Ash'arism which is informed by the insights of the **Mu'tazilites**, Isma'ilis and **Aristotelian** *falasifa*. *Wrestling with the Philosophers* (*Musara'at al-falasifa*, sometimes just referred to as *Kitab al-musara'a*) works up a thorough-going critique of **Ibn Sina**, albeit one that differs markedly from its more famous (and polemical) predecessor, al-Ghazali's *Incoherence of the Philosophers*. In this work he focuses in particular on the philosopher's conception of the **Necessary Existent**, which according to al-Shahrastani undermines God's absolute **transcendence**. The fullest expression of al-Shahrastani's thought, however, may be found in his Qur'anic commentary *Keys to the Mysteries and the Lights of the Righteous* (*Mafatih al-asrar wa masabih al-abrar*), which remains incomplete.

See **Ash'arites**; **Isma'ilis**; **al-Juwayni**; **al-Tusi**; **theology**
Further reading: al-Shahrastani 1934, 1956, 2001

al-Shahrazuri, Shams al-Din (d. after 687/1288): Al-Shahrazuri was the first major **Illuminationist** thinker after the founder of the school, **al-Suhrawardi**. Indeed, most of what we know about the latter's life comes to us through the former's great biographical history of ancient

Greek and Islamic philosophers, *The Pleasure Place of Spirits and the Garden of Rejoicing* (*Nuzhat al-arwah wa rawdat al-afrah*). Al-Shahrazuri was a prolific writer, penning numerous *ishraqi* treatises, as well as an encyclopedia of **philosophy** and the sciences entitled *The Divine [Metaphysical] Tree* (*al-Shajara al-ilahiyya*). However, he is best known for his formative commentaries on al-Suhrawardi's *Philosophy of Illumination* (*Sharh Hikmat al-ishraq*) and *Intimations* (*Sharh al-Talwihat*), which unfolded the Master's thought in great detail, setting the stage for subsequent *ishraqiyyun* such as **Ibn Kammuna** and Qutb al-Din **al-Shirazi**. Al-Shahrazuri exemplifies the mystical, symbolic and anti-Peripatetic strand of Illuminationist philosophy, which historically proved more influential than Ibn Kammuna's discursive-analytic approach. Although he viewed himself as the 'upholder' (*qayyim*) of the science of lights, he was by no means a mere imitator or dogmatic partisan. His treatments of other philosophers are objective and even-handed, and despite his own intellectual commitments, he defended the importance of studying **Peripatetic** thought at a time when the orthodox **Ash'arite** backlash against the *falasifa* had made such pursuits highly questionable.

See **Ibn Kammuna; Illuminationism; al-Shirazi; al-Suhrawardi**

Further reading: Aminrazavi 1997; Nasr 2006; Walbridge 2000b; Ziai 1990

Shi'ites (*shi'a*): The Shi'ites constitute one of the two main branches of **Islam**. Although historically there have been Shi'ite communities dispersed throughout various areas in the Middle East, Asia and Africa, today they are primarily concentrated in Iran, Pakistan, Iraq, Syria and southern Lebanon. Unlike the more mainstream majority of **Sunni** Muslims, Shi'ites hold that true authority within the community of believers rests only with the 'people of the house' (*ahl al-bayt*), that is, the Prophet **Muhammad** and his descendants. They thus reject the legitimacy of Muhammad's first three successors (Abu Bakr, 'Umar and 'Uthman), who were his companions, and believe that only the fourth, his son-in-law and cousin 'Ali b. Abi Talib, was actually qualified to lead the community. It was because of this that they acquired the name *shi'at 'Ali* ('partisans of 'Ali'), or just *shi'a*. 'Ali and his descendants are typically characterized by Shi'ites as **imams** rather than caliphs. Imams are not only directly related to Muhammad by bloodline, but are actually guided and legitimized by **God**. Thus, unlike the Sunni caliphs (who in practice if not in theory exercised mainly secular power), the imams were invested with both spiritual and temporal authority. Historically, however, these claims to authority were repeatedly frustrated both religiously and politically. The history of the imams is a bloody and tragic one that has given rise to the veneration of their tombs and shrines, as well as repeated calls for repentance and martyrdom. The Shi'ites believe that the last historical imam was not killed but rather went into occultation or concealment (*ghayba*) and will return as the Mahdi (lit. the 'one who is rightly guided') at the end of time to restore true religion and rule justly and wisely over all. There are several divisions within Shi'ite Islam itself, the two most prominent of which are the **Isma'ilis** (or 'Seveners' [*sab'iyya*], as they are sometimes called) and the '**Twelvers**' (*ithna 'ashariyya*). They are divided by the question of which imam went into occultation (the seventh or the twelfth) and by their practical response to this state of affairs (Isma'ilis opting for various degrees of religio-political activism, the Twelvers generally adopting a kind of quietism until the Mahdi's return). Both branches of Shi'ism produced important philosophical figures ranging from **al-Farabi**, to **al-Sijistani** (Abu Ya'qub), to **al-Tusi**, to **Mulla Sadra**.

See **Batinites**; **Isma'ilis**; **Sunnis**; **theology**; **Twelver Shi'ites**

Further reading: Chittick 1981; Halm 1991/2004; Hogson 1974; Watt 1962/85

al-Shirazi, Qutb al-Din (634–710/1236–1311): A man of many interests and talents, Qutb al-Din al-Shirazi was a physician, an astronomer, a judge, a Sufi, a dedicated student of traditional Islamic sciences such as *hadith* (the study of traditions, or reports of Muhammad's sayings and actions) and *tafsir* (Qur'anic commentary), an avid chess player and a musician (he played the *rababa*, a small viol). He was also a philosopher of broad intellectual sympathies. The 'polymath' (*al-mutafannin*), as he was fittingly called, is typically placed within the lineage of **Illuminationist** thinkers, having written what is perhaps the best-known commentary on **al-Suhrawardi**'s *Philosophy of Illumination*. In terms of his intellectual orientation, al-Shirazi might be situated somewhere between his two main *ishraqi* predecessors, **al-Shahrazuri** and **Ibn Kammuna**. On the one hand, he is representative of what Hossein Ziai has called the more 'popular' strain of Illuminationism. In this respect, he has more in common with al-Shahrazuri's mystical-experiential orientation than with the more logically and analytically inclined Ibn Kammuna. On the other hand, al-Shirazi does not share al-Shahrazuri's anti-**Peripatetic** bent. In fact, he was a student of **al-Tusi**, and as a result, acquired a deep understanding and profound respect for Aristotelian thought and for **Ibn Sina** in particular. Al-Shirazi's main independent philosophical text, the encyclopedic and very influential *Pearly Crown* (*Durrat al-taj*), was arguably the first work to attempt a thorough harmonization of *mashsha'i* methodology and **meta-physics** with *ishraqi* **epistemology** and **psychology**. Into this synthesis he also added **Ibn al-'Arabi**'s monistic **Sufism**, thus setting the stage for the even more ambitious gnostic syntheses of the **School of Isfahan**.

See **Aristotle; Ibn al-'Arabi; Ibn Kammuna; Ibn Sina; Illuminationism; Mir Damad; al-Shahrazuri; al-Suhrawardi; al-Tusi**

Further reading: Aminrazavi 1997; Nasr 2006; Walbridge 1992, 2000b

shirk (lit. 'sharing' or 'associating'): Worshipping other deities or creatures alongside **God** (i.e. polytheism). This is the worst form of disbelief and, according to the **Qur'an**, the one sin that cannot be forgiven. This is because it flies in the face of Islam's fundamental tenet, 'There is no god but God' (*la ilaha illa Allah*), effectively denying God's existence as such. The accusation of *shirk* occurs as a common polemical denunciation against theological and philosophical opponents, where it can be employed rather loosely, based on the potential, unforeseen implications of a position rather than explicit claims. For instance, in the controversy concerning **free will** and predestination, both **Mu'tazilites** and **Ash'arites** accused each other of committing *shirk* (the Mu'tazilites because they attribute to the human being a creative power comparable to God's, the Ash'arites because their doctrine of acquisition involves an association between God and the human being).

See **God** (also: anthropomorphic descriptions of; imitation of; unity of); **Islam; Qur'an**

al-Sijistani, Abu Sulayman Muhammad (d. c. 375/985): The foremost figure of the much-celebrated '**humanist**' movement during the Buyid dynasty in Baghdad, al-Sijistani formed a circle of intellectuals whose lively meetings (*majalis*) ranged over **philosophy, religion, science,** politics and cultural issues. His own philosophical lineage traces back to **al-Farabi** and Abu Bishr Matta by way of the Christian logician Yahya **ibn 'Adi.** Only a few of his own works are extant, most notably the *Cupboard of Wisdom* (*Siwan al-hikma*), although he is said to have produced numerous commentaries on **Aristotelian logic** as well (hence his nickname, *al-mantiqi*, the 'Logician'). On the whole, however, al-Sijistani favored teaching and discussion over writing. Thus, most of what we know about him comes down to us from his student **al-Tawhidi,** who acted as a secretary of sorts at the sessions and recorded his teacher's ideas in the books *Borrowed Lights* (*al-Muqabasat*) and *Book of Pleasure and Conviviality* (*al-Imta' wa al-mu'anasa*). From these works we get a picture of al-Sijistani's quasi-Aristotelian and **Neoplatonic** views on **God,** the **soul** and **reason.** His primary concern was the relation between philosophy and religion, which he saw as independent and irreconcilable sources of truth, characterized by different methods and aims. He was consequently scornful of attempts to harmonize the two (e.g. by the **Brethren of Purity**) and saw the *kalam* theologians as crypto-dogmatists, whose self-proclaimed commitment to reason was at best disingenuous. Although a deeply religious man himself, al-Sijistani was convinced that reason was capable of leading us to **knowledge,** virtue, salvation and **happiness.** Al-Sijistani's importance in the Islamic philosophical tradition lies less with his own profundity or originality than with the fact that, perhaps more than any other figure of the fourth/tenth century, he consolidated, epitomized and disseminated the collective wisdom of his time.

See **al-Farabi; humanism; Ibn 'Adi; philosophy; rationalism; al-Tawhidi; theology**

Further reading: Kraemer 1986a/93, 1986b; Nasr with
Aminrazavi 1999; Netton 1992/99

al-Sijistani, Abu Ya'qub (d. c. 361/971): Al-Sijistani is gener-
ally viewed as one of the most important early Persian
Isma'ili philosophers. A substantial number of his works
have been preserved, among them the *Unveiling of the
Hidden* (*Kashf al-mahjub*) and the *Book of Wellsprings*
(*Kitab al-yanabi'*). Building upon the formative work
of his predecessor al-Nasafi, al-Sijistani elaborated a
Neoplatonic cosmology that differed from those of the
falasifa in certain important respects. First, unlike **al-
Farabi** and **Ibn Sina**'s systems, there are no imported
Aristotelian elements such as the **'active intellect'** and
so forth. Second, al-Sijistani emends the traditional
Neoplatonic model of **emanation** (*fayd*) by distinguishing
between **origination** (*ibda'*) and procession or manifestation (*inba'atha*, *inbi'ath*) in order to preserve **God**'s
absolute **transcendence** and uniqueness. According to
this model, God the 'Originator' (*mubdi'*) creates only
one thing directly through his timeless command, 'Be!'
This is **intellect** (*'aql*), the first originated being (*al-
mubda' al-awwal*), which, like a seed, contains implicitly
within it the entirety of the universe. The emergence of
the universe from intellect is from that point on a matter
of 'procession' rather than origination. In this process of
emanation, intellect gives rise to **soul** (which, in its quest
for perfection, initiates motion and time), soul gives rise
to nature, and nature gives rise to the physical world,
within which the human soul is entangled. Al-Sijistani's
main practical concern is with the reversal of this process:
our return or ascent, which begins when the embodied
soul looks back towards its spiritual origin and attempts
to comprehend it. But towards this end, unaided, universally distributed human reason is simply not sufficient.

Only divine **law,** a manifestation or incarnation of intellect, can activate human beings' implicit **knowledge** of their true nature and origin. This is revealed through the prophets (who function as deputies of intellect in the physical world), and then interpreted and taught by the **Shi'ite imams** (who are uniquely endowed with the intellectual capacity to grasp its true meaning). In this way the soul's return to its intellectual origin is initiated. Yet on al-Sijistani's account, God Himself is above and beyond all intelligibility. The only way to talk about God is by means of double negation (*nafyun wa nafyu nafyin*) (i.e. God is not a thing, but also *not* not a thing). Similarly, concepts such as firstness, substance, intellect, being and cause cannot, strictly speaking, apply to the Divine. Theologians and philosophers have rightly resisted the attribution of physical qualities to God, but unwittingly remain mired in **anthropomorphism** by attributing to Him residual intellectual properties. Al-Sijistani avoids this error by distinguishing God, not only from creation (which on his account proceeds from intellect), but from intellect itself, which is still just the first originated being. Intellect thus functions in al-Sijistani's thought as a kind of 'fire wall' between the emanated universe and God. It can, through its selective manifestation as **prophecy,** tell us how we should live and what we should believe. It can even enable us to rise up from our embodiment in the material world and return to our intellectual origin, but it cannot give us knowledge of God the Originator, who remains forever on the other, inaccessible side of intellect.

See **God (anthropomorphic descriptions of); Isma'ilis; al-Kirmani; Nasir-i Khusraw; Neoplatonism; psychology; Shi'ites; theology**

Further reading: Nasr with Aminrazavi 2001; Walker 1993, 1994, 1996

Socrates (Suqrat) (470–399 BCE): Although Socrates is viewed as the 'father' of **philosophy** in western histories, he occupies a somewhat more peripheral intellectual status in the Islamic tradition. His philosophy is generally not distinguished from **Plato**'s, and he is typically cast as an austere figure of great moral integrity. This is primarily a function of the transmission of sources from Greek to Arabic. First, only a few Platonic dialogues were available in the Islamicate context. Prominent among them was the *Phaedo*, an unusually ascetic dialogue in which the dying Socrates argues for the immortality and general superiority of the soul over the body. Second, the popular portrait of Socrates passed down through later Greek biographies and wisdom texts was profoundly influenced by the Cynics and Stoics, whose philosophical schools were selectively modeled upon the more rigorous and demanding aspects of Socrates' life. In this literature, Socrates is virtually indistinguishable from the Cynic Diogenes, who scorned worldly pleasures, social conventions and political power. Third, certain biographical details of Socrates' personality resonated powerfully with the religious ideals of the Muslim community, prompting further selective emphasis. Islamic authors generally viewed Socrates as a moral exemplar who teaches us philosophy as a way of life (e.g. **al-Kindi** and Abu Bakr **al-Razi**) or as a pre-Muslim forebear who tacitly exemplifies certain Muslim qualities, or even as a kind of prophet (**al-Tawhidi** and **Ibn Sina**). On the whole, he functions more as a symbol of ethical integrity and the demands and rewards of the philosophical life, than as a substantive thinker in his own right.

See **ethics**; **al-Kindi**; **Plato**; **al-Razi (Abu Bakr)**

Further reading: Alon 1991; Plato 1997; al-Razi 1993

soul (*nafs*): see **psychology**

Sufism (*tasawwuf*): Sufi or mystical Islamic **philosophy** rests on the basic distinction between the inner and the outer, the **esoteric** and the exoteric, the hidden and the open. Mundane sense experience and even the conclusions of **reason** give us only superficial **knowledge**, and we need to go deeper if we are really to know anything significant. A frequent Qur'anic passage quoted by the Sufis is *fa aynama tuwallu fa tamma wajh Allah* ('Wherever you turn, there is the face of God' – 2.115). When we become aware of the real truth we feel at peace and the contradictions and confusions of everyday life are resolved. This is easier to say than to do, since for this feeling to arise we have to bring together things which are very different from each other, such as the one and the many, the present and the past and future, the same and the other, the transcendent and the immanent, the finite and the infinite. As one might expect, as the Sufi becomes more adept at resolving these contradictions, the scope for **language** to describe the process becomes progressively less feasible. Language is after all very much built on these dichotomies.

Sufism does not see itself as an alternative to other ways of philosophizing, but more as a supplement. There is nothing wrong with finding things out by using our senses, nor with extending our knowledge by reasoning. We should use these faculties to their furthest extent. A number of philosophers in the classical period were also Sufis, and they argued that one has to work up to **mysticism** by first mastering the lower forms of thought. Only when these were perfected could one hope to move further along the path of knowledge to contact with what lies behind and beyond us ordinarily. Sufism places emphasis on the importance of realizing not only intellectual awareness of God but *dhawq* or taste, where there is actually a felt experience of nearness to the Deity, and they contrast this closer state of being to the more restricted level of awareness reached by the **Peripatetics** when they talk of coming into contact with the **active intellect**. There are many varieties of Sufism, some ecstatic in form while others are very much opposed to such behavior. Most Sufis accept the need for a guide, for spiritual preparation along a path and for the systematic and gradual increase in the sort of gnosis (*'irfan*) that brings one closer to God.

See **epistemology; al-Ghazali; Ibn al-'Arabi; Ibn Masarra; Ibn Sab'in; mysticism**

Further reading: Arberry 1950/90; Chittick 1989; al-Ghazali 1980/2004; Nasr 1981, 2006; Schimmel 1975; Sells 1994, 1996

al-Suhrawardi, Shihab al-Din Yahya [Persian: Sohravardi] (549–587/1154–91): Within the Islamic philosophical tradition, al-Suhrawardi's status is perhaps second only to **Ibn Sina**. Although he was notoriously executed at the age of thirty-eight (on the orders of the Ayyubid sultan Salah al-Din, better known to the West as Saladin), in the course of his short life the 'Slain Master' (*al-shaykh al-maqtul*) gave birth to the celebrated '**philosophy** of **Illumination**' (*hikmat al-ishraq*), a school of thought that would effectively change the course of Islamic intellectual history. In many ways, Illuminationist (*ishraqi*) philosophy can be seen as a response to the perceived shortcomings and inadequacies of **Peripatetic** (*mashsha'i*) thought, particularly as exemplified by Ibn Sina. Throughout philosophical works such as *The Intimations* (*al-Talwihat*), *The Oppositions* (*al-Muqawamat*), *The Paths and Havens* (*al-Mashari' wa al-mutarahat*) and *The Philosophy of Illumination* (*Hikmat al-ishraq*), as well as a number of symbolic-allegorical narratives, al-Suhrawardi sought to replace – or at least supplement – the excessively discursive and deductive (*bahthiyya*) character of Aristotelian thought with a more intuitive, experiential and mystical **wisdom** (*al-hikma al-dhawqiyya*). Yet his philosophy is never thereby vague, obscurantist or wildly speculative; indeed, his criticisms of Peripatetic **logic** and **metaphysics** are often sharp and analytical.

One of the more important points on which al-Suhrawardi takes issue with **Aristotle** and his followers is the theory of definition as the basis of scientific knowledge. He argues that the Aristotelian project of definition is doomed to failure, because (1) a complete definition would have to include all the constituents of the thing defined, which is impossible, and (2) defining cannot actually proceed from the known to the unknown, as Aristotle pretends, since the constituents of the thing to be defined are no more known than the thing itself. Any attempt at definition, then, opens up an infinite regress in which the unknown is perpetually defined in terms of the unknown. Further, our inability to know definitively if we have hit upon a complete catalogue of essential constituents gives rise to the problem of induction, which undermines the Peripatetics' ability to make universal claims. Indeed, for all his emphasis on syllogistic demonstration, Aristotle himself recognizes that scientific knowledge depends ultimately upon primary, necessarily true premises which themselves cannot be deduced. In a way, it is this foundation that al-Suhrawardi seeks to disclose through a kind of direct, unmediated, certain intuition, which is more fundamental than conceptual-discursive knowledge. He calls this knowledge by presence (*al-'ilm al-huduri*), and its most basic mode is the luminescent self-manifestation or self-awareness of consciousness (not entirely unlike the preconceptual, intuitive, reflexive knowledge of one's own existence that Ibn Sina points up in his **floating man argument**).

Al-Suhrawardi conceives of consciousness as more akin to an illuminative lamp than a passively reflecting mirror; indeed, he describes self-aware beings as pure, simple lights. Yet more radically truth-disclosing mystical experiences can be cultivated through spiritual exercises, which reveal all of reality as a hierarchy of self-manifesting, luminescent beings of varying degrees of intensity or gradation, all of whom ultimately receive their emanated being from **God**, 'the Light of Lights' (*nur al-anwar*). Al-Suhrawardi's metaphysics of illumination or 'science of lights' (*'ilm al-anwar*), as he calls it, is enormously complex, with a vertical hierarchy of immaterial 'victorious lights' that emanate from God, in turn giving rise to a horizontal array of 'regent' lights, which are somewhat akin to Platonic forms (each being the 'lord' of a species), and the interactions between these two kinds of luminescent beings finally produce the bodies of the lower physical world, each of which is a kind of boundary or isthmus (*barzakh*) between light and darkness. Between the divine lights and the physical world, al-Suhrawardi also posits an imaginal realm (*'alam al-mithal*, *'alam al-khayal*), within which such immediate, intuitive, mystical knowledge is disclosed.

One consequence of al-Suhrawardi's metaphysics is the so-called **'primacy of essence'** (*asalat al-mahiyya*) over **existence** (*wujud*). Although he himself never actually uses this expression, existence is far less important to his system than it is to the Peripatetics (and Ibn Sina in particular); indeed he views it as a mere conceptual abstraction, a secondary intelligible universal with no reality outside the mind. Like **Ibn Rushd**, he argues that to posit the existence of existence above and beyond particular existents is redundant and results in an infinite regress, since existence would then become another existent, which would again require existence as a generality to make it real. Further, if (as Ibn Sina seemed to suggest) existence is an 'accident' ('*arad*) superadded to an essence, then the essence would presumably have to exist already, before the accident could be added to it, thus rendering the general attribute of existence superfluous. **Mulla Sadra** famously disagreed with al-Suhrawardi's general position on this question, arguing for the **primacy of existence** (*asalat al-wujud*) over essence, even though he would appropriate many other aspects of his predecessor's metaphysics.

The question of al-Suhrawardi's intellectual sources is a difficult one. He saw his Illuminationist philosophy as being part of a long, distinguished lineage which was traceable back to ancient eastern and western sages such as Hermes Trismigistus, Zoroaster, Pythagoras and **Plato**. While his philosophy clearly has pronounced Mazdean and (Neo-) Platonic elements, this genealogy is probably somewhat fanciful. A more immediate and concrete historical influence is Ibn Sina, despite al-Suhrawardi's views concerning the inadequacies of *mashsha'i* logic and metaphysics. It is possible to identify **Sufi** influences in his epistemology and ontology as well (see, for example, **al-Ghazali**'s *Niche of Lights* [*Mishkat al-anwar*]). His effect on subsequent thinkers is much less ambiguous: among those whose philosophies would have been impossible without al-Suhrawardi, one may count such great figures as **al-Shahrazuri, Ibn Kammuna**, Qutb al-Din **al-Shirazi, al-Dawani, Mir Damad** and **Mulla Sadra**, not to mention the many *ishraqi* thinkers active today in Iran. In addition to this, al-Suhrawardi had a considerable influence on later Sufi and Peripatetic thinkers, most notably **Ibn al-'Arabi** and **al-Tusi**.

See **epistemology; essence and existence; Ibn Sina; Illuminationism; Mulla Sadra; mysticism; Neoplatonism; Sufism**

Further reading: Aminrazavi 1997; Corbin 1998; Ha'iri Yazdi 1992; Nasr 1964; al-Suhrawardi 1982/99, 1998, 1999; Walbridge 1992, 2000b, 2001; Ziai 1990

sunna (customary practice, tradition): see **Sunnis; traditionalism**

Sunnis (*sunniyyun*): Followers of the *sunna*, the 'trodden path' or customary practice of the Prophet **Muhammad**, the Sunnis constitute the 'orthodox' majority of **Islam**. They are traditionally known as the 'people of custom and community' (*ahl al-sunna wa al-jama'a*). Sunni Islam comprises numerous legal movements and theological schools, and has taken on various forms as it adapted itself to fit diverse historical, cultural and political contexts. However, at least two commonly held views can be identified, which distinguish it from **Shi'ism**, the other main branch of Islam. First, Sunnis believe that religious authority comes down from the Prophet Muhammad and his companions (specifically, the four 'Rightly Guided Caliphs' who followed him: Abu Bakr, 'Umar, 'Uthman and 'Ali), rather than from the Prophet's specific family line (i.e. only Muhammad and 'Ali, as the Shi'ites maintain). Second, by extension, they hold that any male Muslim who is of age and of good standing in the community can legitimately rule as caliph (*khalifa*, lit. 'successor' of the Prophet Muhammad). Sunnism arose out of early theologico-religious disputes regarding what makes a true Muslim and who is qualified to be the spiritual and secular leader of the community. It represents a consolidation of tradition in response to the many theoretical and practical innovations that emerged in Islam's formative years, especially the Shi'ite movement and the **Mu'tazilite** inquisition (*mihna*) of the third/ninth century. Sunni Islam often casts itself as a 'middle way' in response to the difficult questions that beset the Muslim community. Perhaps because of its penchant for **traditionalism**, the Sunnis' contributions to Islamic philosophy have come primarily in the form of philosophical **theology** (e.g. **Ash'arite** thinkers such as **al-Ghazali** and Fakhr al-Din **al-Razi** and **Hanbalites** such as **Ibn Taymiyya**) and philosophical **mysticism** (e.g. **Sufis** such as **Ibn al-'Arabi**).

See **Ash'arites; al-Ghazali; Hanbalites; Ibn Taymiyya; Islam; Mu'tazilites; al-Razi (Fakhr al-Din); Shi'ites; Sufism; theology**

Further reading: Hodgson 1974; Watt 1962/85

T

Ta'limites (*ta'limiyya*): see **Batinites; Isma'ilis**

tasawwuf (Sufism): see **Sufism**

tawhid (oneness, unity): see **God (unity of)**

al-Tawhidi, Abu Hayyan (d. 414/1023): One of the towering figures of Islamic **humanism**, al-Tawhidi was a student of both Yahya **ibn 'Adi** and Abu Sulayman Muhammad **al-Sijistani**. He earned his living as a scribe and secretary and was one of the most famous courtiers in the cultural renaissance of fourth/tenth-century Baghdad. His best-known work – which preserves the flavor of those heady times – is *Pleasure and Conviviality* (*al-Imta' wa al-mu'anasa*), a kind of philosophical *Arabian Nights* which recounts the intellectual soirees of his then-beneficiary, Ibn Sa'dan. Al-Tawhidi's main philosophical work is *Borrowed Lights* (*al-Muqabasat*), which provides much insight into the ideas circulating in his teacher al-Sijistani's influential *majilis* at that time. In addition to numerous other technical and popular works, he engaged in a correspondence with **Miskawayh**, collected under the title *Rambling and Comprehensive Questions (al-Hawamil wa al-shawamil)*. Al-Tawhidi's philosophy often hews closely to the views of al-Sijistani, wedding a Neoplatonic cosmology to **Platonic psychology** and **Aristotelian ethics**. Like other thinkers in his philosophical lineage (typically traced back to **al-Farabi**), he links the attainment of **knowledge** with salvation and **happiness**.

Despite his familiarity with the *adab* tradition of social refinement and ethical perfectionism, al-Tawhidi was by most accounts a flawed and difficult man. Moving among the innermost circles of the famous, the powerful and the learned, he is said to have been a gossip, a fault-finder, a tactless guest and something of a political naïf. However, he was cognizant of his own shortcomings and did encounter numerous obstacles and disappointments in the course of his career which probably hardened his instinctive pessimism into spite and bitterness. Like **al-'Amiri**, he had a strong mystical bent, and in his old age he retreated to the **Sufi** center of al-Shiraz, where he burned all his books in an expression of piety. Despite al-Tawhidi's many great contributions to the Islamic intellectual tradition, his life was not a particularly happy one and he died a disappointed man. One might say that his personal character and political fortunes were intimately bound up with the mood of his philosophical humanism. Muhammad Arkoun characterizes him as the 'indignant humanist' (as compared to Miskawayh, the 'serene' humanist), and Joel Kraemer elegantly sums up the tenor of al-Tawhidi's thought and life when he remarks that 'His humanism was not a joyful celebration of man's grandeur but a sober acceptance of man's ambiguity.'

See *adab*; humanism; Ibn 'Adi; Miskawayh; al-Sijistani (Abu Sulayman Muhammad)

Further reading: Kraemer 1986a/93, 1986b; Netton 1992/99

theology (*kalam*): *'Ilm al-kalam* – lit. 'the science of the word' (or speech or discussion) – comprises a tradition of dialectical argumentation and speculative thought that attempts to explain, clarify and defend the fundamental theological doctrines of Islam. Early disputes in this tradition revolved around essentially practical questions such as who should lead the Muslim community and whether or not sinners who are nonetheless believers should still be considered Muslims. However, these issues soon gave way to more speculative concerns such as the tension between predestination and **free will**, the question of whether the **Qur'an** as the word of **God** is created or uncreated, and the relation between God's various traditional **attributes** and His essential **unity**. The two most influential schools of *kalam* are the **Mu'tazilites** and the **Ash'arites**. The Mu'tazilites emphasized God's unity and justice, strongly advocated the use of reason in the interpretation of Qur'anic doctrines and were defenders of human free will. The Ash'arites emphasized God's omnipotence (sometimes at the expense of human free will) and in general staked out a middle ground between Mu'tazilite **rationalism** and staunchly **traditionalist** theologico-juristic schools such as the **Hanbalites** and **Zahirites**, who generally rejected the use of **reason** and **interpretation** in favor of the literal truth of the Qur'an and the sayings of **Muhammad** and his companions. For political as well as doctrinal reasons, Ash'arism eventually overshadowed Mu'tazilism, and for many came to represent the mainstream of Islamic theological thought. Both schools, however, produced numerous resourceful proofs for the **creation** of the world, articulated a distinctly Islamic form of **atomism**, and were severe and implacable critics of the philosophers. Indeed, by the end of the twelfth century, *kalam* had overshad-owed and marginalized Greek-influenced philosophy within the **Sunni** milieu, at least – although not without being enriched by its concerns, methods and insights.

See **Ash'arites; creation vs. eternity of the world; free will and predestination; al-Ghazali; God (also: arguments for the existence of; attributes of; unity of); Hanbalites; Jabrites; Kharijites; Murji'ites; Mu'tazilites; occasional-ism; philosophy; Qadarites; Qur'an; rationalism; tradi-tionalism; Zahirites**

Further reading: Abrahamov 1998; Arberry 1957; van Ess 2006; Morewedge 1979; Watt 1948, 1962/85

time (*dahr*): see **creation vs. eternity of the world**

traditionalism: An influential theological and legal tendency that identifies tradition (*naql*) rather than **reason** (*'aql*) or considered opinion (*ra'y*) as the preeminent source of human **knowledge**. Traditionalists (*ahl al-hadith*, lit. 'people of tradition') typically privilege **revelation** (the **Qur'an**), the actions and sayings of the Prophet **Muhammad** (*sunna*, lit. 'well-followed path', i.e. cus-tomary practice or tradition) and consensus (*ijma'*). They place great stock in traditional reports of Muhammad's actions and sayings (*ahadith*; sing: *hadith*) and revere those who collect and transmit these reports (*muhaddith* or 'traditionists'). In general, they are opposed to figura-tive interpretations of the Qur'an and hostile to any kind of rational speculation or disputation about questions left unclear by revelation. They see pure reason as an unstable, unreliable device that gives rise to **innovation** and deviation from the truths provided by the sources mentioned above, leading to heresy and even **unbelief**. Not surprisingly, they are implacable critics of rationalist theologians and philosophers. However, traditionalists disagree about how best to respond to those who privilege reason. Pure or extreme traditionalists prohibit rational argumentation altogether and completely dissociate themselves from those who engage in it, branding them as unbelievers and in some cases even persecuting them. Moderate traditionalists engage with and attempt to refute advocates of reason, using not only traditional proofs but rational arguments themselves (turning reason on itself, as it were, to highlight its own limitations and inadequacies). This points up a certain ambivalence about the status of reason within traditionalism. While extreme traditionalists (e.g. the **Zahirites**) often seem to reject rational argumentation and interpretation altogether, moderate traditionalists (e.g. the **Hanbalites**) accept the use of reason so long as it is confirmed by tradition. Thus, figures like Ibn Hanbal and **Ibn Taymiyya** will employ reason to defend tradition and refute their rationalist adversaries (indeed, their arguments can be surprisingly resourceful), but ultimately assign it a subordinate role. In short, reason is answerable to tradition, but not vice versa.

See **Ash'arites; Hanbalites; Ibn Hazm; Ibn Taymiyya; rationalism; theology**

Further reading: Abrahamov 1998; Arberry 1957; Hallaq 1993

transcendence (*tanzih*): see **God (anthropomorphic descriptions of)**

al-Tusi, Nasir al-Din (597–672/1201–74): It is often claimed that **philosophy** effectively came to an end in the Islamic world with the death of **Ibn Rushd** at the close of the twelfth century. This is certainly an exaggeration, in part because of the various non-**Peripatetic** movements that continued to flourish well beyond that time (the **Isma'ilis**, the school of **Illumination**, philosophical **Sufism**, the philosophical **theology** of the 'modern' **Ash'arites** and the **Twelver Shi'ites**). But it is also false because of thinkers like the Persian scientist-philosopher al-Tusi (also known as Khwaja Nasir), who was arguably the towering intellectual figure of the thirteenth century, as well as the great defender and reviver of Peripatetic thought in the East. Brought up as a Twelver Shi'ite, al-Tusi benefited from an unusually broad, ambitious and non-sectarian education. He studied the rational or 'ancient' sciences (logic, philosophy, mathematics, natural **science**) as well as the traditional Islamic sciences and had the opportunity to familiarize himself with Isma'ili doctrines (his later writings show a knowledge of, and respect for, Sufism and Illumination as well). In his early thirties, he joined the Isma'ilis, and even lived for twenty years in their storied mountain fortress of Alamut. However, when the Mongol invasion of Iran smashed the Isma'ili *da'wa*, al-Tusi converted back to Twelver Shi'ism and even became advisor to the Mongol conqueror Khan Hülegü, who prized his astronomical expertise quite highly. Hülegü brought al-Tusi along during his conquest of Baghdad (which brought about the end of the 'Abbasid caliphate), put him in charge of religious endowments and affairs, and placed considerable scholarly and scientific resources at his disposal, most notably the famous astronomical observatory at Maraghah, which the Khan had built for the philosopher. There is some disagreement about the depth of al-Tusi's commitment to Isma'ilism; it may have been a function of political expediency, much as some of his subsequent choices were. Yet during that period, he used the extensive library at Alamut to produce many of his most important theological, philosophical and scientific works, and scholars have detected residual Isma'ili doctrines in his later, ostensibly post-Isma'ili works (e.g. the **imam's** authoritative teaching [ta'lim] and the unchangeability of God's will concerning the designation [nass] of the imam). Al-Tusi's chief presentation of Isma'ili doctrines can be found in the *Paradise of Submission* (*Rawda-yi taslim*); another key work is his autobiographical *Contemplation and Action* (*Sayr wa suluk*). His most important contribution to Twelver thought is the enormously influential *Abstract of Belief* (*Tajrid al-i'tiqad*), which revitalized Imami theology by introducing rigorous new metaphysical terminology and arguments. His most essential work of Peripatetic philosophy is the *Commentary on the Directives and Remarks* (*Shahr al-Isharat wa al-tanbihat*, also known as the *Hall mushkilat al-Isharat*), a devastating response to an earlier, critical commentary on **Ibn Sina**'s *Isharat* by the Ash'arite theologian Fakhr al-Din **al-Razi**. It is considered the decisive statement of Ibn Sina's thought and has deeply influenced the way he is read in the tradition. Later, after al-Tusi repudiated his Isma'ili affiliations, he responded in a similar vein to **al-Shahrastani**, who had written an Isma'ili-tinged critique of Ibn Sina entitled *Wrestling with the Philosophers* (*Musara'at al-falasifa*). Al-Tusi's polemical rejoinder, cleverly titled *The Floorings of the Wrestler* (*Masari' al-musari'*), might be seen as a more successful historical counterpart to Ibn Rushd's *Incoherence of the Incoherence* (which, compared to its own target – **al-Ghazali**'s *Incoherence of the Philosophers* – was virtually ignored in the Islamic world). Al-Tusi also produced several ethical works, the most important being *The Nasirean Ethics* (*Akhlaq-i Nasiri*), which builds upon the ethical thought of **Miskawayh**, the economic insights of Ibn Sina (as well as the Neopythagorean Bryson's *Oikonomikos*) and the political philosophy of **al-Farabi**. It is one of the most highly regarded works of Islamic moral philosophy written in Persian. Among his numerous logical works, the

Foundations of Inference (Asas al-iqtibas) is the most important; it is considered second only to the comparable section in Ibn Sina's *Healing*. Finally, al-Tusi produced numerous mathematical and scientific works that made significant original contributions to arithmetic, geometry, trigonometry and astronomy. The most well-known of these is the *Ilkhani Tables (Zij-i ilkhani)*, the result of his fruitful research at the Maraghah observatory – and more generally of the institutionalization of the rational sciences, which until then had been almost entirely dependent upon private patronage or individual initiative.

See **Aristotle; Ibn Sina; Isma'ilis; Neoplatonism; (Fakhr al-Din) al-Razi; science; al-Shahrastani; Twelver Shi'ites**

Further reading: Daftary 1990; Nasr 1996; Nasr with Aminrazavi 1999; al-Tusi 1964, 1992, 1997

Twelver Shi'ites (*ithna 'ashariyya*): The 'Twelvers', or Imamis (*imamiyya*) as they are also known, constitute the largest sect of **Shi'ite Islam**. With the development of Twelver Shi'ism, the **imam** became an increasingly elevated figure. Not only was he identified as a blood descendant of **Muhammad**'s family, he was endowed with divinely inspired **knowledge** and was seen as sinless and without error (*'isma*). Twelvers believe that the twelfth imam went into occultation (*ghayba*) and will return at the end of time as the Mahdi ('the rightly guided one') to rule justly over all. In the meantime, they have traditionally espoused a kind of political quietism, one aspect of which is the practice of *taqiyya*, or precautionary **dissimulation**, according to which the imam and his followers are permitted to conceal their religious beliefs for the sake of survival in times of danger and persecution. In the realm of **jurisprudence**, the Twelver Shi'ites recognize the same sources or roots (*usul*) as most **Sunnis** do: the Qur'an, *sunna* (custom as reported in tradition [*hadith*]), consensus (*ijma'*) and analogy (*qiyas*). However, there are a few noteworthy differences. First, the Twelvers' accepted *hadith*s often have different lines of transmission (due to their privileging of Muhammad's family lineage and their consequent rejection of the authority of the first three caliphs). Second, their notion of consensus is closely linked to the imams rather than just legal experts. Third, Twelver jurists typically give more leeway to analogy than the Sunnis do, since they reject *taqlid* ('**obedience**', or unquestioning acceptance of authority) and retain the right to considered, **independent judgement** in their attempt to discern the actual intentions of the imams. Theologically, the Twelvers are influenced by the **Mu'tazilites** on a number of key points: (1) they are great defenders of **God**'s absolute, transcendent **unity**, (2) they interpret scripture figuratively when necessary (e.g. **anthropomorphic** descriptions of God, but also some eschatological passages), (3) they hold that the Qur'an is created and not an eternal expression of God's essence (accordingly, it is not immutable and may be modified by an inspired imam), and (4) they place great emphasis on reason, although they typically see it as justified by the Qur'an and *hadith*, rather than as self-legitimating. The tradition of Twelver Shi'ism produced numerous important philosophers, among them **al-Tusi, Mir Damad, Mulla Sadra** and **al-Sabzawari**.

See **Isma'ilis; law; Mir Damad; Mulla Sadra; Mu'tazilis; al-Sabzawari; Shi'ites; Sunnis; al-Tusi**

Further reading: Halm 1991/2004; Momen 1987; Watt 1962/85

unbelief (*kufr*): see **belief**

unity (*tawhid*): see **God (unity of)**

universal and particular (*kulli*; *juz'i*): see **God's knowledge; metaphysics**

Wali Allah, Shah (1114–76/1703–62): Qutb al-Din Ahmad ibn 'Abd al-Rahim, known more commonly by his honorific title Shah Wali Allah, was perhaps the greatest Muslim scholar in the Indian subcontinent. He benefited from a wide-ranging, sophisticated education in the traditional and rational sciences and later, after he went on his pilgrimage (*hajj*) to Mecca and Medina, extensively studied reports of the Prophet's deeds and sayings with traditionists there. He was a teacher and ultimately the principal of the prestigious Madrasa Rahimiyya, which his father had founded. Shah Wali Allah was also, it should be added, a **Sufi**, who recorded his numerous mystical visions. As a broadly educated man of many perspectives, living in a time of decline and disintegration for the Muslim (Mughal) empire in India, Shah Wali Allah's chief concerns were two-fold. The first was the reestablishment and revivification of **Islam** through reform. Shah Wali Allah sought to return Islam to a purer, less corrupt and more rational form by directing Muslims back to the **Qur'an**, which he famously translated into Persian in order to further its accessibility. However, although he was a *traditionist* (i.e. a scholar of *hadith*), he was by no means a **traditionalist**; like a number of other modernist Muslim thinkers who sought to breathe new life into the Islam of their pious forebears, Shah Wali Allah's approach to scripture and tradition was a thoroughly rational one. Second, in order to preserve the essential unity of Islam, he focused in particular on the reconciliation (*tatbiq*) of apparently conflicting claims wherever they arose. In religio-political terms, he endeavored to reconcile the **Sunnis** and **Shi'ites** in their quarrel over the legitimacy of the caliphs. With regard to the **interpretation** and application of Islamic **law**, he attempted to reconcile the four major schools of **jurisprudence**, and was a staunch defender of the necessity and justifiability of **independent judgement**, which most schools had long since closed off. As can be seen by the specific nature of his return to the Qur'an, he sought to harmonize **reason** and **revelation** as well. But perhaps his most interesting and resourceful rapprochement was his attempt to defuse the long-standing tensions between **mysticism** and **theology** concerning the **unity** of **God**. Specifically, he was concerned with a dispute of sorts between two philosophical Sufis, **Ibn al-'Arabi** and Shaykh Ahmad Sirhindi. The former famously posited a fundamental unity of all beings in God insofar as they are manifestations of the divine names. This ontological model, which subsequent writers would name the '**oneness of existence**' (*wahdat al-wujud*), was frequently interpreted as disturbingly monistic and even pantheistic by more traditionalist sensibilities. In response to this, Shaykh Ahmad Sirhindi acknowledged that existence is indeed one and that it is God, yet denied that God and creation are one and the same. On his account, creation is simply a shadow or reflection of the divine names and attributes in the mirrors of their opposite non-beings (*a'dam al-mutaqabila*). This in effect is the doctrine of the 'oneness of witnessing' (*wahdat al-shuhud*). Shah Wali Allah's peace-making intervention on the question of the unity of existence or witnessing showed that when the ambiguous metaphors and similes are stripped away from either position, it becomes clear that they are essentially saying the same thing. Beyond reconciling two rival metaphysical camps, this made the doctrine of the unity of existence more acceptable to the **kalam** theologians. Shah Wali Allah's treatment of this issue can be found in his *Metaphysical Instruction (Tafhimat al-ilahiyya)*. He composed numerous philosophical works, the greatest of which is *The Conclusive Argument from God (Hujjat Allah al-baligha)*, ranging comprehensively over **metaphysics**, theology, the development of human society, the wisdom behind divine commands and prohibitions, **ethics**, politics, etc. Shah Wali Allah's dim view of sectarianism and rejection of all systems (*fakk kull nizam*) can be seen clearly in this work. In terms of his sociopolitical ideas, Shah Wali Allah was a revolutionary thinker, although his ideas never really took root effectively in his particular historical-political context. Yet he would have a considerable influence upon various later reformist and revivalist movements.

See **Ibn al-'Arabi; Iqbal (Muhammad); traditionalism**
Further reading: Rizvi 1980; Wali Allah 1980, 1982, 1995

wisdom (*hikma*): see **philosophy**

Y

Yahya ibn 'Adi: see **Ibn 'Adi**

Z

Zahirites (*zahiriyya*): A theological-juridical school founded by Dawud ibn Khalaf (d. 270/844), a student of the great jurist al-Shafi'i. The name of the school derives from the word *zahir* ('apparent', 'external') and has to do with its basic interpretive principle: careful privileging of the literal sense of the **Qur'an** and tradition (*sunna*). Restricting consensus (*ijma'*) to that of Muhammad's companions, rejecting juristic discretion (*istihsan*), considered opinion (*ra'y*) and even reasoning by analogy (*qiyas*), the now-defunct Zahirite school of **jurisprudence** was similar in spirit to the **Hanbalites**, but represented an even more extreme form of **traditionalism**. In spite of their low estimation of **reason** and interpretation, however, they rejected *taqlid* (**obedience**, following, imitation) and defended *ijtihad* (in the sense of exerting oneself in the search for a text, rather than *ra'y* or *qiyas* as an exercise of **independent judgement**). The Zahirites could also reach surprisingly cautious, moderate conclusions in the realm of **theology**, if only because of their refusal to engage in substantive exegesis: they recognized the importance of the divine names without **anthropomorphizing God** or positing a multiplicity of **attributes**, they emphasized God's transcendent **unity** without divesting Him of attributes, and they affirmed the free power of human beings over their actions. The most influential and original thinker among the Zahirites was the Andalusian polymath, **Ibn Hazm**.

See **Ibn Hazm; independent judgement; interpretation; law; obedience; traditionalism**

Further reading: Goldziher 1971; Hallaq 1997; Schacht 1964/83

Bibliography

'Abduh, M. [1966] (2004), *The Theology of Unity*, trans. I. Musa'ad and K. Cragg, London: George Allen and Unwin.

Abed, S. B. (1991), *Aristotelian Logic and the Arabic Language in Alfarabi*, Albany: State University of New York Press.

Abrahamov, B. (1998), *Islamic Theology: Traditionalism and Rationalism*, Edinburgh: Edinburgh University Press.

Adams, C. C. (1933), *Islam and Modernism in Egypt*, Oxford: Oxford University Press.

Adamson, P. (2003), *The Arabic Plotinus: A Philosophical Study of the Theology of Aristotle*, London: Duckworth.

— (2006), *Al-Kindi (Great Medieval Thinkers)*, Oxford: Oxford University Press.

— and Taylor, R. (eds) (2005), *The Cambridge Companion to Arabic Philosophy*, Cambridge: Cambridge University Press.

Addas, C. (1993), *The Quest for Red Sulphur; The Life of Ibn 'Arabi*, trans. P. Kingsley, Cambridge: Islamic Texts Society.

Ali, A. (1993), *Al-Qur'an: A Contemporary Translation*, Princeton, NJ: Princeton University Press.

Alon, I. (1991), *Socrates in Medieval Arabic Literature*, Leiden: Brill.

Altmann, A. and Stern, S. M. [1958] (1979), *Isaac Israeli: A Neoplatonic Philosopher of the Early Tenth Century*, Oxford: Oxford University Press.

Amin, O. (1953), *Muhammad 'Abduh: Essay on his Philosophical and Religious Ideas*, trans. C. Wendell, Washington, DC: American Counsel of Learned Societies.

Aminrazavi, M. (1997), *Suhrawardi and the School of Illumination*, Richmond: Curzon.

Arberry, A. J. [1950] (1990), *Sufism: An Account of the Mystics of Islam*, London: Routledge.

— [1955] (1996), *The Koran Interpreted*, trans. A. J. Arberry, New York: Touchstone.

— (1957), *Revelation and Reason in Islam*, London: George Allen and Unwin Ltd.

Aristotle (1984), *The Complete Works of Aristotle: The Revised Oxford Translation*, ed. J. Barnes, Princeton, NJ: Princeton University Press.

Arnaldez, R. (2000), *Averroes: A Rationalist in Islam*, trans. D. Streight, Notre Dame, IN: University of Notre Dame.

al-Ash'ari (1953), *The Theology of al-Ash'ari*, trans. R. J. McCarthy, Beirut: Imprimerie Catholique.

Asín Palacios, M. [1972] (1997), *The Mystical Philosophy of Ibn Masarra and His Followers*, trans. E. H. Douglas and H. W. Yoder, Leiden: Brill.

Atiyeh, G. [1966] (1977), *Al-Kindi: Philosopher of the Arabs*, Chicago: Kazi Publications.

al-Azmeh, A. [1981] (2003), *Ibn Khaldun: An Essay on Reinterpretation*, Budapest and New York: Central European University Press.

Bakar, O. (1991), *Tawhid and Science: Essays on the History and Philosophy of Islamic Science*, Kuala Lumpur: Secretariat for Islamic Philosophy and Science.

— (1992), *Classification of Knowledge in Islam*, Kuala Lumpur: Institute for Policy Research.

Bearman, P. J. et al. (eds) (1960–2005), *Encylopedia of Islam*, New Edition, 12 vols, Leiden: Brill.

Bello, I. (1989), *The Medieval Islamic Controversy between Philosophy and Orthodoxy*, Leiden: Brill.

Berman, L. (1961), 'The Political Interpretation of the Maxim: The Purpose of Philosophy is the Imitation of God', *Studia Islamica* 15: 53–61.

al-Biruni (2003–5), 'Ibn Sina–al-Biruni Correspondence' (in six installments), trans. R. Berjak and M. Iqbal, *Islam and Science* vol. 1, no. 1 – vol. 3, no. 2.

Black, D. (1990), *Logic and Aristotle's* Rhetoric *and* Poetics *in Medieval Arabic Philosophy*, Leiden: Brill.

Brethren of Purity (1978), *The Case of the Animals vs. Man Before the King of the Jinn: A 10th Century Ecological Fable of the Pure Brethren of Basra*, trans. L. E. Goodman, New York: Twayne Publishers.

Buijs, J. A. (ed.) (1988), *Maimonides: A Collection of Critical Essays*, Notre Dame, IN: University of Notre Dame.

Burrell, D. (1986), *Knowing the Unknowable God: Ibn Sina, Maimonides, Aquinas*, Notre Dame, IN: University of Notre Dame.

— (1993), *Freedom and Creation in Three Traditions*, Notre Dame, IN: University of Notre Dame.

— and McGinn, B. (eds) (1990), *God and Creation: An Ecumenical Symposium*, Notre Dame, IN: University of Notre Dame Press.

Butterworth, C. E. (ed.) (1992), *The Political Aspects of Islamic Philosophy: Essays in Honor of Muhsin S. Mahdi*, Cambridge, MA: Harvard University Press.

— and Kessel, B. (eds) (1994), *The Introduction of Arabic Philosophy into Europe*, Leiden: Brill.

Calder, N. et al. (eds) (2003), *Classical Islam: A Sourcebook of Religious Literature*, London: Routledge.

de Callataÿ, G. (2005), *Ikhwan al-Safa': A Brotherhood of Idealists on the Fringe of Orthodox Islam*, Oxford: Oneworld.

Carr, B. and Mahalingam I. (eds) (1997), *Companion Encyclopedia of Asian Philosophy*, London: Routledge.

Chejne, A. G. (1982), *Ibn Hazm*, Chicago, IL: Kazi Publications.

Chittick, W. (ed.) (1981), *A Shi'ite Anthology*, Albany, NY: State University of New York Press.

Chittick, W. (1989), *The Sufi Path of Knowledge: Ibn al-'Arabi's Metaphysics of Imagination*, Albany, NY: State University of New York Press.

— (1997), *The Self-Disclosure of God: Principles of Ibn al-'Arabi's Cosmology*, Albany, NY: State University of New York Press.

— (2001), *The Heart of Islamic Philosophy: The Quest for Self-Knowledge in the Teachings of Afdal al-Din Kashani*, Oxford: Oxford University Press.

Chodkiewicz, M. (1993), *An Ocean Without Shore: Ibn 'Arabi, the Book and the Law*, trans. D. Streight, Albany, NY: State University of New York Press.

Choueiri, Y. M. [1990] (1997), *Islamic Fundamentalism*, London and Washington, DC: Cassell-Pinter.

Colmo, C. (2005), *Breaking With Athens: Al-Farabi as Founder*, Lanham, MD: Lexington Books.

Conrad, L. I. (ed.) (1996), *The World of Ibn Tufayl: Interdisciplinary Studies on Hayy Ibn Yaqzan*, Leiden: Brill.

Cooper, J., Nettler, R. and Mahmoud, M. (eds) (2000), *Islam and Modernity: Muslim Intellectuals Respond*, London: I. B. Tauris.

Corbin, H. [1960] (1980), *Avicenna and the Visionary Recital*, trans. W. Trask, Princeton, NJ: Princeton University Press.

— [1969] (1998), *Alone With the Alone: Creative Imagination in the Sufism of Ibn 'Arabi*, trans. R. Mannheim, Princeton, NJ: Princeton University Press.

— (1993), *History of Islamic Philosophy*, trans. L. and P. Sherrard, London: Kegan Paul International.

— (1998), *The Voyage and the Messenger: Iran and Philosophy*, trans. J. Rowe, Berkeley, CA: North Atlantic Books.

Craig, E. (ed.) (1998), *Routledge Encyclopedia of Philosophy*, London: Routledge.

Daftary, F. (1990), *The Isma'ilis: Their History and Doctrines*, Cambridge: Cambridge University Press.

Daiber, H. (1999), *Bibliography of Islamic Philosophy*, 2 vols, Leiden: Brill.

Davidson, H. (1987), *Proofs for Eternity, Creation, and the Existence of God in Medieval Islamic and Jewish Philosophy*, Oxford: Oxford University Press.

— (1992), *Alfarabi, Avicenna, and Averroes on Intellect: Their Cosmologies, Theories of Active Intellect and Theories of the Human Intellect*, Oxford: Oxford University Press.

al-Dawani [1839] (1977), *Practical philosophy of the Muhammadan People . . ., being a translation of the Akhlaq-i Jalaly . . . from the Persian of Fakir Jany Muhammad Asaad . . .*, London: Oriental Translation Fund of Great Britain and Ireland.

Deutsch, E. and Bontekoe, R. (eds) (1997), *A Companion to World Philosophies*, Oxford: Blackwell.

Dillon, J. M. and Gerson, L. P. (2004), *Neoplatomic Philosophy: Introductory Readings*, Indianpolis, IN and Cambridge: Hackett Publishing Company.

Druart, T. A. (ed.) (1988), *Arabic Philosophy and the West*, Washington, DC: Center for Arab Studies, Georgetown University.

— (1993), 'Al-Kindi's Ethics', *Review of Metaphysics* 47: 329–57.

Esposito, J. [1991] (2004), *The Straight Path*, Oxford: Oxford University Press.

— and Voll, J. O. (2001), 'Hasan Hanafi: The Classical Intellectual', in *The Makers of Contemporary Islam*, Oxford: Oxford University Press.

van Ess, J. (2006), *The Flowering of Muslim Theology*, trans. J. M. Todd, Cambridge, MA: Harvard University Press.

Euben, R. (1999), *Enemy in the Mirror: Islamic Fundamentalism and the Limits of Modern Rationalism*, Princeton, NJ: Princeton University Press.

Fakhry, M. (1958), *Islamic Occasionalism and its Critique by Averroes and Aquinas*, London: Allen and Unwin.

Fakhry, M. [1970] (2004), *A History of Islamic Philosophy*, New York: Columbia University Press.

— (1991), *Ethical Theories in Islam*, Leiden: Brill.

— (2002), *Al-Farabi, Founder of Islamic Neoplatonism: His Life, Works and Influence*, Oxford: Oneworld Publications.

al-Farabi (1963), *The Political Regime*, trans. F. Najjar, in Mahdi and Lerner.

— [1969] (2002), *The Philosophy of Plato and Aristotle*, trans. M. Mahdi, Ithaca, NY: Cornell University Press.

— (1973), 'The Letter Concerning the Intellect', trans. A. Hyman, in Hyman and Walsh (eds).

— (1985), *Al-Farabi on the Perfect State: Abu Nasr al-Farabi's Mabadi' ara' ahl al-madinah al-fadilah*, ed. and trans. R. Walzer, Oxford: Oxford University Press.

— (2001), *The Political Writings: Selected Aphorisms and Other Texts*, trans. C. E. Butterworth, Ithaca, NY: Cornell University Press.

Frank, D. and Leaman, O. (eds) (1997), *History of Jewish Philosophy*, London: Routledge.

Frank, R. (1978), *Beings and their Attributes: The Teaching of the Basrian School of the Mu'tazila in the Classical Period*, Albany, NY: State University of New York Press.

— (1994), *Al-Ghazali and the Ash'arite School*, Durham, NC: Duke University Press.

Galston, M. (1990), *Politics and Excellence: The Political Philosophy of Alfarabi*, Princeton, NJ: Princeton University Press.

Gersonides (Levi ben Gerson) (1984), *The Wars of the Lord*, 2 vols, trans. S. Feldman, Philadelphia, PA: Jewish Publication Society.

— (1992), *The Logic of Gersonides: A Translation of the Sefer ha-Heqqesh ha-Yashar*, trans. C. H. Manekin, Dordrecht: Kluwer Academic Publishers.

al-Ghazali [1980] (2004), *Deliverance from Error: Five Key Texts Including His Spiritual Autobiography, al-Munqidh min al-Dalal*, trans. R. J. McCarthy, Louisville, KY: Fons Vitae.

— [1997] (2000), *The Incoherence of the Philosophers: A Parallel English-Arabic Text*, trans. M. E. Marmura, Provo, UT: Brigham Young University Press.

Goldziher, I. (1971), *The Zahiris: Their Doctrine and their History*, ed. and trans. W. Behn, Leiden: Brill.

Goodman, L. E. (1969), 'A Note on Avicenna's Theory of the Substantiality of the Soul', *Philosophical Forum* 1, 547–54.

— [1992a] (2006), *Avicenna*, Ithaca, NY: Cornell University Press.

—(ed.) (1992b), *Neoplatonism and Jewish Thought*, Albany, NY: State University of New York Press.

— (1999a), 'Razi vs. Razi—Philosophy in the *Majlis*', in *The Majlis: Interreligious Encounters in Medieval Islam*, ed. H. Lazarus-Yafeh et al., Wiesbaden: Harrassowitz Verlag.

— (1999b), *Jewish and Islamic Philosophy: Crosspollinations in the Classic Age*, Edinburgh: Edinburgh University Press.

— (2003), *Islamic Humanism*, Oxford: Oxford University Press.

Gutas, D. (1975), *Greek Wisdom Literature in Arabic Translation: a Study of the Graeco-Arabic Gnomologia*, New Haven, CT: Yale University Press.

— (1988), *Avicenna and the Aristotelian Tradition: Introduction to Reading Avicenna's Philosophical Works*, Leiden: Brill.

— (1998), *Greek Thought, Arabic Culture*, London: Routledge.

— (2000), *Greek Philosophers in the Arabic Tradition*, Aldershot: Ashgate Variorum.

Gwynne, R. (2004), *Logic, Rhetoric, and Legal Reasoning in the Qur'an: God's Arguments*, New York: Routledge Curzon.

Hahn, L., Auxier, R. and Stone, L. (eds) (2001), *The Philosophy of Seyyed Hossein Nasr*, La Salle: Open Court.

Ha'iri Yazdi, M. (1992), *The Principles of Epistemology in Islamic Philosophy: Knowledge by Presence*, Albany, NY: State University of New York Press.

Halevi, Judah (1964), *The Kuzari: An Argument for the Faith of Israel*, trans. H. Hirschfeld, New York: Schocken Books.

Hallaq, W. B. (1993), *Ibn Taymiyya against the Greek Logicians*, Oxford: Oxford University Press.

— (1997), A *History of Islamic Legal Theories*, Cambridge: Cambridge University Press.

— (2005), *The Origin and Evolution of Islamic Law*, Cambridge: Cambridge University Press.

Halm, H. [1991] (2004), *Shi'ism*, trans. J. Watson, Edinburgh: Edinburgh University Press.

Hassan, R. (ed.) (1977), *The Sword and the Sceptre*, Lahore: Iqbal Academy.

Hawi, S. [1974] (1997), *Islamic Naturalism and Mysticism: A Philosophic Study of Ibn Tufayl's Hayy Bin Yaqzan*, Leiden: Brill.

Hodgson, M. G. S. (1974), *The Venture of Islam*, vols 1–3, Chicago, IL: University of Chicago Press.

Hourani, G. (1971), *Islamic Rationalism: The Ethics of 'Abd al-Jabbar*, Oxford: Clarendon Press.

— (ed.) (1975), *Essays on Islamic Philosophy and Science*, Albany, NY: State University of New York Press.

— (1983), *Arabic Thought in the Liberal Age 1798–1939*, Cambridge: Cambridge University Press.

— (1985), *Reason and Tradition in Islamic Ethics*, Cambridge: Cambridge University Press.

Houtsma, M. T. et al. [1913–36] (1993), *First Encyclopedia of Islam*, 9 vols, Leiden: Brill.

Hunsberger, A. (2000), *Nasir-i Khusraw, the Ruby of Badakhshan: A Portrait of the Persian Poet, Traveller and Philosopher*, London: I. B. Tauris.

Hurvitz, N. (2002), *The Formation of Hanbalism*, London: Routledge.

Hyman, A. and Walsh, J. (eds) (1973), *Philosophy in the Middle Ages*, Indianapolis, IN: Hackett Publishing Company.

Ibn 'Adi (2002), *The Reformation of Morals* (parallel English-Arabic edition), trans. S. H. Griffith, Provo, UT: Brigham Young University Press.

Ibn al-'Arabi (1980), *The Bezels of Wisdom*, trans. R. W. J. Austin, New York: Paulist Press.

— (2002), *The Meccan Revelations*, 2 vols, ed. M. Chodkiewicz, trans. W. Chittick et al., New York: Pir Press.

Ibn Bajja (1963), *The Governance of the Solitary*, trans. L. Berman, in Mahdi and Lerner.

Ibn Gabirol (1962), *The Fountain of Life*, trans. H. E. Wedeck, New York: Philosophical Library.

Ibn Hazm [1953] (1997), *The Ring of the Dove*, trans. A. J. Arberry, London: Luzac Oriental.

— (1990), *In Pursuit of Virtue: The Moral Theology and Psychology of Ibn Hazm al-Andalusi*, trans. M. Abu Layla, London: Ta-Ha Publishers.

Ibn Kammuna (1971), *Ibn Kammuna's Examination of the Three Faiths: A Thirteenth Century Essay in the Comparative Study of Religion*, trans. M. Perlmann, Berkeley, CA: University of California.

— (2002), *Al-Tanqihat Fi Sarh Al-Talwihat: Refinement and Commentary on Suhrawardi's Intimations*, ed. and intro. H. Ziai and A. Alwishah, Costa Mesa: Mazda Publishers.

Ibn Khaldun [1950] (1987), *An Arab Philosophy of History: Selections from the Prolegomena of Ibn Khaldun of Tunis*, ed. and trans. C. Issawi, Princeton, NJ: Darwin Press.

— [1958] (1967), *The Muqaddimah: An Introduction to History*, 3 vols, ed. and trans. F. Rosenthal, Princeton, NJ: Princeton University Press.

Ibn Rushd [Averroës] [1954] (1978), *Tahafut al-Tahafut (The Incoherence of 'The Incoherence')*, 2 vols, trans. S. Van Den Bergh, London: Luzac.

Ibn Rushd [Averroës] [1974] (2005), *Averroes on Plato's Republic*, trans. R. Lerner, Ithaca, NY: Cornell University Press.

— (1977), *Averroes' Three Short Commentaries on Aristotle's 'Topics,' 'Rhetoric,' and 'Poetics'* trans. C. E. Butterworth, Albany, NY: State University of New York Press.

— [1983] (1998), *Averroes' Middle Commentaries on Categories and De Interpretatione*, trans. C. E. Butterworth, South Bend, IN: St Augustine Press.

— (1984), *Ibn Rushd's Metaphysics: A Translation with Introduction of Ibn Rushd's Commentary on Aristotle's Metaphysics, Book Lam*, trans. C. Genequand, Leiden: Brill.

— (1999), *Averroes' Middle Commentary on Aristotle's Poetics*, trans. C. E. Butterworth, South Bend, IN: St Augustine Press.

— (2001a), *Decisive Treatise and Epistle Dedicatory* (parallel English/Arabic text), trans. C. E. Butterworth, Provo, UT: Brigham Young University Press.

— (2001b), *Faith and Reason in Islam: Averroes' Exposition of Religious Arguments*, trans. I. Najjar, London: Oneworld Publications.

— (2002), *Middle Commentary on Aristotle's De anima* (parallel English/Arabic text), trans. A. Ivry, Provo, UT: Brigham Young University Press.

— (2007), *Long Commentary on the De Anima of Aristotle*, trans. R. C. Taylor, New Haven, CT: Yale University Press.

Ibn Sina [Avicenna] (1951), *Avicenna on Theology*, ed. and trans. A. J. Arberry, London: J. Murray.

— [1952] (1981), *Avicenna's Psychology: An English Translation of Kitab al-Najat, Book II, Chapter VI*, trans. and ed. F. Rahman, Oxford: Oxford University Press.

— [1973] (2001), *The Metaphysica of Avicenna (Ibn Sina)*, ed. and trans. P. Morewedge, Binghamton, NY: Global Scholarly Publications.

— (1974), *The Life of Ibn Sina: A Critical Edition and Annotated Translation*, ed. and trans. W. Gohlman, Albany, NY: State University of New York Press.

— (1984), *Remarks and Admonitions, Part One: Logic*, trans. S. Inati, Toronto: Pontifical Institute for Mediaeval Studies.

— (1985), 'Essay on the Secret of Destiny', trans. G. Hourani, in Hourani (1985).

— (1996), *Ibn Sina and Mysticism: Remarks and Admonitions, Part 4*, trans. S. Inati, London: Kegan Paul International.

— (2005), *The Metaphysics of 'The Healing'*, parallel English/Arabic text, trans. M. E. Marmura, Provo, UT: Brigham Young University Press.

Ibn Tufayl [1972] (2003), *Hayy Ibn Yaqzan: A Philosophical Tale*, trans. L. E. Goodman, 4th edn, Los Angeles: Gee Tee Bee.

Iqbal, M. [1908] (1964), *The Development of Metaphysics in Persia*, Cambridge: Cambridge University Press.

— (1930), *The Reconstruction of Religious Thought in Islam*, Lahore: Shaikh Muhammad Ashraf.

— (1950), *The Secrets of the Self*, trans. R. A. Nicholson, Lahore: Shaikh Muhammad Ashraf.

— (1953), *The Mysteries of Selflessness*, trans. A . J. Arberry, Lahore: Shaikh Ghulam Ali and Sons.

— [1966] (2003), *Javid-Nama*, trans. A. J. Arberry, Ajman, UAE: Islamic Books.

al-Jabiri (1999), *Arab-Islamic Philosophy: A Contemporary Critique*, trans. A. Abbassi, Austin, TX: Center for Middle Eastern Studies, University of Texas.

Janssens, J. (2006), *Ibn Sina and his Influence on the Arabic and Latin World*, Aldershot: Ashgate Variorum.

Kamal, M. (2006), *Mulla Sadra's Transcendent Philosophy*, Aldershot: Ashgate.

Katz, S. (ed.) (1980), *Saadiah Gaon*, New York: Arno Press.

Keddie, N. (1968), *An Islamic Response to Imperialism*:

Political and Religious Writings of Sayyid Jamal al-Din al-Afghani, Berkeley, CA: University of California.

— (1972), *Sayyid Jamal al-Din al-Afghani: A Political Biography*, Berkeley, CA: University of California Press.

Kedourie, E. (1966), *Afghani and 'Abduh: An Essay on Religious Unbelief and Political Activism in Modern Islam*, London: Frank Cass and Co. Ltd.

Kemal, S. (1991), *The Poetics of Alfarabi and Avicenna*, Leiden: Brill.

Kennedy-Day, K. (2003), *Books of Definition in Islamic Philosophy: The Limits of Words*, London: Routledge.

Kholeif, F. (1966), *A Study on Fakhr al-Din al-Razi and his Controversies in Transoxania*, Beirut: Dar El-Machreq.

al-Khumayni, R. (1981), *Islam and Revolution*, trans. H. Algar, Berkeley, CA: Mizan Press.

al-Kindi (1974), *Al-Kindi's Metaphysics: A Translation of the Treatise on First Philosophy*, trans. A. Ivry, Albany, NY: State University of New York Press.

— (2002), 'The Epistle of Ya'qub ibn Ishaq al-Kindi on the Device for Dispelling Sorrows', trans. G. Jayyusi-Lehn, *British Journal of Middle Eastern Studies* 29 (2): 121–35.

Kogan, B. (1985), *Averroes and the Metaphysics of Causation*, Albany, NY: State University of New York Press.

Kraemer, J. [1986a] (1993), *Humanism in the Renaissance of Islam: The Cultural Revival During the Buyid Age*, Leiden: Brill.

— (1986b), *Philosophy in the Renaissance of Islam: Abu Sulayman al-Sijistani and his Circle*, Leiden: Brill.

Lameer, J. (1994), *Al-Farabi and Aristotelian Syllogistics: Greek Theory and Islamic Practice*, Leiden: Brill.

Leaman, O. [1985] (2002), *An Introduction to Classical Islamic Philosophy*, Cambridge: Cambridge University Press.

— [1988] (1998), *Averroes and His Philosophy*, Richmond: Curzon.

— (1990), *Moses Maimonides*, London: Curzon.

— (1995), *Evil and Suffering in Jewish Philosophy*, Cambridge: Cambridge University Press.

— (1997), 'Logic and Language in Islamic Philosophy', in Carr and Mahalingam, 950–94.

— (1999), *A Brief Introduction to Islamic Philosophy*, Oxford: Polity.

— (2000), 'Islamic philosophy and the attack on logic', *Topoi* 19: 17–24.

— (2004), *Islamic Aesthetics: An Introduction*, Notre Dame, IN: University of Notre Dame Press.

— (ed.) (2006a), *The Qur'an: An Encyclopedia*, London: Routledge.

— (ed.) (2006b), *Biographical Encyclopaedia of Islamic Philosophy*, London: Thoemmes Continuum Press.

Lerner, R. and Mahdi, M. (eds) (1963), *Medieval Political Philosophy: A Sourcebook*, Ithaca, NY: Cornell University Press.

Mahdi, M. [1957] (1964), *Ibn Khaldun's Philosophy of History: A Study in the Philosophic Foundation of the Science of Culture*, Chicago: University of Chicago Press.

— (1970), 'Language and Logic in Classical Islam', in G. E. von Grunebaum (ed.), *Logic in Classical Islamic Culture* (Wiesbaden: Harrasowitz), 51–83.

— (2001), *Alfarabi and the Foundation of Political Philosophy*, Chicago: University of Chicago Press.

Maimonides [Ibn Maymun] (1963), *The Guide of the Perplexed*, 2 vols, trans. S. Pines, Chicago: University of Chicago Press.

— [1976] (1984), *Rambam: Readings in the Philosophy of Moses Maimonides*, trans. and commentary L. E. Goodman, Los Angeles: Gee Tee Bee.

Margoliouth, D. S. (1905), 'The Discussion Between Abu Bishr Matta and Abu Sa'id al-Sirafi on the Merits of Logic and Grammar', *Journal of the Royal Asiatic Society*, 79–129.

Marmura, M. E. (2005), *Probing in Islamic Philosophy:*

Studies in the Philosophies of Ibn Sina, al-Ghazali and Other Major Muslim Thinkers, Binghamton, NY: Global Academic Publishing.

Martin, R., Woodward, M. and Atmaja, D. (1997), *Defenders of Reason in Islam: Mu'tazilism from Medieval School to Modern Symbol*, Oxford: Oneworld.

al-Mawdudi, S. [1932] (1980), *Towards Understanding Islam*, Beirut: The Holy Koran Publishing House.

McAuliffe, J. (2001–6), *Encyclopedia of the Qur'an*, 6 vols, Leiden: Brill.

— (2001), 'Debate and disputation', in McAuliffe, vol. 1, 511–14.

Miskawayh [1968] (2002), *The Refinement of Character*, trans. C. K. Zurayk, Chicago: Kazi Publications.

Momen, M. (1987), *An Introduction to Shi'i Islam: The History and Doctrines of Twelver Shi'ism*, New Haven, CT: Yale University Press.

Morewedge, P. (ed.) (1979), *Islamic Philosophical Theology*, Albany, NY: State University of New York Press.

— (1982), 'Greek Sources of Some Islamic Philosophies of Being and Existence', in P. Morewedge (ed.), *Philosophies of Existence*, New York: Fordham University Press, 285–336.

— (ed.) (1992), *Neoplatonism and Islamic Thought*, Albany, NY: State University of New York Press.

Mulla Sadra (1982), *The Wisdom of the Throne*, trans. J. W. Morris, Princeton, NJ: Princeton University Press.

— (1992), *The Metaphysics of Mulla Sadra*, trans. P. Morewedge, New York: Society for the Study of Islamic Philosophy and Science.

— (2002), *The Elixir of the Gnostics*, parallel English/Arabic text, trans. W. Chittick, Provo, UT: Brigham Young University Press.

Nasir-i Khusraw [1993] (2001), *Make a Shield from Wisdom: Selected Verses from Nasir-i Khusraw's Divan*, trans. A. Shimmel, London: I. B. Tauris.

— (1998), *Knowledge and Liberation: A Treatise on Philosophical Theology*, trans. F. M. Hunzai, London: I. B. Tauris.

Nasr, S. H. [1964] (1993), *An Introduction to Islamic Cosmological Doctrines*, Albany, NY: State University of New York Press.

— (1964), *Three Muslim Sages*, Cambridge, MA: Harvard University Press.

— [1968] (1997), *Man and Nature: The Spiritual Crisis in Modern Man*, Chicago: Kazi Publications.

— (1968), *Science and Civilization in Islam*, Cambridge, MA: Harvard University Press.

— (1976), *Islamic Science: An Illustrated Guide*, Westerhem: Westerhem Press Limited.

— (1978), *Sadr al-Din Shirazi and His Transcendent Theosophy: Background, Life and Works*, Tehran: Imperial Academy of Philosophy.

— (1981), *Knowledge and the Sacred*, Edinburgh: Edinburgh University Press.

— (1989), 'Existence (*wujud*) and Quiddity (*mahiyyah*) in Islamic Philosophy', *International Philosophical Quarterly* 29 (4): 409–28.

— (1993), *The Need for a Sacred Science,* Albany, NY: State University of New York Press.

— (1996), *The Islamic Intellectual Tradition in Persia*, ed. M. Aminrazavi, Richmond: Curzon.

— (1997), *Religion and the Order of Nature*, Oxford: Oxford University Press.

— (2006), *Islamic Philosophy from Its Past to the Present: Philosophy in the Land of Prophecy*, Albany, NY: State University of New York Press.

— with Aminrazavi, M. (eds) (1999, 2001), *An Anthology of Philosophy in Persia*, 2 vols, Oxford: Oxford University Press.

— and Leaman, O. (eds) (1996), *History of Islamic Philosophy*, London: Routledge.

Netton, I. R. [1982] (1991), *Muslim Neoplatonists: An Introduction to the Thought of the Brethren of Purity (Ikhwan al-Safa')*, Edinburgh: Edinburgh University Press.

— [1989] (1995), *Allah Transcendent: Studies in the Structure and Semiotics of Islamic Theology, Philosophy, and Cosmology*, London: Routledge.

— [1992] (1999), *Al-Farabi and His School*, London: Routledge.

Ormsby, E. (1984), *Theodicy in Islamic Thought*, Princeton, NJ: Princeton University Press.

Parens, J. (2006), *An Islamic Philosophy of Virtuous Religions: Introducing Al-Farabi*, Albany, NY: State University of New York Press.

Peters, F. E. (1968a), *Aristotle and the Arabs*, New York: New York University Press.

— (1968b), *Aristoteles Arabus: The Oriental Translations and Commentaries of the Aristotelian Corpus*, Leiden: Brill.

Pines, S. [1979] (2000), *Studies in Abu'l-Barakat Al-Baghdadi: Physics and Metaphysics* (Collected Works, vol. I), Jerusalem: Magnes Press.

— [1986] (2000), *Studies in Arabic Versions of Greek Texts and in Mediaeval Science* (Collected Works, vol. II), Jerusalem: Magnes Press.

— (1995), *Studies in the History of Arabic Philosophy* (Collected Works, vol. III), ed. S. Stroumsa, Jerusalem: Magnes Press.

— (1997), *Studies in Islamic Atomism*, ed. T. Langermann, trans. M. Schwarz, Jerusalem: Magnes Press.

Plato (1997), *Complete Works*, ed. J. M. Cooper and D. S. Hutchinson, Indianapolis, IN and Cambridge: Hackett Publishing Company.

Pourjavady, R. and Schmidtke, S. (2006), *A Jewish Philosopher of Baghdad: 'Izz al-Dawla Ibn Kammuna (d. 683/1284) and His Writings*, Leiden: Brill.

Qutb, S. (1990), *Milestones*, trans. A. Z. Hammad, Indianapolis, IN: American Trust.

Rahman, F. (1958), *Prophecy in Islam: Philosophy and Orthodoxy*, London: George Allen and Unwin.

— (1975), *The Philosophy of Mulla Sadra Shirazi*, Albany, NY: State University of New York Press.

— (1979), *Islam*, 2nd edn, Chicago: University of Chicago Press.

— [1980] (1994), *Major Themes of the Qur'an*, Minneapolis: Bibliotheca Islamica.

— (1982), *Islam and Modernity: Transformation of an Intellectual Tradititon*, Chicago: University of Chicago Press.

al-Razi (1950), *The Spiritual Physick of Rhazes*, trans. A. J. Arberry, London: John Murray.

— (1993), 'The Book of the Philosophical Life', trans. C. E. Butterworth, *Interpretation* 20.3: 227–36.

Rizvi, S. (1980), *Shah Wali Allah and His Times*, Canberra: Ma'rifat Publishing House.

Rosenthal, E. I. J. [1958] (1985), *Political Thought in Medieval Islam*, Cambridge: Cambridge University Press.

Rosenthal, F. (1970), *Knowledge Triumphant: The Concept of Knowledge in Medieval Islam*, Leiden: Brill.

— (ed.) [1975] (1994), *The Classical Heritage in Islam*, London: Routledge and Kegan Paul.

— (1990), *Greek Philosophy in the Arab World* (Variorum Collected Studies Series), London: Ashgate.

Rowson, E. [1988] (1996), *A Muslim Philosopher on the Soul and its Fate: al-'Amiri's Kitab al-Amad 'ala l-abad*, Chicago: Kazi Publications.

Saadia Gaon (1948), *The Book of Beliefs and Opinions (Amanat wa-al-i'tiqadat)*, trans. S. Rosenblatt, New Haven, CT: Yale University Press.

— (1988), *The Book of Theodicy: Translation and Commentary on the Book of Job by Saadiah Ben Joseph al-Fayyumi*, trans. L. E. Goodman, New Haven, CT: Yale University Press.

al-Sabzawari (1983), *The Metaphysics of Sabzawari*, trans. I. Toshihiko and M. Mohaghegh, Delmar, NY: Caravan.

Saflo, M. (1974), *Al-Juwayni's Thought and Methodology, with a Translation of and Commentary on Luma' al-Adilla*, Berlin: Klaus Schwarz Verlag.

Schacht, J. [1964] (1983), *An Introduction to Islamic Law*, Oxford: Oxford University Press.

Schimmel, A. (1963), *Gabriel's Wing: A Study into the Religious Ideas of Sir Muhammad Iqbal*, Leiden: Brill.

— (1975), *Mystical Dimensions of Islam*, Chapel, NC: University of North Carolina Press.

— (1992), *Islam: An Introduction*, Albany, NY: State University of New York Press.

Sells, M. (1994), *Mystical Languages of Unsaying*, Chicago: University of Chicago Press.

— (1996), *Early Islamic Mysticism: Sufi, Qur'an, Mi'raj, Poetic and Theological Writings*, New York: Paulist Press.

al-Shahrastani (1934), *The Summa Philosophiae of Al-Shahrastani: Kitab Nihayatu'l-Iqdan fi Ilmi'l-Kalam* (The Furthest Steps in the Science of Theology), ed. and trans. A. Guillaume, Oxford: Oxford University Press.

— (1956), *Muslim Sects and Divisions: The Section on Muslim Sects in Kitab al-Milal wa'l-Nihal*, London: Kegan Paul.

— (2001), *Struggling with the Philosopher: A Refutation of Avicenna's Metaphysics*, ed. and trans. W. Madelung and T. Mayer, London: I. B. Tauris.

Sharif, M. M. (ed.) [1961] (1999), *A History of Muslim Philosophy*, 2 vols, Delhi: LPP.

Shehadi, F. (1964), *Al-Ghazali's Unique Unknowable God: A Philosophical Critical Analysis of Some of the Problems Raised by Ghazali's View of God as Utterly Unique and Unknowable*, Leiden: Brill.

— (1982), *Metaphysics in Islamic Philosophy*, Delmar, NY: Caravan Books.

Siddiqi, M. Z. (1993), *Hadith Literature: Its Origin, Development and Special Features*, Cambridge: The Islamic Texts Society.

Silman, Y. (1995), *Philosopher and Prophet: Judah Halevi, the Kuzari and the Evolution of His Thought*, Albany, NY: State University of New York Press.

Singh, I. (1997), *The Ardent Pilgrim: An Introduction to the Life and Work of Mohammed Iqbal*, Delhi: Oxford University Press.

Sirat, C. (1985), *A History of Jewish Philosophy in the Middle Ages*, Cambridge: Cambridge University Press.

Smith, J. I. and Haddad, Y. Y. (1981), *The Islamic Understanding of Death and Resurrection*, Albany, NY: State University of New York.

Strauss, L. [1945] (1977), 'Farabi's Plato', in *Essays in Medieval Jewish and Islamic Philosophy*, ed. A. Hyman (New York: KTAV Publishing House), 391–427.

Stroumsa, S. (1999), *Freethinkers of Medieval Islam: Ibn al-Rawandi, Abu Bakr al-Razi, and their Impact on Islamic Thought*, Leiden: Brill.

al-Suhrawardi [Sohravardi] [1982] (1999), *The Philosophical Allegories and Mystical Treatises*, trans. W. Thackston, Costa Mesa: Mazda.

— (1998), *The Book of Radiance*, trans. H. Ziai, Costa Mesa: Mazda.

— (1999), *The Philosophy of Illumination*, parallel English/Arabic text, trans. J. Walbridge and H. Ziai, Provo, UT: Brigham Young University Press.

Toshihiko, I. (1971), *The Concept and Reality of Existence*, Tokyo: Keio Institute of Cultural and Linguistic Studies.

al-Tusi (1964), *The Nasirean Ethics*, trans. G. M. Wickens, London: George Allen and Unwin.

— (1992), *The Metaphysics of Tusi*, trans. P. Morewedge, New York: Institute of Global Cultural Studies.

— (1997), *Contemplation and Action*, trans. S. J. H. Badakhchani, London: I. B. Tauris.

Urvoy, D. (1991), *Averroes*, trans. O. Stewart, London: Routledge.

Vahid, S. A. (1959), *Iqbal: His Art and Thought*, London: John Murray.

Walbridge, J. (1992), *The Science of Mystic Lights: Qutb al-Din Shirazi and the Illuminationist Tradition of Islamic Philosophy*, Cambridge, MA: Harvard University Press for Center of Middle Eastern Studies of Harvard University.

— (2000a), 'Logic in the Islamic Intellectual Tradition: The Recent Centuries', *Islamic Studies* 39: 55–75.

— (2000b), *The Leaven of the Ancients: Suhrawardi and the Heritage of the Greeks*, Albany, NY: State University of New York Press.

— (2001), *The Wisdom of the Mystic East: Suhrawardi and Platonic Orientalism*, Albany, NY: State University of New York Press.

Wali Allah, Shah (1980), *Sufism and the Islamic Tradition: The Lamahat and Sata'at of Shah Waliullah*, trans. G. Jalbani, London: Octagon Press.

— (1982), *The Sacred Knowledge*, trans. G. Jalbani, London: Octagon Press.

— (1995), *The Conclusive Argument from God: Shah Wali Allah of Delhi's Hujjat Allah Al-Baligha*, trans. M. K. Hermansen, Leiden: Brill.

Walker, P. (1993), *Early Philosophical Shi'ism: the Isma'ili Neoplatonism of Abu Ya'qub al-Sijistani*, Cambridge: Cambridge University Press.

— (1994), *The Wellsprings of Wisdom: A Study of Abu Ya'qub al-Sijistani's Kitab al-Yanabi, Including a Complete English Translation With Commentary and Notes*, Salt Lake City, UT: University of Utah Press.

— (1996), *Abu Ya'qub al-Sijistani: Intellectual Missionary*, London: I. B. Tauris.

— (1999), *Hamid al-Din al-Kirmani: Ismaili Thought in the Age of al-Hakim*, London: I. B. Tauris.

Walzer, R. (1962), *Greek into Arabic: Essays on Islamic Philosophy*, Cambridge, MA: Harvard University Press.

Wan Daud, W. M. N. (1989), *The Concept of Knowledge in Islam*, London: Mansell.

Watt, W. M. (1948), *Free Will and Predestination in Early Islam*, London: Luzac.

— [1962] (1985), *Islamic Philosophy and Theology*, 2nd edn, Edinburgh: Edinburgh University Press.

— (1963), *Muslim Intellectual: A Study of al-Ghazali*, Edinburgh: Edinburgh University Press.

— (1973), *The Formative Period of Islamic Thought*, Edinburgh: Edinburgh University Press.

Wisnovsky, R. (ed.) (2001), *Aspects of Avicenna*, Princeton, NJ: Markus Wiener Publishers.

— (2003), *Avicenna's Metaphysics in Context*, Ithaca, NY: Cornell University Press.

Wolfson, H. A. (1976), *The Philosophy of the Kalam*, Cambridge, MA: Harvard University Press.

Yarshater, E. (ed.) (1985 ff.), *Encyclopedia Iranica*, London: Routledge Kegan and Paul.

Zaid, A. (2003), *The Epistemology of Ibn Khaldun*, London: Routledge Curzon.

Ziai, H. (1990), *Knowledge and Illumination: A Study of Suhrawardi's Hikmat al-ishraq*, Atlanta, GA: Scholars Press.